D0153367

THE MESS IN WASHINGTON

THE MESS IN WASHINGTON

MANPOWER MOBILIZATION IN WORLD WAR II

GEORGE Q. FLYNN

Contributions in American History, Number 76

GREENWOOD PRESS
Westport, Connecticut • London, England

331.11
F64m

Library of Congress Cataloging in Publication Data

Flynn, George Q.
  The mess in Washington.

  (Contributions in American history ; no. 76
ISSN 0084-9219)
  Bibliography: p.
  Includes index.
  1. Labor supply--United States--History.
2. World War, 1939-1945--Manpower--United States--
History. I. Title.
HD5724. F57   331.1'1'0973   78-4027
ISBN 0-313-20418-7

Copyright © 1979 by George Q. Flynn

All rights reserved. No portion of this book may be
reproduced, by any process or technique, without the
express written consent of the publisher.

Library of Congress Catalog Card Number: 78-4027
ISBN: 0-313-20418-7
ISSN: 0084-9219

First published in 1979

Greenwood Press, Inc.
51 Riverside Avenue, Westport, Connecticut 06880

Printed in the United States of America

10 9 8 7 6 5 4 3 2 1

for   DOROTHY S. FARRELL

UNIVERSITY LIBRARIES
CARNEGIE-MELLON UNIVERSITY
PITTSBURGH, PENNSYLVANIA 15213

CONTENTS

PREFACE

Mobilizing to fight World War II was a complex enterprise for the United States. While the exciting military and diplomatic dimensions of the war have drawn considerable attention, the prosaic process of mobilizing the home front has been slighted by historians. Clearly the war was a dividing line in American foreign policy, in the shift from unilateralism to internationalism. Some students see the conflict as a watershed in domestic developments, through the growth of a federal bureaucracy and rapid social change. The war, William Manchester writes, provided a "tremendous impetus to egalitarianism." In 1946 Allen Nevin stated that the war had a revolutionary effect upon the civil population. But Richard Polenberg seems closer to the truth when he insists that the war had only a limited effect in the area of social change. By ending the depression the war allowed the federal government to attack other social issues in the postwar world, such as aid to education, civil rights, and medical insurance.[1]

All of these arguments assume that the war did contribute to the acceptance by Americans of the new, active role of the federal government in society. The generation which fought both the depression and the war found the power of the federal state new and impressive. Many citizens still saw the expansion of the government's role as an exceptional reaction to an exceptional problem—an economic crisis followed by a foreign crisis. But did the war convert Americans to the beneficence of big government?

No program seemed better designed to lose support for big government than manpower mobilization. No program seemed better proof of how government bureaucracy could confuse the lives of citizens than the techniques employed to mobilize manpower during World War II. Such is the conventional wisdom of contemporaries, a wisdom which has been ratified by historians who have derided the attempts by Franklin Roosevelt and War Manpower Commissioner Paul McNutt to bring order to this field.[2] Yet few programs were as important—if we measure importance by the number of lives affected. The manpower problem proved to be the most "delicate and complicated of all the problems of home front administration."[3] As manpower was "the ultimate limiting resource of an economy," the topic deserves more attention than it has heretofore received. Five years after the end of the war a scholar wrote that "the complete story of the administration of manpower allocation would furnish a fascinating study of American economic and political institutions."[4]

Historians, least of all the present author, seldom write complete stories, on manpower or anything else. But the subject requires some attempt at historical analysis, some effort to achieve perspective. Under the pressure of a world war the federal government made an unprecedented venture in mobilizing society. The achievements and failures of this experiment reveal the impact of the war on domestic institutions and illustrate the uncertain growth of bureaucracy in the midst of conflict. Manpower mobilization tells part of the story.

No one but the author is responsible for any errors which follow, but several others deserve acknowledgment for their generous assistance. James Patterson of Brown suggested the study when we were temporarily colleagues in Bloomington, Indiana. Several of my colleagues in the history department at Texas Tech University have read and commented on parts of the study. While traveling from one archival center to another I benefited greatly from the hospitality extended by Norman Melun and Lawrence Henneberger in Washington, D.C., and Paul Reising, Jr., in Boston. Paul Young and his reference staff at Texas Tech University Library were tireless in tracing down obscure information. This same spirit of service revealed itself at the following institutions: the University of Miami

Library, the Lilly Library of Indiana University, Clemson University Library, the Franklin D. Roosevelt Library, the Schlesinger Library at Radcliffe College, the Military History Institute at Carlisle Barracks, Pennsylvania, the Yale University Library, the Manuscript Room at the Library of Congress, the National Archives in Washington, D.C., and the Huntington Library in San Marino. My research was made possible due to the generosity of faculty grants from the Arts and Science Council of Texas Tech University and by a special grant from the Eleanor Roosevelt Institute of Hyde Park, New York.

The preparation of the manuscript benefited from the typing of Joan Weldon and Donna Aldridge. My wife, Mary Reising Flynn, once again provided assistance in proofreading and managed my home with Teutonic efficiency and Gallic charm.

Notes

1. William Manchester, *The Glory and the Dream*, 2 vols. (Boston: Little, Brown, 1973), p. 355; Allan Nevins, "How We Felt about the War," in Paul Goodman, ed., *While You Were Gone* (New York: Simon and Schuster, 1946), p. 7; Richard Polenberg, *War and Society: The United States, 1941-1945* (Philadelphia: J.B. Lippincott, 1972), p. 98.

2. For generally negative estimates of manpower mobilization see the following: Jack E. Babcock, "Evolution of Industrial Mobilization Planning Technique, 1920-1945 (Ph.D. dissertation, Georgetown University, 1955), pp. 188-89; Robert K. Murray, "Government and Labor during World War II," *Current History* 37 (September 1959), p. 151; Jim F. Heath, "Domestic America during World War II: Research Opportunities for Historians," *Journal of American History* 58 (September 1971), p. 404; Eliot Janeway, *Struggle for Survival* (New Haven: Yale University Press, 1951), p. 89; Henry F. Pringle, "The War Agencies," in *While You Were Gone,* p. 184; Lester V. Chandler and Donald H. Wallace, eds., *Economic Mobilization and Stabilization* (New York: Holt, Rinehart, Winston, 1951), pp. 58, 137; Byron Fairchild and Jonathan Grossman, *The Army and Industrial Manpower* (Washington, D.C.: U.S. Department of the Army, 1959), pp. 196-200; Paul A. C. Koistinen, "Mobilizing the World War II Economy: Labor and the Industrial-Military Alliance," *Pacific Historical Review* 42 (November 1973), pp. 443-78.

3. Janeway, *Struggle for Survival*, p. 157.

4. Herman M. Somers, *Presidential Agency: OWMR, Office of War Mobilization and Reconversion* (Cambridge: Harvard University Press, 1950), p. 140.

George Q. Flynn

THE MESS IN WASHINGTON

CHAPTER 1

The Mandate Bestowed

For most Washingtonians Sunday meant church and professional football. On December 7, 1941, the Redskins expected a close game from the Philadelphia Eagles, a regional rival. The game would be close but the natives had confidence because of their premier quarterback, "Slinging" Sammy Baugh. A stripper down at the Gayety Theater even tried to bolster attendance by adopting the quarterback's name, but slinging things other than footballs. As the crowd drove through Washington a few people passing the Japanese Embassy noticed smoke rising from the lawn. While officials raced in and out with documents for a recently kindled fire, one curious bystander heard a man say it was probably old love letters being destroyed. There may have been some symbolic truth to this guess; love was not a popular emotion in another part of the world as Japanese planes raced to their rendezvous with American ships in Pearl Harbor. After news of the sneak attack reached Washington, embassy officials expressed faith in the fairness of the American people. The officials did not expect mobs to attack the delegation. To make sure, detectives hired from the Burns Agency took up positions around the building.[1]

I

The entire scene in Washington on that fateful Sunday bespoke the unpreparedness of Americans for war. One economist estimated that the country was wasting as much as one-third of its total manpower in areas marginal to the economy as late as 1940. War had been raging in Europe since September 1939. Through Lend Lease and other steps the nation had become increasingly involved. But the American economy seemed reluctant to convert from private production to war production. With war orders arriving from Europe, the American economy showed signs of recovering from the 1937 recession, but manufacturers saw little merit in committing all of their production facilities to a European war. Conversion to war production meant retooling, which meant temporary layoffs. Unions had no more enthusiasm than management. In Washington, planners struggled over the problem of distinguishing between a potential defense industry and a pure civilian industry. The distinction was difficult in such an interconnected economy as America's. Others worried over how mobilization would affect union-management relations. The 1930s had seen the rise of organized labor to a new position of power. Significant segments of management had yet to adjust to labor's new status. Even if new war plants were designed, disagreement arose over whether they should be built near labor sources or where they would be isolated from enemy attack.[2]

In seeking answers to these questions and others in preparing the American economy for war, Franklin Roosevelt seemed indecisive. A few liberals saw the mobilization experience as an opportunity to extend the New Deal. Such men shook their heads as they observed the old enemies of the New Deal, the captains of industry, returning to Washington with Roosevelt's blessing to assume control of mobilization. Instead of a more equitable distribution of economic power, mobilization might lead to more concentration of wealth and power. The industrialists were not only welcomed to Washington, but the administration garnished their return with a variety of spices. Incentives ranged from liberal amortization provision for expansion of plants to a moratorium on antitrust prosecution, from federal plant construction to a cost-plus-a-fixed-fee contract.[3]

Although such liberal criticism of Roosevelt's mobilization actions seems unreasonable, the President had himself to blame. His actions appeared to many to be reminiscent of the baffling, experimental approach which characterized the early New Deal. Once again a complex and overlapping series of agencies appeared by grace of executive orders. In August 1939 the President appointed a

War Resources Board consisting of Sumner Welles, Edward R. Stettinius, and others to study the problem of economic mobilization and make recommendations. This group soon suggested that Roosevelt appoint a super mobilizer, but the President demurred. Instead, on September 8, 1939, he created what came to be called the Office of Emergency Management, a gesture designed to keep the reins of mobilization in presidential hands. By May 1940 Roosevelt had taken yet another step with the creation of a National Defense Advisory Committee (NDAC), using as his authority war powers granted to Woodrow Wilson in 1916. The NDAC consisted of such industrial and labor leaders as William S. Knudsen, Sidney Hillman, Edward R. Stettinius, and Chester Davis. When German troops swept over the Low Countries in early 1940, Roosevelt met with this new board and called for a massive program of plane and tank production. Such calls were useless, however, because the authority of the NDAC was vague and its responsibilities divided. The mobilization plan remained without central direction. Hopes were raised when Donald Nelson, former executive manager with Sears Roebuck, received presidential authority to control the priorities of production orders. But Nelson soon disappointed his subordinates by refusing to use his power. Instead, he delegated responsibility to the military.[4]

Months passed and the Selective Service Act became law in September 1940. Thousands of young men were withdrawn from the civilian economy. Still no clear mobilization plan appeared in Washington. Some people suspected that Roosevelt had no intention of delegating authority and was merely going through a charade for the sake of public opinion. A more likely explanation, and one more consistent with Roosevelt's past administrative habits, is that he continued to experiment, seeking the right combination of men and duties, as he had done in 1933. In January 1941 he decided upon another approach by establishing the Office of Production Management (OPM) under White House direction. The OPM was headed by William S. Knudsen and Sidney Hillman. The appointment of Hillman as associate director was belated recognition of the importance of labor in any mobilization plan. Battered by the same vagueness of mission, by the same rivalry from the military and internal dissension that plagued earlier efforts, the OPM struggled with its task.[5] But not for long. By August 1941 Roosevelt decided to refine production mobilization again by creating the Supply, Priorities and Allocations Board. This agency was revamped into the War Production Board (WPB) in January 1942. At this point in what appeared to be a game of musical chairs, the President realized that in addition to organizing material and plants he would need someone to oversee manpower, an increasingly crucial factor in the mobilization equation.

This realization came late for several reasons. Back in 1941 the President and the men around him exuded confidence about the availability of manpower for mobilization. Even earlier, a War Department report of 1930 stated: "It is almost impossible to assume a situation where our population would be in danger of suffering actual hardships in war due to lack of personnel to produce the necessaries of life." Military men always felt optimistic because they argued that the civilian sector could be squeezed tighter for men to increase the size of the army. Such optimism also evolved naturally from the depression experience of the 1930s and the evidence of long lines of unemployed men seeking work. After all of the work-relief activities of the New Deal up to June 1940, some 8.5 million people were reported unemployed out of a total work force of fifty-five million. Few observers realized that such national statistics could be misleading as an answer to defense mobilization. No one asked if these unemployed individuals were in the right area and if they possessed the right skills. In New York, the Buffalo-Niagara area contained considerable defense industry. Yet the area reported a potential labor surplus of only 27,000 men in 1940. Such a surplus would quickly evaporate when defense mobilization accelerated in 1941.[6]

The availability of manpower became a critical factor in determining the pace of mobilization. Some insight into this problem emerged in May 1940 as the President launched his National Defense Advisory Commission and announced new production goals. Secretary of Labor Frances Perkins immediately informed Roosevelt of the need for close monitoring of manpower. She called for holding the line on work-safety standards, for establishing a special standard for women workers, for the creation of labor-management committees in plants, for stabilizing hiring and priorities, for main-

tenance of the forty-hour week, and for the immediate appoint-
ment of two national labor leaders on the advisory committee. The
President anticipated this last request by creating a Labor Policy
Advisory Committee under NDAC with Sidney Hillman as chairman.[7]

Hillman took charge of manpower mobilization. He did not fit
the stereotype of the typical Washington bureaucrat. Born in
Zagare, Lithuania, in 1887, he was chased out of Russia for political
reasons and went to England. He emigrated to the United States in
1907 and became the leader of the Amalgamated Clothing Workers
of America. An active supporter of pragmatic unionism, he soon
became the confidant of Roosevelt and an enthusiastic supporter of
the New Deal. By 1940 he was the most important union leader in
the Roosevelt coalition.

In his new post Hillman wasted little time in attacking the problem of anticipated labor shortages. In July 1940 he recruited Owen
Young and Isador Lubin to assist him in developing an industrial
training program. Within days Young announced that industrial
and labor leaders had agreed that the best source of new labor
would be unemployed skilled workers. Next in line for jobs would
be men working in training programs within industry. This Training Within Industry program became the responsibility of Lubin.
The training was run on a local level by joint labor-management
councils. By the time of the Pearl Harbor attack more than 1.5
million workers had passed through the program. Simultaneously,
Hillman promoted labor stabilization through special industrial
committees of management and labor to control basic wage rates,
work rules, and grievance machinery.[8]

These efforts appeared barely adequate. Acting Secretary of War
Louis Johnson announced to the press before the Pearl Harbor
attack that some 300,000 skilled mechanics were needed immediately
in armament production. Johnson implied that the war effort was
already being hampered by a lack of labor. The military leaders of
the nation would continue to repeat this litany until V-E Day in
1945. On this first occasion Secretary of Labor Perkins decided to
call the military's bluff, thereby establishing another trend which
would reappear during the war years. She immediately wrote to
Johnson asking for specifics of the cities and firms where these
300,000 workers were needed. Johnson, who had been engaging in

simple bombast, lamely replied that he had been misunderstood. What he really said was that if the military received new funds for war production a labor shortage might develop.[9]

Despite the vigorous efforts of Perkins, Hillman, and his aides, manpower continued to be a source of concern to the President during 1941. Undoubtedly, the major cause of labor problems revolved around the dynamics of mobilization itself and was not subject to tight government management. Some 5.5 million workers entered defense industry during 1941. But in the same year more strikes occurred than in any prior year during the past decade except for 1937. Altogether 2.3 million workers lost some twenty-three million man-days through strikes. Organized labor, making great headway in achieving recognition at the Ford Motor Company, Little Steel, and other bastions of the open shop willing to sacrifice principle for war contracts, cooperated with Roosevelt's mobilization plan when it suited them. Hillman became a target for union criticism because of his total commitment to the President.[10]

Workers entered defense industry at an unprecedented rate, but strikes continued. Fast was not fast enough for the military, and the President continued to hear complaints. To Hillman, Roosevelt wrote that he was "disturbed about the number of defense industries that are claiming they cannot get enough skilled workers or supervisors to work full complements of labor on second and third shifts." Assuming that the problem stemmed from lack of support for Hillman by others on the OPM, Roosevelt gave the Labor Division full responsibility for putting workers into plants. This gesture revealed Roosevelt's vague view of the problem of manpower mobilization. Hillman had adequate support, but it is doubtful if anyone, even with total emergency power, could have controlled the spontaneous movement of labor into an expanding job market. National data on labor skills, labor potential, migration trends and hundreds of other facts were simply not available. The President again revealed his naïveté by blandly suggesting "that if arrangements were made for transfers of workers from consumer goods industries . . . together with a diligent search for properly trained workers plus an adequate emergency training program," the problem of manpower would be solved. The suggestion reflected Roosevelt's desperate desire to do something. The strikes were exasperating. After much consultation he used 2,500 troops with fixed bayonets to break a strike at North American Aviation Company in California in June 1941. Something more seemed needed and fast.[11]

Improvising as usual, the President thought to assist Hillman by placing at his disposal the labor placement facilities of the United States Employment Service. This agency, which was really a federal overseer to forty-eight state-run employment services, operated out of the Federal Security Agency (FSA) headed by Paul McNutt. McNutt had no objection to placing the office under the control of Hillman, but such a step would do little good unless the entire network of employment placement was federalized. In December 1941 the President requested that all states transfer their employment offices to the federal government so that the labor needs of national defense could be met. Some 1,500 local offices, covering every industrial community in the nation, now came under direct control of the FSA and Hillman. These local offices were to register, recruit, and place workers in war jobs. Comprehensive information on the national labor supply could now be obtained through the registration activities at a local office. Here at last might be the key to scientific control and placement of American labor to aid military production.[12] But it was too late for Hillman. As this key tool of manpower mobilization became available, his star faded. Partially the result of poor health and partially the consequence of union animosity, Hillman had outstayed his usefulness at the White House. A new star arose to confront the imbroglio of manpower.

II

World War II spelled tragedy for some Americans, opportunity for others. Paul V. McNutt of Indiana did not serve at the front but was nonetheless a professional casualty of the war. Few men in America seemed to have as promising a future as McNutt in 1941. He had burst on the national scene after a brilliant career in the Midwest. Born in 1891, the son of a judge, McNutt attended Indiana University and later took his law degree from Harvard. He returned to Bloomington, first as a professor and then as dean of the law school at the modest age of thirty-four. By 1932 he had entered politics and been swept into the governor's chair by Roosevelt's landslide. During the 1930s he moved into national prominence. Roosevelt appointed him a High Commissioner to the Philippines, and in 1939 he took over the direction of the newly established Federal Security Agency. At the 1940 Democratic convention several dozen delegates put his name forward for second place on the ticket. This move proved abortive, but McNutt appeared a likely candidate for 1944.[13]

McNutt had all of the necessary ingredients for a successful political career. He combined intelligence with a hard-boiled sense of political realism. As a Democrat in a Republican area, he knew the advantages of compromise. Few national figures cut as dashing an appearance. Tall and well built, he carried his physique with grace. His blue eyes, black brows, and white hair impressed not only the ladies, but also crusty Harry Truman of Missouri, who remarked: "Isn't he a hell of an attractive-looking man?" Accomplishment and achievement shone from his Phi Beta Kappa Key and his solid gold cigarette case.[14] Gregarious by nature as well as from political necessity, McNutt enjoyed a good drink and an exciting sports event. He willingly stood in for the President to throw out the first ball of the baseball season. Still more remarkable, he stayed to watch the Philadelphia Athletics beat the Senators by a score of seven to five. Confident, handsome, well appointed, McNutt seemed destined to assume the leadership of his party once Roosevelt retired. The competition, as represented by Jimmy Byrnes and Henry Wallace, appeared second class. Unfortunately, World War II turned out to be more of a briar patch than a rose garden for the handsome Hoosier.[15]

McNutt deserved a better fate. During the war he would be frequently criticized, sometimes fairly, but often unfairly. His personality explains a few of the problems he encountered. A big man with a big mouth, he had the unfortunate habit of appearing to lecture his peers rather than conversing with them. He frequently imagined himself back behind the podium at Indiana University when addressing fellow members of the cabinet. A few critics complained because he was a dedicated politician, as though such a vocation were unique to government and precluded meritorious work. But McNutt's reputation had been tarnished while he was governor of Indiana. The press had uncovered a system of monetary kickbacks, contributions into the Democratic campaign fund, by state appointees. McNutt had done nothing illegal but he shared a weakness of most politicians, the inability to view the future outside of public office. He knew how to plan a speech for its broadest and vaguest impact and how to clear appointments with powerful senators and with the Democratic National Committee. Among party stalwarts, his reputation remained high. But these characteristics hardly distinguished him from thousands of others around the country. Under McNutt young liberals such as Wayne Coy entered government. Party leaders, including Roosevelt himself, applauded McNutt's sportsmanship when he lost the vice-presidential spot in 1940. At no time did he compromise personal integrity for personal gain during the war years.[16]

McNutt believed in Franklin Roosevelt and New Deal liberalism. For McNutt, as for millions of citizens, the New Deal represented the height of democracy in action. The National Youth Administration, for example, was "a marvelous contribution . . . to the youth of the United States." As the labor policies of the New Deal had led to a vigorous unionism, McNutt rejected any suggestion that labor should give up the social and economic gains made during the 1930s because of economic mobilization in the 1940s.[17]

As the nation mobilized for war, people expected regimentation and centralization by government. Instead, McNutt preached the faith of Thomas Jefferson. Two principles guided McNutt's rhetoric and action throughout the war years: localism and voluntarism. He believed strongly that decision-making on manpower mobilization should be as close to the worker's home as possible. "The only place to solve a problem is where it is," said McNutt, "and the place where things happen to people . . . is in their own home towns." On another occasion he repeated: "Most jobs are best done nearest the people." After assuming direction of the manpower program he sought to live up to this Jeffersonian idea by delegating vast amounts of power to area and regional assistants. As McNutt saw it, the manpower problem consisted not in one national problem but in thousands of local and community conundrums. One solution would not work for all communities.[18]

McNutt realized that traditional American resentment of government restriction would impede mobilization attempts. This belief in the power of American individualism led him to stress continually the voluntary dimension of his work. He agreed that war mobilization would mean the curtailment of some sacred traditions. He hoped it might mean the permanent end of such unholy practices as racial and sexual discrimination in hiring. But most of the restrictions, especially those involving labor mobility, would be only temporary irritations. McNutt played up the American tradition of fair play and team play. He hoped these sentiments would come to the forefront during the mobilization crisis. "Cooperative democracy" should be the basis of national defense. Naturally, when McNutt spoke of voluntary cooperation he did not imply that every citizen was free to cooperate or not as he chose. Such rugged individualism amounted to "planless chaos." In McNutt's mind, "voluntary cooperation refers to the democratic process by which the controls are established." Presumably, he meant that citizens became involved in the process each election day, not that they continuously ran the government. Rules were needed if manpower control was to succeed, but McNutt always displayed a humanistic appreciation that his actions and directives would have an effect on real human beings. Labor statistics represented flesh and blood. When a colleague suggested the forced transfer of workers, McNutt replied that "the people are not wooden chessmen. There are human values and emotions to be considered."[19]

McNutt hardly fit the stereotype of a federal manipulator of the masses, as pictured in conservative rhetoric. As was the case with several administrators, including the President, McNutt combined an almost reactionary commitment to the preservation of traditional values with a vision of the war as a new beginning. He warned against mobilization leading to an "unhealthy concentration of men and machines in a few industrial centers," and called for the protection of the small town and village. In selecting methods of mobilization, he preferred to "try to find methods which will do the minimum damage to our essential values." Yet before the war ended, McNutt would also express the hope that mobilization experience might lead to significant changes in American values and institutions. Above all, he argued that the mobilization experience should create a permanent change in the willingness of management and labor to cooperate and promote full production and full employment. Even here, however, his stress on cooperation rather than competition between interest groups should be seen as a desire to return to the idealized harmony of a small village, a desire to turn away from an acrimonious broker state. Repeatedly in his speeches during the war McNutt insisted that the final victory should also include a triumph over the type of economic depression which had characterized the 1930s. This modest idealism, shared by President Roosevelt, had the ironic result of leading critics to complain that McNutt was attempting to use mobilization for war as a vehicle for continuing the fancy reforms of the New Deal.[20]

In foreign policy McNutt echoed the ideological commitment of Roosevelt and progressivism. Along with Roosevelt, McNutt preached American intervention before Pearl Harbor. "A free world is locked in a death struggle with the powers of darkness," he wrote in 1941. "In that struggle there can be no compromise." As the United States entered the war, McNutt saw no reason to reevaluate his views and insisted that "our democracy is on the march by the side of its allies." All of mankind, it seemed to him, was fighting for democracy and human dignity, including the Russians. Again echoing the President, McNutt tied the Allied cause to the will of Providence. "Our faith and hope, based on our unshakeable belief in a living God, have worked the miracle" against pagan forces. He expected victory in war to lead to a new age of tolerance and democracy.[21] He supported the Zionist cause in Palestine. "The right of Jews to freedom and security in their own homeland," he wrote in 1943, "is a true expression of the fundamental principles of those who fight to preserve our democratic system of government." Throughout the war, McNutt identified the cause of the Zionists with the cause of the Allies, to the discomfiture of the British.[22] In his hatred of the enemies of America, McNutt went even beyond the position of unconditional surrender and called for the total elimination of the Japanese race.[23]

Filled with Jeffersonian ideals of localism and cooperation and possessing an ideological commitment to the war, McNutt appeared to be the logical successor for Hillman to direct manpower mobilization. As early as November 28, 1940, the Council of National Defense had designated McNutt coordinator of health, welfare, medical, nutrition, recreation, and other fields affecting national

defense. As head of the Federal Security Agency he already played
a role in mobilization. One of his most important duties in 1941 fit
nicely with his personality. Like a cheerleader, he roamed the country, speaking out in defense of Roosevelt's policies in tones that
belied America's nonbelligerent status. Time and again he warned
local communities to prepare for an expansion of services to accommodate an explosion of the labor force through migration
from other parts of the country. He testified before congressional
committees on small business on the problems of labor pirating.
Although he urged the public to do more to prepare, his tone was
optimistic when he spoke of manpower. At commencement exercises
at Louisiana State University in June 1941 he reported to apprehensive graduates that the employment situation was good. Government training programs awaited them.[24]

III

During the first year of American belligerency the manpower
problem remained perplexing. Gallup polls reported that 79 percent
of the work force indicated that their jobs were not connected with
the war. Yet almost 60 percent of the work force said it would take
defense jobs regardless of the pay scale. Within the administration
a confused chorus of voices could be heard. In March McNutt publicly praised the work of the newly federalized USES and the labor
control devices of the War Production Board.

Privately, however, McNutt had doubts. He always doubted the
wisdom of placing manpower management under the control of a
production-oriented committee such as the WPB. As early as December 1939 he had urged Roosevelt to create a "Manpower Mobilization Board." On January 26, 1942, McNutt again pressed the
President for such a board. General Lewis Hershey, head of the
Selective Service System, also called for an "appropriate agency
[to] decide where the individual may best serve his Nation in total
war rather than to leave that decision to the individual. . . ." Hershey
had no doubt that "this device is found in the Selective Service
System." Even Donald Nelson and General Frank J. McSherry of
the War Production Board realized that a new approach was needed
because the manpower task no longer meant finding work for the
unemployed, but rather finding skilled workers for new jobs. But

the man most responsible for pushing the President into creating a new manpower commission was Sidney Hillman. He knew more than anyone about the problem and argued that all phases of labor and utilization should be under a separate agency.[25]

By early 1942 several important government officials saw the need for a manpower commission, but Franklin Roosevelt was not one of them. As was often the case with new government agencies, Roosevelt had to be pushed into creating the War Manpower Commission (WMC). Several drafts of an executive order creating the WMC began circulating in the White House. McNutt, Hillman, and Hershey all had their own ideas. Roosevelt instructed Harold Smith, the Director of the Budget and one of the most sensible bureaucrats in Washington, to staff these drafts with various officials, including the ever-sensitive Secretary of Labor, Frances Perkins, who desperately wanted to control any new manpower agency. As Smith began work he concluded that Roosevelt was in no hurry for action and that he did "not realize how urgent the problem was becoming."[26]

When newspaper reporters, alerted by various sources in February, asked the President about rumors of a new agency, Roosevelt replied vaguely and coyly that he was still mulling over the idea. In fact, the administrative details of the new agency had been worked out, but the President now faced the delicate task of selecting the commissioner to head it. Hillman had strong support within the administration for the job. Isador Lubin, a labor economist and advisor to the White House, wrote Samuel Rosenman, Roosevelt's speech writer, that the appointment of McNutt would be the equivalent of executing Hillman as a failure. But Hillman's friends were balanced by the numerous enemies he had made during his term in office, including elements of organized labor. Union leaders such as Phillip Murray of the Congress of Industrial Organizations (CIO) and William Green of the American Federation of Labor (AFL) preferred McNutt to Hillman. These labor leaders pressed their view on Roosevelt who continued to hesitate.[27]

Weeks went by and on April 10, 1942, Roosevelt informed reporters that he doubted that a completely new manpower agency was needed, what with the USES, the NYA, and the Labor Division of the WPA already working. Roosevelt wanted to keep everyone happy. Organized labor preferred a new agency under either

McNutt or Perkins, but management refused to accept the expansion of the Labor Department under the guise of mobilization. Businessmen believed that a separate war agency would be easier to dismantle after the emergency. Finally, on the afternoon of April 16, the President held an off-the-record meeting with Smith, Rosenman, and two other advisors—Justice William O. Douglas and Anna Rosenberg of New York City. Roosevelt rolled into the meeting late and in an ugly mood. He had just come from a lengthy duel with his dentist. Only the day before both Murray and Green had been to the White House and had urged that McNutt be appointed. Roosevelt now seemed ready to agree provided no one objected. Anna Rosenberg announced that Murray and Green had already informed McNutt that he had the job. No one objected as McNutt seemed to have the least number of enemies, was familiar with the problem, was available, and was eagerly seeking the job. Happy at the consensus, the President lifted his phone and informed McNutt of his new job. At the request of Justice Douglas, Roosevelt sent a soothing telegram to Hillman who had recently been hospitalized.[28]

Two days later Roosevelt signed Executive Order no. 9139, based on authority granted by the First War Power Act of 1941. The new order created a War Manpower Commission (WMC) with McNutt as chairman and with representatives from the following departments: War, Navy, Agriculture, Labor, Selective Service, Civil Service, and the WPB. The chairman's duties encompassed formulating plans and programs to establish national policies to assure effective mobilization and maximum utilization of manpower in the prosecution of the war. The WMC was supposed to help the chairman establish requirements of manpower for industry and to review the needs of the military and agricultural sectors. After collecting data on the labor market, the commission had the responsibility of directing both civilian and governmental agencies on the proper allocation of available manpower. All policies and regulations on recruiting labor by both private and public agencies had to get clearance from the WMC. The commission provided policies and regulations for all federal recruiting, training, and placing of workers. Finally, the WMC had the task of formulating a legislative program for effective mobilization and utilization of manpower. Within the next few months, additional powers were added to

McNutt's organization. On September 17, 1942, Executive Order no. 9247 officially transferred the USES, NYA, Apprenticeship Training, and Training Within Industry programs to the WMC. In December another executive order placed the Selective Service under McNutt. Roosevelt had created a manpower czar with extraordinary power.[29]

The power loomed imposing on paper, but paper power bound few in the Byzantine bureaucracy of wartime Washington. The members of the commission represented some of the strongest figures in government. As chairman, McNutt was joined by Secretary of Labor Perkins, Secretary of War Henry Stimson, Secretary of the Navy Frank Knox, Donald Nelson of the WPB, Secretary of Agriculture Claude R. Wickard, General Lewis Hershey of the Selective Service, Arthur S. Flemming of the Civil Service Commission, and John B. Blandford of the National House Agency. The original executive order provided for the commission to advise the chairman. McNutt was granted full power to act even if the commission objected. No member of the commission objected to this language because everyone, including McNutt, realized that acting without a consensus of the WMC would insure the director's removal by Roosevelt. Significantly, whatever the problems which emerged later in the war, at this early stage both commission members and McNutt seemed in agreement that the new agency should adopt a voluntary and decentralized approach to manpower mobilization.[30]

Under the chairman a bewildering array of support agencies blossomed. Some of these had only nominal allegiance to McNutt. For example, the Management-Labor Policy Committee (MLPC) provided an opportunity for management, labor, and agriculture to monitor and even anticipate McNutt's decisions. The Selective Service maintained total independence under Hershey. A Women's Advisory Committee, established to help with the recruiting of female labor, did little more than act as a showcase. The major operating agencies were the following bureaus: Planning and Review, Placement, Training, Utilization, Reports and Analyst. Although a few names changed before the end of the war, the responsibilities remained the same. In keeping with the principles of localism and decentralization, the action agencies were spread throughout the country. Twelve regional manpower directors covered the entire nation. The directors included educators such as Bowman F. Ashe who served in Atlanta, and political workers such as Anna Rosenberg who covered New York. Below the regional directors sat area directors, appointed to handle small problem areas. Their numbers varied from sixty to more than 200 at different times. Each area director had personnel to handle utilization and training. By 1943 state directors were also working with the responsibility of directing labor to shortage areas. As the area director operated only in certain designated, critical locations, responsibilities frequently overlapped. Finally, at the bottom, making actual contact with potential workers, were the 1,500 offices of the United States Employment Service. These USES offices received regulations and policies from Washington, but they enjoyed a surprising degree of autonomy, much as did the local draft boards.[31]

In keeping with the military analogy, the WMC provided for an appeal system for any worker who disliked a decision made by the local USES affecting his employment status. In most cases the worker sought to appeal orders freezing him in a job as a consequence of policies developed later in the war. An appeal system, staffed by voluntary members of management-labor committees, paralleled the entire WMC organization. The national MLPC made recommendations to McNutt, whose decision was final. Overall, the appeal system seemed rather effective. Taking the period from May 1943 to November 1944 as a base, one study revealed that the vast majority of appeals were based on grounds of personal hardship. No national statistics on appeal action were kept but one estimate is that reversals of local freeze restrictions occurred in about 50 percent of all cases which were appealed. McNutt usually went along with the recommendation of the MLPC. Although it took an average of ninety-six days to appeal to Washington, little criticism of the system emerged.[32]

IV

Precisely at 10:30 A.M. on April 20, 1942, reporters crowded into Room 5554 of the Social Security Building to hear the new manpower czar explain what he expected to do with the vast array of power dumped into his lap by the President. McNutt, characteristically, disdained modest objectives and goals. "The War Manpower Commission," he pontificated as newsreel cameras whirled, "will be the great clearing house for all the wartime labor needs—civilian and military. In terms of the war production goals, it will set priorities of jobs, just as priorities have been set for metals, chemicals, and other materials." When a reporter asked about a possible labor draft, McNutt repeatedly insisted that he would use a voluntary approach but might consider exerting pressure by threatening the withdrawal of war contracts, a move which would hurt both worker and employer. Anticipating President Roosevelt by several months, McNutt also claimed control over the entire Selective Service System. In language which must have amused the strongly entrenched Hershey, McNutt spoke of authority over local draft boards. He correctly foresaw that no manpower program could work without control of the Selective Service which was vacuuming up thousands of men from key jobs each day. He also saw that certain labor shortages resulted from blatant discrimination against women, blacks, and aliens. Reporters filed out impressed with McNutt's sense of authority but with little insight into the steps he would use to find the needed thirteen million workers for war jobs before the end of the year.[33]

Members of the WMC had similar questions at their first meeting with McNutt on May 6. He opened the meeting with a bland request for close cooperation with other government agencies. Nelson spoke for all by replying "that goes without saying." With this innocuous exchange the new manpower mobilization program was under way. During the next few months the WMC met regularly but accomplished little. McNutt looked upon the commission as mere window dressing while the real work unfolded out of his office. Gradually, the commission met less frequently; second-line officials substituted for the big names. Only Frances Perkins contributed anything constructive. She asked Nelson to produce a list of essential war industries to assist Hershey in preparing deferments. She also wanted a list of essential occupations in these plants. Nelson was pessimistic.[34]

No commission could run the manpower program. McNutt soon produced a program and went about executing it with little reference to the commission. It included the following objectives: To bring order to manpower mobilization he needed a careful inventory of the needs of the services, of war industry, of agriculture, and other essential civilian industry. An inventory of the labor supply had to be obtained through the USES with the aid of information furnished to local draft boards. After this information was in hand the WMC could see to it that additional workers were trained in the right skills, that available skilled labor went to the most critical areas, that men worked at their highest skill level, that hiring was orderly with minimum pirating, that the draft deferred critical workers, and that war contracts were placed in areas of labor surplus. On top of this formidable list of objectives, and much more difficult, McNutt sought to create a mobile labor force for emergency duty and also hoped to remove the existing barriers of race and sex to full employment.[35]

In short, all McNutt required to complete his task was an economic and social revolution in traditional patterns of American behavior. He hoped that the revolution could be conducted on a voluntary basis with emphasis on decentralization. Some program; some problem.

Notes

1. Scott Hart, *Washington at War: 1941-1945* (Englewood Cliffs, N.J.: Prentice-Hall, 1970), pp. 1, 16-17, 22.

2. Richard Polenberg, *War and Society: The United States, 1941-1945* (Philadelphia: J. B. Lippincott, 1972), pp. 10, 11, 19; Leonard P. Adams, *Wartime Manpower Mobilization* (Ithaca, N.Y.: Cornell University Press, 1951), pp. 20-21; Joel Seidman, *American Labor from Defense to Reconversion* (Chicago: University of Chicago Press, 1953), pp. 41-42.

3. For an extreme interpretation of this dimension of mobilization see Bruce Catton, *The War Lords of Washington* (New York: Harcourt, Brace, 1948), pp. 4, 26-27; Polenberg, *War and Society,* p. 12.

4. Donald Nelson, *Arsenal of Democracy: The Story of American War Production* (New York: Harcourt, Brace, 1946), pp. 58-86, 87-107 passim; Eliot Janeway, *Struggle for Survival* (New Haven: Yale University Press, 1951), pp. 45, 49, 193; Jim F. Heath, "Domestic America during World War II: Research Opportunities for Historians," *Journal of American History* 58 (September 1971), pp. 393-94.

5. Nelson, *Arsenal,* pp. 116, 139; Janeway, *Struggle,* p. 121; Catton, *War Lords,* pp. 52-65; Polenberg, *War and Society,* p. 8, says munition production rose by 225 percent in 1941. For a recent discussion of Roosevelt's problems of administration on the home front see James M. Burns, *Roosevelt: The Soldier of Freedom* (New York: Harcourt Brace Jovanovich, 1970), especially chaps. 1, 8, 11, 14, 15. Another recent and sympathetic study is John M. Blum, *V Was for Victory: Politics and American Culture during World War II* (New York: Harcourt Brace Jovanovich, 1976).

6. Quotation is from Byron Fairchild and Jonathan Grossman, *The Army and Industrial Manpower* (Washington, D.C.: U.S. Department of the Army, 1959), p. 7; David Hinshaw, *The Home Front* (New York: Putnam, 1943), p. 82; Seidman, *American Labor*, pp. 30-31, 152-53 for statistics. The American labor growth rate exceeded by 7.3 million the normal labor rate expected under peacetime conditions by 1945. Teenagers in the work force exceeded expectations by 2.8 million and women over 35 by 1.9 million. Adams, *Wartime*, pp. 11, 18-19.

7. Carol Riegelman, *Labour-Management Co-operation in United States War Production* (Montreal: International Labour Office, 1948), p. 9; Perkins to Roosevelt, May 25, 1940, file 302, Harry Hopkins Papers, Franklin Roosevelt Library, Hyde Park, N.Y.; congressional memo to Roosevelt, June 21, 1940, file 302, *ibid.*; W. Y. Elliott to Roosevelt, June 3, 1940, *ibid.*

8. Nelson, *Arsenal*, pp. 96, 312-13; Robert K. Murray, "Government and Labor during World War II," *Current History* 37 (September 1959), p. 146; Janeway, *Struggle*, p. 245.

9. Perkins to Johnson, July 1, 1940, file 302, Hopkins Papers; Johnson to Perkins, July 2, 1940, *ibid.*

10. Seidman, *American Labor*, pp. 28, 52-53.

11. Minutes of Office of Production Management, February 18, 1941, and May 29, 1941, box 12, Donald Nelson Papers, The Huntington Library, San Marino, Calif.; Roosevelt to Hillman, May 28, 1941, file 324, Hopkins Papers; Seidman, *American Labor*, p. 48; Rosenberg to Roosevelt, August 23, 1941, President's personal file 8101, Franklin Roosevelt Papers, Hyde Park, N.Y.; diary of Henry Morgenthau, 4,976 (October 23, 1941), Roosevelt Library.

12. Office of Production Management Council minutes, July 8, 1941, box 12, Nelson Papers; Roosevelt to Byrnes, June 11, 1941, President's personal file 2816, Roosevelt Papers; Adams, *Wartime*, p. 22.

13. For a popular biography of McNutt see I. George Blake, *Paul McNutt: Portrait of a Hoosier* (Indianapolis: Central Publishing Co., 1966); also file of June 1944, Paul V. McNutt Papers, The Lilly Library, Indiana University, Bloomington, Ind.

14. Allen Drury, *A Senate Journal, 1943-1945* (New York: McGraw-Hill, 1963), p. 189; see *Business Week*, December 12, 1942, p. 15, for a photograph.

15. Jonathan Daniels, *White House Witness* (Garden City, N.Y.: Doubleday, 1975), p. 253; *New York Times*, April 21, 1943, p. 37; file of October 22, 1943, McNutt Papers.

16. General file, 1940-1941, McNutt Papers; Philip S. Broughton to McNutt, January 10, 1944, *ibid.*; Marvin McIntyre to Roosevelt, January 29, 1943, official file 4905, Roosevelt Papers; Robert B. Hamblett to Roosevelt, March 17, 1942, *ibid.*; Daniels, *White House Witness*, p. 29. Undersecretary of War Patterson disagreed with and fought McNutt for three years but could still write of him in April 1946: "He has performed his duties with great distinction and ability. . . . His character, integrity and professional ability are of the highest order." Affidavit enclosed in Patterson to McNutt, April 5, 1946, box 20, Robert Patterson Papers, Library of Congress, Washington, D.C.; Roosevelt to McNutt, August 3, 1940, PPF 2836, Roosevelt Papers.

17. McNutt to Eleanor Roosevelt, May 6, 1944, file 919, Eleanor Roosevelt Papers, Roosevelt Library, Hyde Park, N.Y.; *New York Times*, April 20, 1941, p. 1.

18. Speech file of March 6, 1941, April 30, 1941, and June 21, 1943, McNutt Papers; *New York Times*, January 21, 1944, p. 10.

19. Speech files of February 25, 1941, July 14, 1942, October 21, 1942, June 18, 1942, October 11, 1943, and November 20, 1942, in McNutt Papers; testimony before Senate Military Affairs Committee, October 21, 1942, *ibid.*

20. Quote from testimony before Senate Committee on Small Businesses, December 18, 1941, McNutt Papers; review of W. Beveridge, *Full Employment. . . .*, February 5, 1945, *ibid.*; Paul McNutt, "3,765,000 Jobs for Pennsylvania," October, 1945, *ibid.*; clipping from *Detroit Free Press*, November 30, 1943, and file of November 30, 1943, in McNutt Papers. Edward O'Neal of the American Farm Bureau Federation complained about McNutt's socialistic ideas in the *New York Times*, October 29, 1942, p. 1.

21. McNutt to Andrew Kalpaschnikoff, September 11, 1941; statement in *Opinion*, January 10, 1943; statement to United Jewish War Effort, June 12, 1943; press release, June 22, 1943; statement for International Council of Religious Education, August 6, 1943; press release, September 18, 1944, all in McNutt Papers.

22. Press release to Zionist Organizations of America, September 8, 1943; McNutt to Rabbi Elmer Berger, April 13, 1944; McNutt to Israel Goldstein, October 11, 1944; McNutt to Harry A. Goldstein, April 25, 1945, all in McNutt Papers.

23. John B. Babcock to McNutt, April 7, 1943, box 1-29, record group 211, National Archives, Washington, D.C. This retired colonel suggested to McNutt that the air force might drop huge bombs into the volcanoes dotting the Japanese home islands. The resulting explosions would sink the entire island chain. Eleanor Roosevelt to McNutt, April 12, 1945, file 943, Eleanor Roosevelt Papers; press release by McNutt, April 12, 1945, McNutt Papers.

24. See files of January 22, 1941, January 28, 1941, May 25, 1941, August 26, 1941, and September 1, 1941, and L. S. U. commencement speech, June 2, 1941, in McNutt Papers.

25. *New York Times*, March 14, 1942, p. 32; files of March 8, 1942, and April 30, 1942, McNutt Papers; *New York Times*, March 29, 1942, sec. 4, p. 5; Hershey to Secretary of War Stimson, January 12, 1942, staybacks, 1942, General Lewis Hershey Papers, Military History Research Collection, Carlisle Barracks, Pa.; digest of War Production Board minutes, March 3, 1942, Nelson Papers; Clara Beyer to Frances Perkins, March 11, 1942, A 159, folder 111, Beyer Papers, Schlesinger Library, Radcliffe College, Cambridge, Mass.; digest of WPB minutes, March 10, 1942, Nelson Papers; Murray, "Government and Labor," p. 150.

26. Diary of Harold Smith, 13, February 7, 1942, Roosevelt Library.

27. *Complete Presidential Press Conferences of Franklin D. Roosevelt*, 25 vols. in 12 books (New York: Da Capo Press, 1972), 19: 254-56 (April 3, 1942), hereafter cited as *PPC*; Smith Diary, Presidential Conference no. 13, February 7, 1942, February 14, 1942, March 4, 1942, April 16, 1942.

28. *PPC*, 19: 273-75 (April 10, 1942); William D. Hassett, *Off the Record with F.D.R.* (New Brunswick, N.J.: Rutgers University Press, 1958), pp. 36, 38; *New York Times*, April 11, 1942, p. 1.

29. Copy of Executive Order no. 9139, April 18, 1942, box 20-73, RG 211; copy of Executive Order no. 9247, September 17, 1942, *ibid.*; See also *Federal Records of World War II*, 2 vols. (Washington, D.C.: National Archives, 1950-1951), p. 525. Executive Order no. 9301 of February 9, 1943, made McNutt responsible for administering the forty-eight-hour work week and Executive Order no. 9328 of April 8, 1943, gave the WMC responsibility for a national economic stabilization program. See Riegelman, *Labour-Management Co-operation*, p. 16, note 1.

30. Riegelman, *Labour-Management Co-operation*, p. 98; minutes of War Manpower Commission, 1942, box 5-100, RG 211.

31. See especially box 1-29, RG 211 and May-June 1943 files, and July 1942, files of McNutt Papers for organizational information of the WMC. The 12 regions were as follows:

    I—Conn., Me., Mass., N.H., R.I., Vt.

    II—N.Y.

    III—Del., N.J., Pa.

    IV—D.C., Md., N.C., Va., W.V.

    V—Ky., Mich., Ohio

    VI—Ill., Ind., Wis.

    VII—Ala., Fla., Ga., Miss., S.C., Tenn.

    VIII—Iowa, Minn., Neb., N.D., S.D.

    IX—Ark., Kan., Mo., Okla.

    X—La., N.M., Tex.

    XI—Colo., Idaho, Mont., Utah, Wyo.

    XII—Ariz., Calif., Nev., Oreg., Wash.

32. Riegelman, *Labour-Management Co-operation*, pp. 29, 129, 133, 140, 147-152.

33. Minutes of press conference by McNutt, April 20, 1942, McNutt Papers; *New York Times*, April 21, 1942, p. 16.

34. Minutes of WMC, May 6 and 13, 1942, box 5-100, RG 211, National Archives.

35. Files of May 4 and 6, 1942, McNutt Papers; *Monthly Labor Review*, August 1942, pp. 223-26.

CHAPTER 2

Problems and Programs

In the early, intoxicating days of his new office McNutt expected the WMC to develop the precision and efficiency to locate in twenty minutes a bacteriologist who had researched *Endamoeba histolytica* and was fluent in Hindustani. Presumably, such an individual might be needed if American troops came down with diarrhea while on the Indian subcontinent. He soon found more pedestrian problems to occupy his time. His entire agency was underfinanced and understaffed from the beginning. The USES was supposed to be expanding its responsibility but it suffered from demoralized and underpaid workers, the latter condition no doubt contributing to the former. Where McNutt estimated a need for 150 area manpower offices, Congress budgeted for twenty-five. Even if McNutt had been a genius at streamlining and decentralizing his agency, the WMC would still have been underfinanced. With a keen sense of understatement, he wrote his father that much work remained for the regional and area organizations of the WMC.[1]

I

His first year was his hardest. The entire manpower mandate still appeared vague. Roosevelt had been skeptical of the need for a separate commission as late as April 1942. As the year progressed, military demands on the civilian population increased. Labor short-

ages developed in key segments of the economy despite the intro-
duction of a forty-eight-hour week and continuous shifts. McNutt's
agency seemed to be having little impact. Leaders in Congress became disturbed at the conflicting testimony and overlapping responsibilities of presidential agencies. As the WMC attempted to
compile adequate information on the labor situation, the Selective
Service, the War Production Board, and the military continued to
operate independently. Hershey continued to draft workers. When
reporters asked the President who had the final say over production
problems, including manpower, he replied: "I guess the answer is
that they work it out together." Roosevelt knew that the WMC,
with its limited mandate and voluntary, decentralized approach,
could not solve all manpower problems. But he remained cautious
in having the government assume too much power over something
as sacred as a man's right to a job. He kept hoping that McNutt
could make up for inadequate funding and authority with hard
work and political finesse. These hopes began to fade by the fall of
1942.[2]

Superficially, the President and McNutt continued to cooperate.
When McNutt asked for more power, Roosevelt appointed him a
member of the War Production Board and enlarged the membership of the WMC. On September 17, 1942, a new executive order
transferred all public employment offices and defense training
functions to McNutt's jurisdiction. At his press conference of
October 1, 1942, the President stated that war production "as a
whole through the country is around 94 or 95 percent of the objective." The manpower problem seemed on the verge of resolution.
Yet within a few weeks McNutt faced the possible loss of his job
and a major reshuffling of manpower administration appeared
likely.[3]

Public expressions of harmony hid scenes of a less attractive
drama which was unfolding toward the end of the year. Ironically,
the problem began with Donald Nelson rather than with McNutt.
When the director of the WPB delegated his authority to control
defense contracts to the military, he lost a major instrument for
managing the economy. In the White House a search was under
way, led by Sam Rosenman, for someone to replace Nelson and
purge his agency of rich Republicans. Secretary of the Treasury

Henry Morgenthau, a long-time confidant of Roosevelt's and one of the most suspicious men in the cabinet, agreed that Nelson had made a mess of mobilization. The problems at WPB began to infect manpower and McNutt, adding to existing difficulties.

No single authority controlled the various forces operating on the manpower variable. Nelson had no control over the military which continued, with little understanding or regard for the industrial and civilian economy, to demand men to fight. Hershey continued to supply these men through the largely autonomous local draft boards. Nelson, McNutt, Hershey, Secretary of War Stimson —each had his own assessment of the manpower scene. The editor of *Business Week* finally complained that attempts at manpower control ''have been so haphazard, so unintegrated and so irresolute that, instead of simplifying the problem, they have served to add to its seriousness and to multiply its complexities.'' According to a survey conducted by the Bureau of Public Inquiry of the Office of War Information (OWI), the general public was simply confused on manpower. Local draft boards refused to take a national view in picking men out of industry. Within the White House, presidential aide Mark McCloskey reported that McNutt appeared overwhelmed by his task. Sam Rosenman asked Oscar Cox, a New Deal lawyer now working in the Justice Department, to make a study of the manpower mess. By October 30, 1942, Cox reported back to Harry Hopkins at the White House that firmer manpower controls were needed. In Cox's opinion, the problem required an administrator trusted by the public and more cooperation from organized labor. After hearing this report, Hopkins launched a search for a replacement for McNutt, who seemed to be ''running for office.'' Paradoxically, while Hopkins agreed that part of the manpower problem was poor leadership at the WMC, he also agreed that the new head of such a powerful agency should be a nonpolitical man who enjoyed public confidence. But how could any man with such power and such responsibility remain nonpolitical? Furthermore, just adding new power to the director of the WMC would not solve the problem; a total reorganization of the agency seemed needed. With such opposition growing, McNutt's future seemed insecure. Unless he could quickly convince Roosevelt otherwise, a new manpower czar would appear.[4]

McNutt had not come as far as he had in the Democratic party without developing sensitive antennae. He knew his position was vulnerable. Despite repeated efforts he had failed to establish an effective working relationship with Congress. Congressmen were already denouncing his ruthless political ambition. Congressional committees of both houses, looking into the manpower scene, reported an absence of leadership and general confusion. McNutt proceeded to counterattack with the argument that the solution to these problems required that he have more power, not less. In private conference with Roosevelt and in public, McNutt endorsed the congressional suggestion that all manpower reins be centralized in one man. Within the WMC the MLPC drew up a plan calling for the transfer of Selective Service to McNutt, for an end to all voluntary military enlistments, and for the USES to control all hiring in war industry. In early November McNutt presented this plan to Roosevelt who seemed sympathetic.[5]

In the Department of War rumors of such a plan sent Secretary of War Stimson into apoplexy. But Goldthwaite Dorr, Stimson's manpower expert serving with the WMC, agreed with McNutt that the solution to the manpower problem was more centralization. Dorr and Undersecretary of the Navy James Forrestal recommended that Bernard Baruch be designated as the new manpower czar. Stimson had other ideas. He was totally committed to the absolute priority of military manpower requirements. The Selective Service under Hershey was already carrying out this task. In Stimson's mind any selection of manpower for civilian industry "must be a posterior process and subject to the first." Stimson refused to see the intrinsic connection between military draft calls and the capacity of war industry to provide the material of war. He and his subordinates, Undersecretary Robert Patterson and General Brehon Somervell, remained consistent in this narrow view throughout the war. Any suggestion that Hershey and Selective Service might be controlled by a civilian upset the Secretary. He refused to allow this efficient tool for military manpower to be confused with secondary obligations. Besides, muttered the seventy-five-year-old Stimson, Baruch was too old for the job.[6]

Roosevelt had to take Stimson's opposition seriously. Stimson was already a senior citizen when Roosevelt appointed him Secretary

of War in 1940. But his firm grip, square shoulders, and capacity
for work belied his age. A charter member of the Republican establishment of the Northeast, he had taken his degree at Yale, made an
international reputation as a law partner of Elihu Root, and gone
on to serve as Secretary of War under President Taft and Secretary
of State under Herbert Hoover. As a firm believer in the Teddy
Roosevelt school of physical fitness (he played deck tennis almost
every afternoon) and of big-stick diplomacy, Stimson spoke from a
position of strength within the Franklin Roosevelt administration.
The President had sought him out in 1940 to add a bipartisan tone
to American interventionism.[7]

Now Stimson began a campaign to sabotage McNutt's request
for more power. The Secretary met with Patterson, Knox, and
Forrestal to plot a united front. James Byrnes, newly appointed
Director of the Office of Economic Stabilization, encouraged the
cabal but warned that Roosevelt seemed sympathetic to McNutt's
proposal. On hearing this news Stimson became desperate. He even
accepted the idea of Baruch replacing McNutt. As the President left
a cabinet meeting on October 22, 1942, the Secretary grabbed him
and pleaded for an opportunity to be heard in defense of an independent Selective Service. Following his usual custom, Roosevelt
appeared conciliatory. For the next few days Stimson worked
feverishly on a memorandum to Roosevelt justifying an independent
Selective Service. In his memo Stimson admitted the logic of having
both military and civilian manpower under the same overall supervision, but he feared that under McNutt the local draft boards
would lose their autonomy. Although some critics might argue that
such autonomy was the cause of manpower problems, Stimson disagreed. The local boards had built up a reputation for integrity;
that reputation would be lost if they were forced to enter the arena
of civilian labor needs. After sending his memo to Roosevelt, Stimson worried privately about McNutt who "is ambitious and pushing and has been apparently entrenching himself . . . with the President.'' Such reflections suggest that Stimson's main concern was
less with the autonomy of Selective Service than with the man who
would be given control. In his memorandum to Roosevelt, Stimson stressed the importance of preserving the purity of Selective
Service. He refused to admit that his main fear was that McNutt
would shift priorities from the military to the war plants.[8]

Whatever his motives, Stimson remained a powerful opponent to McNutt's plan. Roosevelt could hardly ignore his own Secretary of War. Stimson, unlike others in the administration, was his own man, a Republican leader who had entered the cabinet on his own terms. Privately, the President reassured Stimson that military manpower needs would naturally have priority in any reform scheme. To newspaper reporters, Roosevelt tried to explain the complexities of staffing an army and simultaneously mobilizing a sophisticated economy. At a November 6 press conference he assumed a favorite professorial pose to lecture the reporters gathered around his desk. Solving the manpower problem, he explained, required much time and study. Besides, with the exception of dairy workers and a few other small businesses, "I don't know of any factory that is shut down because of lack of labor today." He had been studying the problem for months, but he admitted that he did not have an answer to the conflicting claims of industry and the military for manpower; however, he knew that the draft boards had to cooperate to insure proper industrial replacements. In sum, the President appeared indecisive on the future of McNutt's plan. He had recommendations from both McNutt and Stimson, but he had yet to make a decision. Whichever way he moved, he was bound to offend someone.[9]

McNutt and Stimson had made their positions clear. Now Roosevelt heard from other important sources. Congress wanted a change in the manpower program but insisted that civilian control be maintained. At the same time Bernard Baruch, whom Forrestal and Dorr were now pushing as a replacement for McNutt, wrote Roosevelt that no new laws were needed to clear up manpower, just new leadership. This sounded suspiciously like self-advertisement for the job, but Baruch had few new ideas. The Daddy Warbucks of the Democratic party called for a continuation of the voluntary approach, favored putting Selective Service under the WMC, and wanted an end to voluntary enlistments. The only disagreement between Baruch and McNutt was over who should head up the strengthened WMC. By late November the idea of dropping McNutt had been endorsed by Hopkins, Stimson, Baruch, and several others. Roosevelt had to consider this alternative. McNutt, learning of the danger, rushed to the White House. The President was too busy to see him but sent out a note that no war plant should slow down for

lack of workers, that military manpower needs remained paramount, that young men would have to be drafted, and that women
must play a greater role in war plants. McNutt should have suspected
Stimson of drafting this note, so closely did it follow War Department thinking.[10]

II

Roosevelt now calculated the advantages of dropping McNutt
and perhaps giving the Department of Labor overall responsibility
for manpower mobilization. Presidential advisors agreed that there
was too much overlapping of responsibility in manpower. If the
Department of Labor received the job it would provide an excuse
for dropping McNutt. The President thought of shifting McNutt to
the Department of the Interior and giving the manpower mobilization job to Harold Ickes. Incorruptible Harold had been master at
Interior since 1933. An ex-Republican and committed liberal, he
was capable of inspired idealism, as in his advocacy of the cause of
the American Negro, and petty jealousy, as in his constant suspicions
that others in the administration were poisoning the President
against him. Soon Baruch, Forrestal, and Knox began supporting
Ickes for the job. By late November the press was printing stories
of an impending shift of Ickes to head the Department of Labor
augmented with responsibility for manpower mobilization. On
Thanksgiving Day of 1942, Roosevelt tried to recruit Ickes. The
President explained that manpower should go back under the Department of Labor. Frances Perkins, however, wanted to retire.
The President hoped to shift her to head the Federal Security Agency,
put manpower under Labor with Ickes as Secretary, and give McNutt
the job at Interior.

Ickes balked. He had already been told by Abe Fortas what Roosevelt had in mind. But Ickes had no desire to accept what he knew
was a thankless, man-killing job. He was sixty-nine; his wife was in
her twenties. After building up an outstanding reputation at Interior,
he and his wife both feared that he might end his career by falling
victim to the manpower morass. As he manufactured excuses to
avoid the manpower task Ickes focused on the danger of allowing
McNutt to gain control of Interior. Ickes told Roosevelt that McNutt

had a selfish, political attitude toward government service. He would ruin the fine department Ickes had slaved over since 1933. Privately, Ickes admitted to Attorney General Francis Biddle, Ben Cohen, Thomas Corcoran, and Abe Fortas that his main objection to the job was his fear of an inevitable fight with the military over manpower. Echoing McNutt, Ickes argued that any man who hoped to control manpower, had to control the draft. But Hershey had recently admitted to Congress that no one controlled the draft. Local draft boards could ignore 99 percent of the directives from Washington. Ickes thought the problem beyond solution and campaigned to stay at Interior by asking his friends in the oil industry to write the White House, insisting that he was indispensable. Another friend, Irving Brant of the *Chicago Sun*, wrote Roosevelt that "if something has to be done for Paul [McNutt], why not make him Archbishop of Canterbury." Despite his reluctance, Byrnes, Morgenthau, and Baruch continued to urge Ickes to take the new job. Never one to underestimate his own importance, he began to weaken before the blandishments. If McNutt could be kept out of Interior, if the manpower czar would control Selective Service, if he did not have to run the Labor Department, Ickes conceded he would make the sacrifice demanded.[11]

Approaching the White House on December 1, 1942, Ickes felt noble. If Roosevelt insisted, he would take over manpower mobilization and the Department of Labor, but he would insist upon running both jobs from his present position as Secretary of Interior. In his magnanimity, Ickes envisioned an aggrandizement of power which would have created more havoc for Roosevelt's mobilization organization. The Secretary was deflated, however, when Roosevelt seemed in no hurry to make such an appointment. By the end of the interview Ickes realized that the President had changed his mind.

Ickes's anguish seemed wasted. Roosevelt explained that the public-power people, conservationists, and others had all opposed McNutt's appointment to Interior. Roosevelt agreed that Ickes should stay at Interior. Many oil leaders had insisted upon his remaining. As for running manpower from Interior, the President explained that several labor leaders had objected to such an arrangement. Reversing roles, Ickes now sought the job but Roosevelt had changed his mind. Ickes departed furious, convinced that

the Iago who had done him in was none other than Harry Hopkins.
Ickes always had paranoid feelings toward Hopkins, but in this
case, his mood was totally unjustified. Not Hopkins but Harold
Smith, the Director of the Budget, was responsible for saving McNutt
and also pushing through a reorganization of WMC. Anna Rosenberg, a close personal friend of Roosevelt's, also contributed to
McNutt's rescue, but Smith's role was decisive.[12]

Smith had felt partially responsible for the manpower mess because his office had drawn up the original executive order creating
the WMC. In November, he went to see McNutt and afterward
wrote a lengthy memo to Roosevelt. Smith called his talk with
McNutt the "frankest conversation I have ever had with any man
in my entire career in the public service." Smith began by telling
McNutt that he seemed to be running for president instead of running manpower. McNutt, increasingly insecure, felt Smith's accusations unfair. By the end of the conversation McNutt had won
Smith over. Admittedly, McNutt had his faults, Smith told Roosevelt, but he was honest and "thoroughly loyal to you." McNutt
knew when he took the job that it would mean political suicide because it involved the regimentation of Americans. But he had been
loyal. Despite the external bluster that irritated cabinet members,
Smith believed McNutt was really shy and insecure: "His manner
covers up something of an inferiority complex." Overall, Smith
concluded that while McNutt had fumbled the ball, it was not his
fault. He and the WMC "are dealing, in many of these areas, with
delicate human material and terrifically intricate problems, such as
have never faced this country before." Smith argued with Roosevelt that McNutt should be kept on, that the policies of the WMC
were "not far off the beam," that the administrative personnel of
WMC were weak but could be improved, and that McNutt needed
operational as well as advisory power over manpower.[13]

On the morning of December 4, 1943, the President met with
Smith and Sam Rosenman in the Oval Office. After a few minutes
the President turned to the manpower problem and announced that
the Budget Director's memo on the subject was "the best he had
received during his whole administration." Roosevelt had used
Smith's memo to convince Hopkins and Byrnes that McNutt should
remain in charge of manpower. Rosenman and Smith now urged

Roosevelt to give McNutt control of Selective Service. Roosevelt agreed to back McNutt despite Stimson's objections. Privately, Rosenman still had doubts about McNutt but on this occasion he supported Smith. McNutt won a temporary reprieve.[14]

The same afternoon, at the weekly cabinet meeting, McNutt learned of his rescue. As Ickes entered the White House, still irritated over his recent rebuff, he noticed McNutt leaving the President's office looking "as happy as a bride." Roosevelt opened the cabinet meeting and saw that Patterson was substituting for Stimson. The President announced that he had accepted the WMC plan for reorganizing manpower responsibility, and could not resist adding that he was sure the decision would be a disappointment to Stimson. Roosevelt also requested that Dorr be replaced on the WMC because he was too long-winded. Stimson was disappointed at the support for McNutt's plan, but he was furious at Roosevelt's overall behavior which implied a personal feud between the Secretary of War and the Director of Manpower. Stimson had convinced himself that his opposition rested on principles about the integrity of Selective Service. Now McNutt had new power which would require even more cooperation from the military and he was being told that Stimson hated him. Altogether it seemed a rather doleful beginning for the new manpower plan.[15]

Executive Order no. 9279, drafted by Smith and signed by Roosevelt on December 5, 1942, gave McNutt unprecedented power. The Selective Service System, and all functions, powers, and personnel (including the director) and all money were transferred to the WMC, to be supervised by the chairman. The functions, powers, and duties of the Director of Selective Service were transferred to McNutt. The Secretary of War and the Secretary of the Navy had to consult with McNutt before determining the number of men required by the military each month. In addition to these major points, the executive order also provided for an expanded membership of the WMC, for the creation of a reorganized Management-Labor Policy Committee, and for an end to induction of males eighteen to thirty-eight into the service by volunteering. All in all, McNutt could not have asked for more power.[16]

The editor of *Business Week* sensed the new situation by editorializing that Executive Order no. 9279 "may be considered this country's national service act." Roosevelt, in fact, saw the order as a substitute for national service. The order solved several problems. Public opinion was dissatisfied with the manpower program. More importantly, Congress was also dissatisfied. When Senators Harry Truman, Claude Pepper, Harley M. Kilgore, and James E. Murray and Congressman John H. Tolan had visited the White House in November 1942, they had pointed to several congressional reports on labor migration which demonstrated a need for reorganization in manpower mobilization. Military leaders had endorsed a national service act, or labor draft, as the answer. But these congressmen had no desire to take such a drastic step. They wanted to retain a voluntary program, but they also wanted more centralization. McNutt's total commitment to a voluntary program helped to offset charges of his political ambition. Roosevelt sought to bridge the gap between the congressional and military recommendations by retaining McNutt and voluntarism, but adding more power to WMC to control the many-faceted manpower problem.[17]

As McNutt assumed his new responsibilities he confronted several difficulties. The military, in the persons of Stimson, Patterson, Forrestal, and Knox, had little confidence in McNutt's ability. These men were unreconciled to giving a civilian any control over the determination of military manpower needs. But without some control McNutt would be unable to master his problem. Stimson, however, refused to budge and blew his top over the President's presumption to dictate who in the War Department should serve on the WMC. Dorr did leave the WMC, but Patterson replaced him. The question of McNutt's being able to work with the military remained open. He also had to deal with Hershey who had been filling military manpower requests with little coordination from the WMC. McNutt was now in charge of the SSS, but that agency had been established with congressional support in contrast to the mere presidential authority of McNutt's. At the local level McNutt now had the power to force hiring through the USES. But it remained an open question whether his authority superseded the statutory power of the SSS.[18]

Shortly after Roosevelt signed the new order, reporters clambered into WMC headquarters to hear the views of the man who had just "been given more power over the lives and happiness of Americans than any man ever has exercised before," as one reporter wrote. Those who came expecting to see a budding dictator were disappointed. McNutt appeared immaculately dressed and spoke at his desk below a huge oil painting of himself, but his tone was modest. When asked how he would force hiring through the USES he mentioned using the WPB to manipulate war contracts. Most of all he stressed the importance of voluntary cooperation. Women should cooperate by joining the work force. Management and labor should cooperate by promoting better utilization. The military should cooperate by ending volunteer enlistments. Congress should cooperate by allocating enough money to staff the USES so that it could perform its new task. McNutt had a clear view of his task, ambitious as it might be. His success would depend on many factors, but at least he did not underestimate what was needed. A few weeks later Harold Smith reported to Roosevelt that the WMC was now "off dead center and is on the way to getting things done." Perhaps manpower mobilization might still be the vehicle to carry this attractive Hoosier to 1600 Pennsylvania Avenue.[19]

III

This optimism did not stop the generals and admirals from complaining. In their view, the United States refused to mobilize its manpower for total war. Whenever a shortage developed in military units or war plants, no matter how temporary or what the cause, it seemed to these men that McNutt and the WMC were inefficient and inadequate. Contemporary and later criticism reflected a misunderstanding of America's concept of total war and of the obstacles of manpower mobilization.[20]

McNutt was no Hamilton. The Hoosier preferred Thomas Jefferson as a guide to troubled times. Manpower mobilization would be guided by the principles of localism and voluntarism as they seemed best suited to the nature of the problem. The American economy consisted of a variety of local and regional economies rather than a seamless national fabric. The manpower problem was not a national problem but rather a network of thousands of local problems. Across the country, throughout the forty-eight states, the relative degrees of industrialization and unionization presented to the eye the chaos of a Jackson Pollock canvas rather than the order of Andrew Wyeth. One national agency directed manpower mobilization, but down in the states, below Olympus, local power remained impervious to change and immune to challenge. The WMC had to accommodate itself to the reality of local politics in the same way relief agencies during the 1930s had to compromise their idealism to fit regional prejudices.[21]

On the national level few things frightened Congress more than the hint that President Roosevelt might use a war agency, directed by a New Dealer such as McNutt, to promote social reform. This lack of congressional sympathy, to put it mildly, explains a recurring problem for McNutt and his agency—questionable legitimacy. During the war the WMC adopted a variety of sanctions to master the manpower conundrum. The effectiveness of these measures always suffered from the constant drag of illegitimacy. Created by executive order, the WMC operated without the special dispensation associated with statutory action. McNutt lacked the statutory power to force either employer or employee to follow the regulations of the WMC. Indirect sanctions at his disposal, such as the threat of being drafted or the withdrawal of a war contract, worked only if other agencies cooperated. This cooperation by the SSS and the WPB remained unreliable during the war years. As late as December 1944 James Byrnes and the Justice Department argued over the legality of the WPB using its power to enforce WMC regulations. Several sanctions adopted by the WMC prevented an individual from seeking a new job, a restriction which appeared in conflict with constitutional rights. As one corporation lawyer expressed it: "Any rule or regulation by the WMC which, in effect, abrogates or seeks to supersede our local civil service rules is an unconstitutional exercise of power never granted to that Commission by the express language or by clear implication under the Federal constitution."[22]

Despite these difficulties McNutt still achieved a high degree of compliance with WMC rules. Such compliance reflected the willingness of most men to accept authority legitimized by the President during a military crisis. But success was also achieved because McNutt followed the path of decentralization by allowing each community much autonomy in adjusting to the details of a national directive. When faced with a stubborn employer, however, McNutt had limited leverage to enforce obedience. His sanctions were more theoretical than real. To obtain cooperation from the WPB, for example, McNutt had to provide evidence not merely that the employer refused to cooperate but that this refusal was leading to malutilization of material in war production. No wonder McNutt always believed that persuasion remained the best weapon in his arsenal.[23]

Within these constitutional and political parameters McNutt and the WMC went about the task of mobilizing American manpower. Without question the problem McNutt heard about most during the war was the overall shortage of manpower. Most of the difficulties which developed related either directly or indirectly to the simple fact that the American economy had been forced by the war to make a 180-degree turn—from the unemployment and low productivity of the 1930s to the full employment and high productivity of the war years. To say that this shift produced a labor shortage, however, is to say little, because the term was and is a relative one. One man's shortage may be another's surplus, if the second man has better labor utilization. Statements about a labor shortage during the war must always be qualified by the startling fact that from 1940 to 1945 the American economy produced 296,429 warplanes, 372,431 pieces of artillery, 2,455,964 trucks, 87,620 warships, and 20,086,061 small arms, while simultaneously maintaining the highest standard of civilian living in the world. American labor, notwithstanding complaints of shortages, did the job. Such retrospective conclusions, however, fail to explain why Americans in the street and in the corridors of Washington from 1941 to 1945 constantly complained that manpower shortages represented a serious problem in the war economy.[24] Whatever the overall production record of American labor and the difficulty of defining precisely the concept of labor shortage, the issue continued to cause problems during the war years.

IV

Paul McNutt was optimistic about the labor supply during the months before Pearl Harbor. In March 1941 he testified before a House committee investigating labor migration and in confident tones described a bright labor picture. Promising statistics emerged when he analyzed the various regions where defense contracts were concentrated. In the Northeast, defense employment had reached 2,355,000 but the labor supply stood at 3,074,000. In the Great Lakes states defense employment was 770,000 but the labor supply was 2,688,000. In the South and Southwest defense employment stood at 985,000 but 2,560,000 workers were available. Even in the Pacific and mountain regions, where war plants burgeoned, employment had reached 890,000 but the labor supply was 907,000. Regional labor surplus figures were encouraging only if there was some correlation between where the military and the WPB issued contracts and where the surplus labor existed. Although this elementary fact was recognized early, at no time during the war could McNutt force the procurement agencies into synchronization with the reality of manpower. Few contracts went to areas merely because they had a labor surplus.[25]

Bulk numbers of available labor and available defense jobs told only part of the story. An inhibiting influence upon matching labor surplus with war jobs included the character of the labor needed, whether it was skilled or unskilled. By May 1941 McNutt announced that despite the registration of 364,000 workers at local employment agencies a shortage of certain skills had already developed. Of the several thousand occupational skills listed by the USES approximately one-half had a total of no more than one hundred individuals registered. In the aircraft industry and in shipbuilding, two critical defense areas, managers began complaining of a shortage of skilled labor. They complained in vain because at this early date the Roosevelt administration had yet to coordinate manpower mobilization. McNutt spoke out as the head of the Federal Security Agency. In August 1941 he reminded the public that a minimum of 487,400 more workers would be needed in two months, especially in shipbuilding. In September he called for 250,000 workers for 9,900 vital defense plants. Six weeks before Pearl Harbor he pleaded for proper utilization and for employers to release voluntarily their skilled workers for jobs in defense industry.[26]

Defense contracts had been affecting the American economy since 1940, but the transition of labor from peacetime to war standing had proceeded only gradually. First, the economy swallowed up the unemployed of the depression. By December 1941 the United

States labor force totaled some 53,300,000 persons, a figure which made officials optimistic about the future. Once the unemployed had been absorbed into the expanding economy, such officials thought, additional personnel could easily be recruited because of the patriotic fever raised by the sneak attack on Pearl Harbor. Less sanguine individuals worried that these new, patriotic workers might lack needed skills. The depression had done more than throw people out of work; it had also dried up apprenticeship programs. Skills had rusted into obsolescence. Now, with economic expansion, the price of skilled labor began to rise. The combined manufacturing industries had an hourly earning rate in November 1939 of 65.3 cents an hour. By November 1941 the rate had jumped to 78.1 cents. Despite this rise in wage rate, skilled labor became hard to find in certain localities. Aircraft plants in Akron, Ohio, could not recruit skilled workers. Baltimore shipyards faced the same dilemma. In Maryland and in Texas employers compounded their problem by refusing to use women and blacks. In Allentown, Pennsylvania, personnel officers turned away women and elderly workers despite shortages. Mobilization had not yet reached the stage where it threatened to upset existing prejudices. It never would.[27]

Roosevelt created the WMC in 1942 to obtain a clearer picture of national manpower needs. For the first time officials began a systematic search for data. The results were discouraging. McNutt reported in June that serious shortages already existed in shipbuilding and in the aircraft industry. Of the 160 important labor markets in the nation identified by the WMC, shortages existed in thirty-five and were soon predicted for another eighty-one. Officials confronted a maddening lack of uniformity from one region to another. Baltimore and Buffalo had severe shortages but thousands of unemployed roamed the sidewalks of New York. By December McNutt had established a classification system to illustrate the diversity of the national labor picture. Group 1 consisted of areas with the greatest labor shortage. In it were found most of the major industrial centers of the nation: Hartford and Bridgeport, Connecticut; Portland, Maine; Springfield, Massachusetts; Buffalo, Harrisburg, Baltimore, Detroit, Flint, Cleveland, Dayton, Mobile, Houston, Beaumont, Los Angeles, San Francisco, San Diego, Seattle, Spokane. The list went on and on.[28]

A dismal scene, but McNutt insisted that manpower shortages

had not, even at the end of 1942, caused any lag in war production. As he looked to the future, however, he realized that the honeymoon was over. The labor force had expanded by nine million since June 1940 but six million of these workers had come from the ranks of the unemployed, ranks now exhausted. The new production program announced by the President in January 1942 and expanded in May would require an expansion of the work force to sixty-five million in 1943. An additional 5.5 million workers had to enter the labor force. To make the scene more dismal, the military required additional manpower. War contractors could expect to lose as many men to the draft in 1943 as they had lost during the entire preceding period of mobilization. Local USES offices reported difficulty in supplying industrial needs. Some 50 percent of the labor request by employers was not being met. By April 1943 Fowler Harper of WMC reported plans to shift three million workers from civilian to war industry and to add two million new women workers. Even if these plans worked the nation would face a deficit of three million workers by the end of the year. War plants were falling behind schedule.[29]

McNutt floundered around in search of a solution. At a meeting of the War Production Board on April 13, 1943, he admitted that some 3,600,000 more men and women had to be found before July 1944. The army alone expected to add one million new men and women to the enlisted ranks before this date.[30] By August 1943 Roosevelt had approved a new plan calling for the addition of four million to both industry and the military before July 1944. Already one-half of the entire population of 135,000,000 was either in uniform or in industry. Yet 50 percent of the jobs in aircraft assembly and two-thirds of all shipyard jobs needed workers. Some fifty-five areas in the nation suffered from extreme labor shortages. McNutt made the point clear in a nationwide radio address of August 25: "In Seattle last month more flying fortresses were lost than were lost over Hamburg because schedules were not met."[31]

Fortunately, by December 1943, the change in the tide of the war led to a definite slackening of contracts. The pressure on manpower was relieved. Problems continued in 1944 but the overall situation seemed stabilized, despite chronic difficulties in such cities as Chicago and Detroit. In Chicago, McNutt bluntly condemned business and executives for allowing labor pirating, discrimination against blacks and women, and underutilization of labor. These local obstructions aside, McNutt appeared optimistic when reporting to the delegates of the American Federation of Labor in New York City in April 1944. He announced that labor shortages now caused fewer problems in war production than "at any time during the past twelve months." Shortages continued in such support activities as railroads, lumber, coal, and cotton duck, but overall war plant production was on or ahead of schedule.[32]

Military events soon shattered McNutt's optimism. On June 6, 1944, as clouds gathered above the English Channel, General Dwight David Eisenhower launched the massive Allied invasion of continental Europe. This final offensive against Germany had several important implications for the labor scene in the United States. Offensive warfare meant a more rapid use of equipment and ammunition. American military men preferred the expenditure of ammunition to the expenditure of lives. Suddenly the supply requirements rose dramatically. Yet at precisely the same time a peace fever began to infect the home front. After waiting so long for the invasion, Americans viewed the successful landing and General George Patton's dramatic spearhead as a guarantee that the war would soon be over. If the war was about to end American workers needed to find more secure jobs than building tanks and bombs. Although labor supply remained adequate overall, local shortages in foundries and forge shops, in rubber and tire production, in logging and lumbering, and in ship repair caused apprehension among government planners.[33]

Between 1940 and August 1944 the nation's civilian employment and military strength had increased by sixteen million— an impressive figure. But in the fall of 1944, McNutt announced that another labor shortage crisis was at hand. Approximately 200,000 to 300,000 workers had to be found for jobs in the production of heavy artillery, heavy ammunition, ship repair, trucks, tires, radio and radar, textiles, lumber and pulpwood, cotton duck, and aircraft. When McNutt conducted a spot check of his twelve regions he found that acute male labor shortages existed in New England, the North Atlantic region, the Midwest, and the Pacific Coast. He blamed the new shortages on the offensive campaign Eisenhower was waging in Europe. Just as important, but less noticeable, was the influence of normal withdrawal from the work force of temporary summer employees. Some one million students and teachers left industrial jobs in September. By November Lt. General Brehon B. Somervell of the Army Service Forces, a forceful individual who seemed to think that most civilians were fools not to be suffered gladly, announced to the AFL that "at this very hour, production of arms and equipment needed by our troops is lagging on 40 percent of the program."[34]

After three years of war and two years of manpower mobilization American leaders continued to complain about labor shortages. McNutt quickly challenged Somervell's implication that the Allied advance against the Germans was being held up by lack of material. McNutt could not be blamed for his irritation. The decline in employment in munitions industries of 10 percent from November 1943 to September 1944 had been due to initial cutbacks in government contracts and to increased output per worker. Shortages were emerging because of the rapid shifts in requirements by an army on the offensive. In the twelve months preceding September 1944, the total labor force, including the military, had expanded by a half million more than originally planned. These figures had produced McNutt's optimism. Now he was being painted a fool by military critics. Somervell testified before a Senate committee that the nation needed national service. General Eisenhower joined the onslaught by shipping back to the United States a delegation of six beribboned GIs as an "ammunition envoy corps" to visit plants and promote war work. The general now wanted 500 shells for every fifty he had before the invasion. The soldiers, however, admitted to the press that there was no shortage of shells.[35]

When the Allied army suffered a temporary reversal in December 1944 everyone began demanding more manpower for military and production requirements. The military now sought 900,000 more soldiers in the first six months of 1945. New defense contracts were issued requiring an additional 700,000 war workers during the same period. McNutt and Charles Hay of the WMC were optimistic about meeting these demands. The military was releasing 400,000 men during this same period but in most cases they ended up in the wrong area or with the wrong skill. Declining munition production in certain areas created another 200,000 surplus and the natural growth of the labor force insured 500,000. But this still left McNutt projecting a cumulative deficit of 500,000 for both military and industrial needs in the first six months of 1945.[36]

The problem of labor shortages endured throughout the war. By late March 1945 McNutt reported that civilian labor shortages amounted to 350,000. When Germany surrendered in May, McNutt announced that employment had to be expanded by 450,000 workers to meet new procurement programs. In the meantime, almost incidentally, while McNutt continued to be criticized for shortages, the United States had won the war by mobilizing enough of its human resources to fight a two-front war, supply its allies, and maintain a comfortable standard of living at home. This achievement, however, was condemned as a failure as late as May 1945.[37]

V

McNutt failed to solve the shortage problem because it consisted of difficulties that went beyond mere numbers, difficulties which struck at the very root of the American system. Before the United States went to war employers recognized that mobilization would mean a shortage of skilled labor. Managers took steps to make sure that their plants would not suffer. An easy means of insuring a proper supply of labor was to pirate workers from other firms by offering higher pay. Once the labor had been found, a plant would then seek to hoard it in anticipation of expanded production. The 1941 labor scene resembled a free-for-all. Employers scouted out skilled workers throughout the country with a resourcefulness that would later characterize college football recruitment. Personnel agents took to the road. Newspaper ads appeared. Confusion followed. In 1942 a West Coast plane manufacturer sent scouts to Michigan to hire skilled men from another plant producing parts for the same plane. Production lines stalled at both sites. Again, an Illinois cartridge company sent scouts to recruit workers outside the state, only to learn when the labor arrived that local housing was inadequate. A Gulf Coast shipbuilding company reported in July 1942 that of the 1,725 workers it recruited in the last two months some 600 had already been stolen by other companies.

Labor hoarding followed labor pirating. A joint navy, WMC, and WPB study of shipbuilding in the state of Washington in 1943 determined that the shipyards could release from 15,000 to 18,000 men without hurting production. This surplus of labor existed next to the Boeing Aircraft Company which was desperate for labor. General Frank J. McSherry of McNutt's staff wrote letter after letter protesting pirating and hoarding. Employers boasted of throwing his letter away.[38]

McNutt struggled desperately to cure these ills. In May 1942 he warned that piracy could lead to demands for a national service act and a freeze of labor in certain plants. A labor freeze would mean that all hiring had to be done through the USES. Several months later he warned that pirated workers would be reclassified by the Selective Service and drafted. In October the National War Labor Board tried to aid McNutt by prohibiting "an employer from hiring an individual at a rate higher than the one previously established in his plant for workers of similar skill and productive ability." The problem remained unresolved and McNutt continued to threaten and to cajole throughout 1943. On April 8, 1943, President Roosevelt issued Executive Order no. 9238 which froze wages and prices. In the order he authorized McNutt to forbid the "employment by an employer of any new employee or the acceptance of employment by a new employee except as authorized in accordance with regulations which may be issued by the Chairman of the WMC. . . ." Roosevelt piled executive order on top of executive order but pirating continued. War Manpower Commission regulations went ignored and McNutt had no desire to resort to the courts. In August 1943 Governor S. L. Holland of Florida complained to McNutt that Campbell Soup of New Jersey had just stolen 438 Florida laborers.[39]

The problems of absenteeism and turnover also plagued McNutt throughout the war. National statistics on both problems were suspect but in November 1943 the Bureau of Labor Statistics conducted a study which concluded that the quit-rate among war-plant employees had reached a level where the plants had to hire seventeen workers to obtain a net increase of three for every 100 employed. Women quit more often than men. Workers sought new jobs primarily to obtain higher pay.[40]

Absenteeism also generated considerable concern among national officials. In December 1942 the President told reporters that absenteeism was a local problem and he had heard no widespread complaints. In fact, Roosevelt knew very little of the problem because statistics were unavailable. The Bureau of Labor Statistics simply guessed that shortages of material were more important than absenteeism. Secretary of Labor Perkins reassured the cabinet that absenteeism rates were within normal bounds.[41]

Public opinion began to focus on absenteeism because of well-publicized union strikes. Captain Eddie Rickenbacker, a war hero after his raid on Tokyo and a labor-baiter of long standing, expressed the feelings of superpatriots by telling his Los Angeles audience that "there is no absenteeism in the fox-holes of the jungles of the Pacific or the burning sands of Africa, for if attempted there, they would get a bayonet in their bellies from their fellow Americans." As the public outcry increased, Congress began to take up the problem. Senator Harry Truman of Missouri called absenteeism as bad as desertion in the face of the enemy. Soon presidential advisor Sam Rosenman wrote Roosevelt that the issue had become a serious source of discontent among congressmen. Rosenman suggested a special ad hoc executive committee to investigate and take the play away from Capitol Hill. A problem which had lacked urgency in December 1942 had become a hot issue by February 1943.[42]

Undoubtedly, absenteeism began simultaneously with the first job. The problem arose partially from human nature rather than from unions or war. McNutt told a Chamber of Commerce meeting that absenteeism "has its roots in sheer laziness." If such were the case, he had little hope of correcting the evil. But other observers were less fatalistic. The Department of Labor began a study which uncovered other causes. A study of more than 200 war plants disclosed that personal illness accounted for between half and three-fourths of all absences. General Knudsen studied twenty-nine plants and reported that absenteeism occurred in proportion to the amount of overtime pay of the worker. McNutt later admitted that housing shortages, poor transportation, and inadequate community services also contributed to the problem. Women, new employees, and older workers stayed out most often.[43]

As different people had different answers to why absenteeism occurred, so disagreement arose over suggested remedies. Suggestions ranged from improved counseling to Rickenbacker's bayonet.

In Louisville, Kentucky, one plant adopted the policy of sending unsigned checks to chronic absentees. When asked by the worker to explain the nonnegotiable check, the company replied that the paymaster had been absent that day. Other plants requested the help of combat veterans who toured work areas in uniform. A Detroit plant making airplane starters purchased shoes for its workers and provided a Turkish bath complete with masseur. Efficient workers earned a paid vacation in Florida. John M. Baker, regional director for WMC, recommended beer and pretzels for good workers. At the other extreme, War Department officials such as Robert Patterson urged that absentees be drafted. Officials of the Picatinny Arsenal in New Jersey visited the homes of 200 absent workers and fired on the spot those without an excuse.[44]

Congress sympathized with the more severe approach. In February 1943 Congressman Lyndon Baines Johnson of Texas won the support of his colleagues on the House Naval Affairs Committee for a naval appropriation rider which would require all shipyards to turn over the names of absentees to local draft boards every three months. Congressmen themselves enjoyed a draft deferment, but Johnson insisted the rider was essential because "absenteeism sank forty-two liberty ships in December alone." Secretary of the Navy Frank Knox and Undersecretary of War Patterson rushed to testify in favor of the bill. In contrast, Secretary of Labor Perkins denounced the entire idea. She testified that the law attacked symptoms rather than causes. According to her studies 90 percent of all absences reported were due to illness and accidents. McNutt and the WMC agreed that Johnson misunderstood the problem. Both McNutt and Lawrence Appley felt the bill represented an unfair attack against unions. Appley, McNutt, and Perkins agreed that voluntary action by management and labor, rather than legislation, would cure absenteeism.[45]

In August 1944 the WMC presented a six-point program to guide employers. In addition to vacations and bonuses the program called for making available at the war plant such services as groceries, laundries, banking, and automobile repairs. Congress remained unconvinced, but was finally dissuaded from acting by Madame Perkins. She insisted that Congress first appropriate $337,000 for a scientific study of the problem of absenteeism. Few congressmen wanted to provide such a sum, especially for the hands of a New Dealer such as Perkins.[46]

VI

Even if McNutt cured absenteeism, reduced accidents, ended piracy, and filled shortages, he still faced the dilemma of under-utilization of labor. As he never tired of repeating, finding a man for a job was not enough. One had to find the right man for the right job at the right time. For McNutt the effective utilization of labor was "the most important single factor in the whole war effort." In addition to improving efficiency, a study of utilization would also help plant managers compose more sensible requests for oc-cupational deferments. From the beginning of mobilization both the WMC and the Selective Service had a stake in promoting pro-per utilization.[47]

On June 3, 1942, the WMC approved a plan to use manning tables as a means of insuring correct utilization in war plants. These tables amounted to a description of the ideal labor needs of the plant. They listed all jobs by department and described the number and skills of personnel needed to fill such jobs. The listing added up to an analysis of efficiency. Once a plant determined what jobs were most important it could make provisions to protect key work-ers from the draft. Prior to the manning table concept the Selective Service had asked employers to provide a replacement schedule to guide local boards, listing the employees in the order the company would prefer to have them drafted. Although the two approaches had different primary missions—the manning table sought efficient utilization while replacement schedules focused on the draft priority of individuals—they did share many characteristics. Presumably, if the employer used efficiency as his guide on the replacement sched-ule it would reflect the same priorities as the manning table. The manning table, however, reflected an internal estimate of the entire plant conducted by utilization experts of the WMC. McNutt found that employers tended to idealize their tables, calling for inflated labor needs. The replacement schedule, which gave the employer control over the draft date of his workers, reflected management's attitude without any outside review.[48]

Not surprisingly, McNutt believed that the manning table should be used by the Selective Service in determining draft status. General Hershey agreed that the manning table was essential in preventing the draft of vital men while simultaneously providing an inventory of new manpower needs. Hershey sent such manning tables to local boards for their information. But when McNutt moved in the fall of 1942 to have manning tables adopted for the purposes of recruiting labor and determining occupational deferments, he ran into opposition from the War Department. The department urged Hershey, who had no serious objection to using the manning tables, to assert his independence from McNutt by maintaining the re-placement schedules. Both Goldthwaite Dorr and Robert Patterson of the War Department disliked McNutt's attempt to dominate the area of labor utilization. These men feared that the WMC would enter particular plants and infringe upon the responsibilities of War Department procurement agents. McNutt, in response, argued that his presidential mandate required a concern with utilization.[49]

The scene was set for the first of many conflicts between McNutt and the military. The War Department always considered the WMC merely a giant filling station. Employers drove up and ordered so many men which the WMC sought to supply. How these men were to be used, insisted the military, should be left to private inter-ests. At a meeting of the WMC on December 2, 1942, Hershey insisted that manning tables should be voluntary for war plants. He found that employers accepted the replacement schedule but resented manning tables as an attempt to control plant utilization. McNutt and Harper, however, contended that the short-term replacement schedule was not subject to evaluation by utilization experts. Al-though Hershey had no responsibility for promoting utilization, McNutt did. Dorr, in defense of Hershey, responded that all war agencies shared responsibility for promoting good labor utilization. But the WMC was the main action agency, insisted McNutt. He invited Patterson to help with the manning studies. But Patterson, despite the advice of General Hap Arnold and Howard Petersen, rejected the invitation because the War Department had two "con-tradictory interests in manpower." The War Department wanted the efficient production of war material but it also wanted to draft workers. Patterson did not think the department, "through endorsing specific manning tables, [should] lose its freedom of action to criticize Selective Service or the WMC on matters affecting either one of these interests.'' The military would have its cake and eat it too.[50]

Despite Patterson's position, McNutt and Hershey managed to work out a compromise. Employers would be responsible for filing a manning report if they wished to continue to enjoy occupational deferments. General Frank McSherry would oversee compliance, an appointment designed to reassure the War Department. Not everyone was happy, but Dorr thought it was workable. Secretary of Labor Perkins, in contrast, saw the entire manning-table program as another encroachment by the WMC on her territory. Both the Labor Department and the War Department had their own utilization teams. But, with the backing of Roosevelt, McNutt successfully stood his ground.[51]

In February 1943 McNutt established a manpower utilization service within WMC. The new agency worked in the field with management and labor to promote utilization through manning tables. At the invitation of management, WMC officials would enter a plant and determine how manpower was being used by analyzing such things as absenteeism, turnovers, production stoppages, morale, job performance, idleness, and the use of women. Personnel management methods would also be studied. After the study these experts would then draw up an overall program of utilization resting upon occupational analysis, manning tables, and common sense. McNutt urged management to cooperate with this ambitious plan.[52]

As manpower shortages grew in 1943, the utilization program became more and more essential. Working on the local level with a staff of about 175 utilization consultants plus volunteers from the private sector, the Bureau of Manpower Utilization began its job of screening labor schedules, reappraising the use of labor, breaking down job skills, and upgrading workers. Within ten months the bureau made more than 1,500 surveys. By April 1945 a total of 5,000 manpower utilization surveys had been made across the country. Manning tables and replacement schedules ended in August 1944 because of reduced military requirements, but utilization studies continued until the end of the war.[53]

Despite the time and effort which went into the utilization program, its effectiveness was mixed due to a shortage of experts and other things. The WMC lacked the power to force a plant to comply with utilization suggestions. Both management and labor insisted that the WMC's work was merely advisory. In addition, many utilization questions were tied to union-management bargaining and contracts. If McNutt sought to enforce his recommendations by withholding labor, the War Department protested effectively.[54]

In November 1943 McNutt testified before Congress that 20 to 25 percent of the nation's manpower was being malutilized. A survey of thirty-one war plants by the Bureau of Manpower Utilization in the summer of 1943 revealed labor hoarding, anachronistic personnel practices and procedures, and ignorance of government programs for placement and training.[55] Such studies were all very well, but studies alone would not produce workers. Yet everyone from Roosevelt to Stimson agreed that finding workers was McNutt's primary job. His future would be determined by his success in this mission.

Notes

1. McNutt speech, August 17, 1942, Paul V. McNutt Papers, The Lilly Library, Indiana University, Bloomington, Ind.; WMC minutes, July 15, 1942, box 5-100, RG 211, National Archives, Washington, D.C.; Leonard W. A'Hearn to Director of Budget, September 18, 1942, box 20-140, RG 211; memorandum by Felix Morley, November 9, 1942, box 20-140, RG 211; Leonard P. Adams, *Wartime Manpower Mobilization* (Ithaca, N.Y.: Cornell University Press, 1951), pp. 29-30; McNutt to John C. McNutt, July 23, 1942, McNutt Papers.

2. Richard Polenberg, *War and Society: The United States, 1941-1945* (Philadelphia: J.B. Lippincott, 1972), p. 20; *Complete Presidential Press Conferences of Franklin D. Roosevelt*, 25 vols. in 12 books (New York: Da Capo Press, 1972), 20: 255-66 (November 24, 1942), hereafter cited as *PPC*; *Monthly Labor Review*, February 1943, p. 414; *New York Times*, May 26, 1942, p. 1.

3. Roosevelt to Nelson, July 27, 1942, official file 4905, and McNutt to Roosevelt, June 2, 1942, *ibid.*, Franklin Roosevelt Papers, Franklin Roosevelt Library, Hyde Park, N.Y.; McNutt file, November 10, 1943, McNutt Papers; quote from *PPC*, 20: 114-15 (October 1, 1942).

4. *Business Week*, November 7, 1942, p. 104; conversation of Morgenthau and Rosenman, Morgenthau Presidential Diary, Franklin Roosevelt Library, 5: 1154 (August 25, 1942); Cox to Abe Feller, October 29, 1942, daily calendar, Cox Papers, Franklin Roosevelt Library; Cox to Hopkins, October 30, 1942, file 324, Hopkins

Papers, Franklin Roosevelt Library; Isador Lubin to Hopkins, November 11, 1942, *ibid.*; conversation of Morgenthau and Hopkins, November 6, 1942, Morgenthau Presidential Diary, 5: 1191; Clark to Roosevelt, November 4, 1942, official file 4905, Roosevelt Papers; Byron Mitchell to Harold Smith, November 5, 1942, *ibid.*

5. *New York Times*, November 17, 1942, p. 17; McNutt speech file of November 19, 1942, McNutt Papers; daily calendar, November 11, 1942, Cox Papers; *PPC*, 20: 156-57 (October 20, 1942).

6. Diary of Henry Stimson, 40: 160-61 (October 19, 1942), Yale University Library, New Haven, Conn., hereafter cited as Stimson Diary; Stimson Diary, 40: 168 (October 21, 1942).

7. See Richard N. Current, *Secretary Stimson: A Study in Statecraft* (New Brunswick, N.J.: Rutgers University Press, 1954).

8. Stimson Diary, 40:168 (October 21, 1942); *ibid.*, 40: 172 (October 22, 1942); *ibid.*, 41:8(n.d.); *ibid.*, 41:11 (Novemer 5, 1942); *ibid.*, 41:23 (November 7, 1942).

9. Stimson Diary, 40: 172 (October 22, 1942); *PPC*, 20:201-2, 210-11, 213-15 (November 6, 1942).

10. Roosevelt to Senator Elbert D. Thomas, November 11, 1942, OF 4905, Roosevelt papers; *New York Times*, November 10, 1942, p. 17; Bernard Baruch to Roosevelt, November 7, 1942, OF 4905, Roosevelt Papers: memo by General Watson, November 18, 1942, *ibid.*; *New York Times*, November 27, 1942, p. 1.

11. *New York Times*, November 27, 1942, p. 1, November 29, 1942, p. 56, and December 1, 1942, p. 31; diary of Harold Ickes, box 9, pp. 7235, 7248, 7254, 7260 (November 28 and 29, 1942), Library of Congress, Washington, D.C.; Irving Brant to Roosevelt, November 30, 1942, OF 6, Roosevelt Papers: Morgenthau to Ickes, telephone memorandum, December 1, 1942, Morgenthau Presidential Diary.

12. Ickes Diary, box 9, pp. 7268, 7274, 7276 (December 6, 1942).

13. Smith to Roosevelt, November 23, 1942, OF 4905, Roosevelt Papers.

14. Smith Presidential Conference Diary, 13 (December 4, 1942), Franklin Roosevelt Library.

15. *New York Times*, December 4, 1942, pp. 19-20; Ickes Diary, box 9, p. 7285 (December 6, 1942); Stimson Diary, 41: 76 (November 29-December 9, 1942); Patterson to Stimson, December 4, 1942, box 171, Henry L. Stimson Papers, Yale University, New Haven, Conn.

16. *New York Times*, December 6, 1942, pp. 1, 63; copy of Executive Order no. 9279, James Byrnes Papers, Clemson University Library, Clemson, S.C.; see also box 20-73, RG 211, National Archives; Patterson to Stimson, December 4, 1942, box 171, Stimson Papers.

17. *Business Week*, December 12, 1942, pp. 15-16; *New York Times*, December 6, 1942, sec. 4, p. 6; December 7, 1942, pp. 19, 26.

18. Roosevelt to Stimson, December 18, 1942, OF 4905, Roosevelt papers; Cox Daily Calendar, November 23, 1942, Oscar Cox Papers; Adams, *Wartime Manpower*, pp. 44-45; *New York Times*, December 6, 1942, p. 1, and December 30, 1942, p. 22; *Business Week*, December 19, 1942, pp. 15-17.

19. Luther Huston, "Mobilizer-in-Chief," *New York Times Magazine*, December 13, 1942, p. 12; minutes of press conference, December 4, 1942, McNutt Papers;

New York Times, December 13, 1942, sec. 4, p. 10 and sec. 7, p. 12, December 29, 1942, p. 1, and December 30, 1942, p. 1; McNutt, "The Task Ahead," manuscript, December 14, 1942, McNutt Papers.

20. See Herman M. Somers, *Presidential Agency: OWMR, The Office of War Mobilization and Reconversion* (Cambridge: Harvard University Press, 1950); Paul A. C. Koistinen, "Mobilizing the World War II Economy: Labor and the Industrial-Military Alliance," *Pacific Historical Review* 42 (November 1973), pp. 443-78; Richard Polenberg, *War and Society*, for such negative views of the WMC.

21. K. B. Williams to Stark, December 21, 1942, miscellaneous pack 3, James Byrnes Papers.

22. Minutes of Management Labor Policy Committee (MLPC), December 23, 1944, box 5-98, RG 211, National Archives; *New York Times*, October 6, 1944, p. 14.

23. Testimony to subcommittee of House Committee on Appropriations, file of April 26, 1945, McNutt Papers.

24. William Manchester, *The Glory and the Dream*, 2 vols. (Boston: Little, Brown, 1973), 2: 296.

25. File of March 25, 1941, McNutt Papers.

26. *New York Times*, May 28, 1941, p. 14, August 7, 1941, p. 19, August 20, 1941, p. 20, September 21, 1941, p. 37, and November 26, 1941, p. 19; file of October 13, 1941, McNutt Papers.

27. Witt Bowden, "Labor in Transition to a War Economy," *Monthly Labor Review*, April 1942, pp. 843-48, 850, 857; file of July 22, 1942, box 20-87, RG 211, National Archives.

28. McNutt speech, September 6, 1942; file of October 24, 1942; "Manpower and the Job Ahead," November 1942, all in McNutt Papers; Frank J. McSherry to Ferdinand Eberstadt, December 3, 1942, box 20-87, RG 211, National Archives.

29. *New York Times*, January 3, 1943, sec. 9, p. 1; January 9, 1943, p. 11, February 5, 1943, p. 1, and April 15, 1943, p. 16; Major Paul J. Kind to General Hershey, February 4, 1943, index file, General Lewis B. Hershey Papers, Military History Research Collection, Carlisle Barracks, Pa.; Leonard Adams, *Wartime Manpower*, p. 10.

30. See chapter 6 on the farm and manpower. Minutes of War Production Board, April 13, 1943, box 12, Donald Nelson Papers, The Huntington Library, San Marino, Calif.; *New York Times*, July 3, 1943, p. 26.

31. *Monthly Labor Review*, August 1943, iv; *New York Times*, August 22, 1943, sec. 4, p. 2, and August 30, 1943, p. 1; McNutt memorandum, August 6, 1943, McNutt Papers; McNutt radio address, August 25, 1943, McNutt Papers.

32. Files of January 20, 1944, March 3, 1944, and April 13, 1944, McNutt Papers, where McNutt reported that the quit-rate in manufacturing in September 1943 was over six workers per one hundred. By January 1944 it had fallen to fewer than five per one hundred. *New York Times*, January 4, 1944, p. 14, April 14, 1944, p. 36, and April 16, 1944, sec. 4, p. 7.

33. WPB minutes, June 13, 1944, box 12, Nelson Papers; July 29, 1944, file for McNutt Labor Day statement, McNutt Papers; *New York Times*, July 9, 1944, sec. 4, p. 6.

34. *Monthly Labor Review*, August 1944, iii; *New York Times*, August 28, 1944, p. 17, September 6, 1944, p. 9, and October 25, 1944, p. 1, Somervell quoted in November 21, 1944, p. 1; see files of August 23, 1944, September 25, 1944, and September 27, 1944, McNutt Papers.

35. *Monthly Labor Review*, December 1944, p. 1158; *New York Times*, December 1, 1944, p. 8, December 5, 1944, p. 17, and December 7, 1944, p. 19; McNutt article "The Final Battle," manuscript, December 1944; file of November 17, 1944, McNutt Papers.

36. Hay to Byrnes, January 9, 1945, box 184-5, Robert Patterson Papers, Library of Congress, Washington, D.C.; McNutt testimony in file of February 7, 1945, McNutt Papers.

37. Gow to CG, February 20, 1945, box 185, Patterson Papers; *Monthly Labor Review*, February 1945, p. 290, and March 1945, p. 535; McNutt radio address, March 18 and 28, 1945, McNutt Papers; testimony before House Committee on Appropriations, April 26, 1945, McNutt Papers; Gow to Patterson, June 12, 1945, box 184-5, Patterson Papers.

38. Speech files of April 29, 1942, May 20, 1942, and July 3, 1942, McNutt Papers; Paul J. Kind to Hershey, February 4, 1943, index file, Hershey Papers; *New York Times*, August 20, 1943, p. 23. The military was also guilty of hoarding through its cadet aviation program.

39. McNutt article, "Let's Face the Facts about Manpower," files of July 14, 1942, and August 25, 1942, McNutt Papers; *New York Times*, May 28, 1942, p. 1, and August 7, 1943, p. 12; Adams, *Wartime Manpower*, p. 27; *Monthly Labor Review*, September 1942, pp. 460-61; NWLB quoted in *Monthly Labor Review*, February 1943, p. 412; Roosevelt quoted in copy of executive order, April 8, 1943, James Byrnes Papers.

40. *New York Times*, September 24, 1943, p. 16, and November 26, 1943, p. 18.

41. *PPC*, 20: 269-71 (December 1, 1942) and 21: 17-18 (January 8, 1943); Patterson to Stimson, March 4, 1943, box 171, Stimson Papers; Duane Evans, "Problem of Absenteeism in Relation to War Production," *Monthly Labor Review*, January 1943, pp. 1-9.

42. Rickenbacker quoted in David Hinshaw, *The Home Front* (New York: Putnam, 1943), p. 193; *New York Times*, Februry 23, 1943, pp. 1, 18; SIR to Roosevelt, March 4, 1943, box 5, manpower file, Sam Rosenman Papers, Roosevelt Library.

43. McNutt quoted in file of April 27, 1943, McNutt Papers; *New York Times*, December 30, 1944, p. 1; Knudsen report in WPB minutes, July 27, 1943, box 12, Nelson Papers; Hinshaw, *Home Front*, p. 192; Joel Seidman, *American Labor from Defense to Reconversion* (Chicago: University of Chicago Press, 1953), p. 161; *Monthly Labor Review*, February 1943, iv; file of April 10, 1943, McNutt Papers.

44. Robert C. Goodwin to Philip Broughton, December 29, 1943, McNutt Papers; Gow to CG, February 27, 1945, box 185, Patterson Papers; McNutt to Harold B. Dow, September 22, 1944, McNutt Papers; John Dos Passos, *State of the Nation* (Boston: Houghton-Mifflin, 1943), pp. 36-37; *New York Times*, January 6, 1944, p. 13, and February 23, 1943, p. 1; minutes of WMC, March 10, 1943, RG 211; *New York Times*, April 11, 1943, sec. 1, p. 1.

45. *New York Times*, February 17, 1943, p. 8, February 27, 1943, p. 28, March 4, 1943, p. 1, March 9, 1943, p. 14, and March 11, 1943, p. 24; press conference, March 29, 1943, McNutt Papers.

46. *New York Times*, March 16, 1943, p. 38, and August 20, 1944, p. 28; *Monthly Labor Review*, December 1944, p. 1319; Roland Young, *Congressional Politics in the Second World War* (New York: Columbia University Press, 1956), p. 61.

47. Speech by McNutt, January 9, 1942, McNutt Papers. Total disabling industrial injuries from 1941-1943 equaled 6,861,900. Deaths and permanent total disability for the same period totaled 59,200. See *Statistical Abstract of the United States, 1944-1945* (Washington, D.C.: U.S. Government Printing Office, 1945), p. 171.

48. Albert A. Blum, *Drafted or Deferred: Practices Past and Present* (Ann Arbor: University of Michigan Press, 1967), pp. 103-110; Adams, *Wartime Manpower*, pp. 33-34.

49. Blum, *Drafted*, pp. 103-10; Hershey to James McGraw, November 10, 1942, staybacks, 1942-1943, Hershey Papers; WMC minutes, May 27, 1942, box 5-100, RG 211.

50. WMC minutes, December 2, 1942, box 5-100, RG 211; Patterson quoted in Blum, *Drafted,* pp. 101-2.

51. WMC minutes, December 9, 1942, box 5-100, RG 211; Dorr to Patterson, December 3, 1942, box 183, Patterson Papers.

52. *Business Week*, November 7, 1942, pp. 18-19, and February 6, 1943, p. 14; *Monthly Labor Review*, February 1943, p. 414; McNutt, "The Task Ahead," December 14, 1942, file, and speech to American Medical Association, February 10, 1943, McNutt Papers.

53. *Monthly Labor Review*, April 1945, p. 915, and September 1944, pp. 518-19; files of February 1, 1944, January 9, 1945, and August 7, 1943, McNutt Papers.

54. Beyer to Frances Perkins, February 3, 1943, A 159, folder 110, Clara Beyer Papers, Schlesinger Library, Radcliffe College, Cambridge, Mass.; file of February 10, 1943, McNutt Papers; Lester V. Chandler and Donald H. Wallace, eds., *Economic Mobilization and Stabilization* (New York: Holt, Rinehart, Winston, 1951), pp. 146-47.

55. *New York Times*, November 5, 1943, p. 14, and August 10, 1944, p. 30; file of May 25, 1943, McNutt Papers; A. A. Hoehling, *Home Front, U.S.A.* (New York: Crowell, 1966), p. 121; memo by J. Davis, January 12, 1943, box 20-81, RG 211.

CHAPTER 3

Controlling Labor

Recruiting and training labor were the two main tasks which occupied McNutt and the WMC throughout the war. Using every device at his disposal, and a few which went beyond his mandate, McNutt sought labor for the war machine. As he pursued his objective his methods became more and more coercive. Despite his attempts to cover this coercion with semantic quibbling, McNutt seemed to be pushing regimentation without the benefit of legislation. If he failed, despite the gyrations, his political future seemed bleak and the economy of the United States might fall under the control of the military.

I

In fulfilling his primary duty McNutt depended upon the United States Employment Service (USES). Originally a state-controlled operation with only cursory federal supervision, the USES was federalized by Roosevelt in December 1941. The entire operation soon came under McNutt's control, despite the objections and fears of southern governors at this alleged infringement of states' rights. McNutt now had at his disposal a nationwide system of labor registration with 1,500 full-time employees and 3,000 part-time workers, all of whom had experience in job analysis and knew local labor needs. He called the local USES office the "corner grocery of the

American job market.'' This grocery was free and acted as a liaison agency between local needs and the national labor market. An individual seeking work registered at his local USES office, where officials administered a battery of tests and conducted interviews. Employment Service officials asked local employers to project labor needs sixty, ninety, and 180 days in advance of reporting data. Such projected labor needs would then be matched by skill and other factors against the available labor supply file. Early in March General Hershey agreed to a procedure by which some twenty-five million men between the ages of twenty and forty-four received work-skill questionnaires as they registered for the draft. The information went from local Selective Service boards to local USES boards. On paper the system seemed formidable.[1]

Like most of McNutt's program, however, the USES operated with severe handicaps. It could only recommend that workers register, could only urge that workers take jobs, could only suggest that employers hire those sent for interviews. While a potential for national coordination existed, the local USES offices had considerable autonomy, in keeping with McNutt's belief that the manpower problem was a local problem. Ironically, the USES suffered from its own manpower shortage. Congress refused to upgrade the pay of these new federal employees. Demoralization and desertion spread throughout the ranks. Personnel managers were pirated away by high wages from the private sector. In some areas the USES suffered a turnover rate of 80 percent.[2]

Even with these handicaps the USES managed to perform effectively. True, some of its recruitment gimmicks bordered on the bizarre. Agents of the USES in Salt Lake City and Denver made daily visits to the local prisons where they recruited minor offenders for war jobs. Two hundred sixty inmates were placed in two months of recruiting. The program spread throughout the country and a Buffalo judge offered inebriants the option of a war job or a jail sentence. By 1943 some 30,000 inmates of prisons worked part-time on jobs. The USES and the WMC sponsored weekly radio programs to report on labor needs in various areas. Instead of banning all private labor recruiting, McNutt sought to control it. He worked with local USES offices and the press to restrict newspaper ads for critical skills.[3]

Through this combination of eccentricity and orthodoxy the USES made 3,688,383 placements during the first six months of 1942 in both agricultural and industrial jobs. For the entire year placements rose to a total of 10.25 million, of which 68 percent were in industrial jobs. Such figures represented an increase of one-third over all placements in 1941. In 1943 the agency placed some 9.4 million workers in nonagricultural jobs. This figure exceeded 1941 totals by 73.8 percent. Unskilled workers represented more than half of the total 1943 placements. Of the total, some 83.5 percent were white and 35.6 percent were women.[4]

By 1944 labor shortages had been isolated to certain local areas and to certain special skills. Recruiting became a more national enterprise supervised closely by McNutt in Washington. The process still began on the local level, but if an employer found the local USES unable to furnish sufficient labor, he could request a regional campaign. If this campaign failed, the problem was referred to Washington for a national search. Such national campaigns occurred only after a thorough investigation and followed tough guidelines. Interregional recruitment hardly matched the spontaneous migration which occurred in 1940 and 1941 as the unemployed sought out defense jobs in the Midwest and the Pacific Coast.[5] The recruitment worked best when confronted with the need for highly specialized personnel. The National Roster of Scientific and Specialized Personnel, which WMC controlled, managed to place 50,000 persons from June 1940 to December 1944.[6]

II

After recruiting labor, McNutt found that his problem had only begun. His original mandate included a vast program of job training which had begun under Sidney Hillman. The depression years had seen a growing obsolescence of skills.[7] Even before being placed in charge of manpower mobilization, McNutt assumed some responsibility for industrial training. On March 21, 1941, in his role as Federal Security Administrator, he appointed Colonel Frank J. McSherry to head up a new Defense Training Program within the Office of Education (DTP). This program was kept separate from civilian education work. McSherry concerned himself with pre-

employment training, supplementary training for workers already
on the job, training for rural and nonrural youth, vocational training for youth through National Youth Administration projects,
and vocational training in Civilian Conservation Corps camps. At
the same time, in the Office of Production Management, Sidney
Hillman sponsored a Training Within Industry division (TWI). By
the end of the year federal manpower training was divided into
three areas. One program involved short courses for older youths
and adults seeking a specific skill or supplementary training for
men already working. Another program involved preemployment
vocational defense training and supplementary training while on
the job. A third program provided work experience to young people
through the NYA and the CCC. Complementing these programs
was regular college training of engineers in off-campus jobs in
defense industry. Theoretically, these programs were supposed to
be coordinated with the USES.[8]

When Roosevelt established the WMC in April 1942, he gave
McNutt responsibility for supervising the entire training program.
The assignment was consistent with the mandate to recruit labor,
but members of the Department of Labor objected at this further
intrusion into their traditional function. As the formidable nature
of the task unfolded, McNutt probably wished some objections had
been heeded. Although some people, such as Donald Nelson, clung
to the romantic notion that Americans could easily out-produce the
enemy because of our national heritage as tinkerers, in reality, the
labor force lacked training for defense industry. The WMC's new
training programs sought to remedy the deficiencies. In 1942 the
vocational educational program expanded rapidly. By May 1942
total enrollment had increased to more than 3,750,000.[9]

The Training Within Industry program, which McNutt assumed
control over in April, represented another major part of his responsibility. Earlier Hillman had pushed this program and when
the WMC finally took it over some 2,100 plants were participating
and 85,000 apprentices were enrolled. By December 1942 the number of plants participating had grown to more than 6,500 and the
number of workers to six million. Within TWI the Job Instructor
Training program certified supervisors, crew chiefs, and others as
instructors to teach within the plant. The program amounted to a

giant on-the-job training effort under the supervision of the WMC.[10]

During 1942 some 4.5 million workers graduated from training programs and were in jobs. New courses were devised in TWI to train plant directors to diagnose difficulties in their own plants and decide which of the various training programs could best solve the problem. Training-program success came despite the demise of the NYA and the CCC. McNutt had urged the President to continue the NYA because of its role in war training. But the New Deal agency was attacked by conservative congressmen as a luxury during the war. Roosevelt, with the encouragement of Harold Smith, decided the agency was not worth the criticism and ended it in early 1943.[11]

More than most men McNutt appreciated the importance of training scientists for the war economy. In an address to the Massachusetts Institute of Technology on January 31, 1943, he boasted of the thousands of biologists, chemists, and engineers who were taking special training at colleges across the country. Some 200 colleges cooperated in what was called "Engineering, Science, and Management War Training." At M.I.T. alone scholars from seventy-three other schools and forty-three industries were working on the war effort. Chinese and Russian students walked the campus and McNutt optimistically concluded: "May the time soon come when students from the Soviet Union will return to the Institute in greater numbers than ever before."[12]

The training program continued throughout the war. But on May 5, 1945, J. S. Studebaker, Commissioner of Education, wired all state directors of war-training programs that they should close their doors by May 31. As the war ended the government retreated from this responsibility. When the program ended a WMC summary indicated that the total enrollment in all types of federal and state war-production training from July 1940 to the end of 1944 had been more than 14,000,000. Without this training program the war economy would never have produced at such a record level.[13]

III

During the first months of its existence the WMC spent most of its time discovering where the workers were and where the jobs were. By the end of 1942 McNutt had erected a system of classification dividing the nation into four categories. Category 1 indicated an acute labor shortage region. At the other extreme, Category 4 indicated a labor surplus region. Throughout the war McNutt endeavored to have these categories acknowledged by government procurement agencies when granting war contracts. The WMC went to great pains to keep the list up-to-date, dropping and adding areas as new information arrived from the field. The precision of the system emerged when the South Side of Chicago retained its Group 1 label as the rest of the city moved to Group 2. Local officials frequently complained when their area was called a labor-short region because they feared that such a designation might curtail lucrative war contracts. They had little to worry about in practice because McNutt could not obtain cooperation from procurement agencies.[14]

In addition, these geographical designations meant little without some mechanism for controlling the movement of workers. Rampant labor piracy and chaotic migration early in the war had led to the creation of the WMC. The lure of higher wages continued to create shortages faster than the WMC could fill them. As shipyard workers were being laid off because of a lack of material, miners in the West headed toward the coast, anticipating higher wages and easier work building boats. The only sure means of ending such migration was through a labor freeze, forcing a man to remain in his job. Aside from the constitutional tangles of such an action, most Americans in 1942 thought a freeze was too drastic. McNutt agreed, but he decided to experiment with a voluntary freeze. On May 28, 1942, he issued a statement warning that if a worker refused to take a job recommended by the USES, or refused to stay in a war job, his name would be given to the local draft board for induction. Plants which hired workers who ignored USES employment guidelines would be reported to the WPB for possible withdrawal of war contracts and material. This "work or fight" scheme, as it was labeled by the press, had no force of law behind it. McNutt counted on the voluntary cooperation of labor and management for success.[15]

By August 1942 McNutt had established a method by which to test his ideas. He chose Baltimore as his laboratory for labor management. The city presented a challenge to the notion of voluntary manpower control. In August it had a population of 860,000 and twenty-five major war plants. Some 90 percent of all new workers were being hired outside of USES channels. Although blacks comprised 20 percent of the population, few were employed in war plants. Migrant laborers arrived from West Virginia and North Carolina at the rate of 3,500 each month. Seeking to control the situation, the WMC sent in agents to sign up plants for what was called an Employment Stabilization Plan (ESP). Although later translated as controlled referral or priority referral, the system remained largely the same. The heart of the plan revolved around statements or certificates of availability to prevent labor migration. Management agreed not to hire new workers unless they possessed a certificate of availability. This certificate insured that the worker had been processed by a local USES office and that he had not left another war job to seek higher pay. The plan required that plants give up hiring at the gate and that they register vacancies with the USES if they wanted referrals. After eight months of experimentation a survey by the Office of War Information revealed that labor piracy had disappeared in Baltimore, recruitment of women had been stimulated, and some headway had been made in hiring blacks.[16]

McNutt was encouraged. The key to controlling manpower was the local USES office. If the ESP, with its certificate of availability, funneled labor through USES, McNutt might yet master manpower. After evaluating Baltimore and consulting with management and labor advisors, McNutt issued an order extending the ESP to nonferrous metal mining and lumber industries in twelve western states. The new plan would deal with critical industries rather than one city, but the principles remained the same. An employer could not hire a worker unless he possessed a certificate from the USES. All labor recruiting would be controlled by the USES. Normally, the USES would issue a certificate whenever a worker was not working at his highest skill level or when he was moving from a nonessential industry. When a worker sought transfer from one war plant to another to better utilize his skill, the original employer had to upgrade the worker or lose him. The transferred worker retained the seniority rights accumulated with his original employer. If denied a certificate, a worker was entitled to appeal his case.[17]

In quick succession ESPs went into effect for Buffalo on October

15, Louisville on November 9, and Detroit on December 10, 1942. In Detroit the plan covered some thirty-four occupational areas and involved more than 700,000 workers. Montague A. Clark, district director of the WMC for Michigan, admitted that he had no means of enforcing the plan but expected the cooperation of military procurement agencies and public opinion to cut back contracts at plants that refused to cooperate. McNutt also felt confident that the voluntary ESP would work. He had cleared the plan with labor and management representatives at the WMC. All of the contracting agencies in the federal government had agreed to it. Naturally, McNutt would have preferred statutory support for his work. He admitted to the Senate Military Affairs Committee in October 1942 that he foresaw "difficulties in the future so long as we depend on indirect sanctions." Requiring certificates was an infringement on the traditional mobility of American labor. William Green told the Catholic Conference on Industrial Problems on December 14, 1942, that the AFL opposed any attempt to freeze workers in their jobs, especially while women workers remained unemployed.[18]

IV

During the new year, 1943, McNutt reached the peak of his power. For twelve months he controlled the SSS. Domestic manpower mobilization crested and the WMC reached an apogee of activity. Stabilization plans went into effect in forty-four additional problem areas. No region of the country remained unaffected. McNutt continued to expand his control. On February 1, 1943, he ordered persons engaged in certain listed jobs to be considered nondeferrable in the draft. In what amounted to a new and specific work or fight order, McNutt allowed such men until April 1 to find new jobs in war industry or face military induction. The WMC took control of all hiring in Category 1 labor areas. As early as December 1942 the WMC had issued a list of essential activities to guide men seeking work and to guide draft boards. Now, in February 1943, McNutt supplemented this list of activities with a list of particular occupations for which no deferment should be granted. This refinement of controls, with the clear threat of the military draft as a sanction, aroused public criticism by those who saw the move as an attempt to institute national service without the approval of Congress. Males under thirty-eight not already in an essential job were now threatened with the draft.[19]

McNutt had good intentions in adopting a nondeferrable list of jobs for individuals and an essential activity list for companies, but the effect was confusion. Neither the local draft boards nor draftable workers could understand the system. The military and the WPB approved the February activity list although it included such marginal jobs as jewelry work, tailoring academic caps and gowns, manufacturing amusement machines, and jobs in dance, music, theatrical, and art studios—jobs that contradicted America's commitment to total war.[20]

As was usual with WMC regulations, the essential activity list and the nondeferrable list gained definition through interpretations and administration at the regional and local level. Regional directors repeatedly received revised lists of essential activities and guidelines for interpretation. For example, in December 1943 the WMC announced that determining the essentiality of an establishment, which meant it would receive priority treatment by the USES, depended not only on the plant being engaged in an activity included on the National List of Essential Activities, but also on the end-use of the product. When war-essential activities in a plant were inseparable from jobs classified as nondeferrable occupations, the entire plant could be classified as essential if approximately 75 percent of its activities were essential. To provide more flexibility McNutt made provisions in September 1943 for designating an activity as "locally needed." If an area manpower director found a particular trade or service required for the health and welfare of his area, he could assign such a service the same status as an essential activity to insure priority referral of labor by the USES.[21] In addition, regional directors of the WMC were given broad latitude in interpreting the general policy. Ultimately, the essentiality of a particular company was determined by the area WMC or the local USES.[22]

Determining the essentiality of a particular plant in the complex American economy required the wisdom of Solomon. McNutt's self-confidence, although more than adequate, did not extend this far. He did not expect to please everyone; he was not disappointed. Critics appeared when the WMC announced that the production of infants' and children's wear had been included in the List of Essential Activities, and when Louisville grave diggers became qualified. Still, the WMC did turn down the Goldsmith Pickle Company's application because their product was "not so staple a food item as to qualify. . . ." To some Americans the list seemed silly, to others "oppressive and drastic." American chiropractors demanded a place on the list by pleading: "Don't deny to the American people the right to service of their choice." At the War Department, Quartermaster Corps and Ordnance Corps officials complained that the WMC's list excluded important activities.[23]

Everyone agreed that it was a good idea to define precisely the most essential activities in the war economy. Even with the confusion attendant on such a program, the list seemed meritorious because, as Anna Rosenberg wrote, the pressure exerted by defining what was important work and what was unimportant had a beneficial psychological effect on the public. Unfortunately, no one could tell how many individuals actually switched jobs as a direct result of McNutt's order of February 1, 1943. Men took war jobs for many motives.[24]

V

As McNutt tried to control manpower through employment stabilization and priority referral, through lists of essential and nonessential activities, President Roosevelt once again intruded. He conducted an extensive review of the entire problem of manpower mobilization in March 1943 and on April 8, 1943, issued Executive Order no. 9238 which froze all wages and prices. The order affirmed McNutt's authority "to forbid the employment by an employer of any new employee except in accordance with regulations of the Chairman, the purpose being to prevent such employment at a higher wage or salary than that received by the employee in his last employment unless the charge of employment will aid in the prosecution of the war." While Roosevelt expanded McNutt's power with one hand, he contracted it with the other. McNutt now had to obtain approval from James Byrnes, Economic Stabilization Director, before launching new programs.[25] McNutt no longer worked directly for the President; he worked for Byrnes.

Circumstances required changes. Despite the ESP and other actions by McNutt, labor hoarding and pirating continued. In Ohio one airfield reported an 88 percent turnover rate. Underutilization of women persisted. Labor shortages continued.[26] By April 1943 the WMC had stabilization plans operating in 70 different areas. With Roosevelt's support, expressed in the new executive order, and Byrnes's approval, McNutt began to expand his program. On April 16 he issued a new regulation providing that no employer should hire for nonessential work any new worker who, in the preceding thirty days, had worked in an essential job "if the salary or wage rate to be paid by the employer would exceed the rate most recently received during such period by the employee." In areas covered by stabilization plans no certificate of availability could be issued "solely on the basis that a man's wages were substantially less than those prevailing in the locality for the same work." Such actions made it appear that McNutt had effectively frozen twenty-seven million citizens in their war jobs. In carrying out Roosevelt's new order, McNutt was again asserting power indistinguishable from a labor draft. If an employer violated these new rules he was liable to a $1,000 fine and one year in jail, besides losing an income tax deduction.[27]

Once again organized labor and management called McNutt's bluff on this labor freeze. Roosevelt had issued another executive order but without congressional and public support for a labor freeze, McNutt still depended upon voluntary cooperation. He could only enforce his program if plant managers and union chiefs co-operated. Fortunately, local officials of the WMC recognized this need. In Buffalo, New York, Anna Rosenberg worked with management and labor to promote stabilization without threatening punishment from Washington. Within a few months during the summer of 1943 the new manpower program became more acceptable. Local priority committees, staffed by management and labor representatives, worked with the USES to control the flow of manpower into essential industry. Before controlled referral began some fifty-six plants were behind in war-production schedules. Four months later only fourteen plants remained behind schedule.[28]

Such steps by the WMC made Senator Warren R. Austin, who was sponsoring a national service act in the Senate, wonder whether or not McNutt had succeeded in turning a voluntary system into a nonvoluntary system. In response, McNutt denied that his program was compulsory, although he admitted that the distinction between voluntary and compulsory was difficult to judge. He explained that every human action involved some form of compulsion or pressure from the community, the society, and friends. War merely intensified these pressures. The WMC sought "to guide these pressures and to use them as a means to an end that all agree is good—effective mobilization of manpower for war." The employment stabilization or controlled referral plans were voluntary because they were self-imposed restrictions. Inventing a new theorem of political science, McNutt implied that rules adopted through popular participation should not be considered compulsory. His argument confused the origins of a procedure with the effect. In saner moments McNutt acknowledged that his program was compulsory rather than voluntary, but, as he wrote Austin, "we do not worry about definition. . . . Out of the tangled web of week-to-week events, the nation has witnessed the emergence of a community mechanism for solving labor problems—the employment stabilization program."[29]

Senator Austin ignored McNutt's prattle and continued to press for a national service law. But McNutt believed that his regulations reflected local desires. His commitment to Jeffersonianism led him to exaggerate the grass-roots origin of labor control plans. He explained carefully to critics how every worker and every employer had an opportunity to appeal every decision, how every citizen in each town was supporting the stabilization plan. On a national radio broadcast in August 1943 he announced to the nation that "the people acting through the wartime government has now adopted standards governing the hiring and transfer of workers. . . ."[30] McNutt refused to concede that he had frozen workers in their jobs.

VI

A severe airplane production crisis on the West Coast during the summer of 1943 prompted the next manpower innovation. A few plants were experiencing disastrous turnover rates, with four out of every ten men departing inside of twelve months. Employment stabilization plans had little effect on this turnover. If a worker desired release to seek another job he merely stopped paying his union dues. As union contracts required a dismissal for nonpayment of dues, the worker had little trouble obtaining a certificate of availability from his employer. To make things even easier, local stationery stores did a land-office business selling copies of USES forms; forgery became a major problem. By August the War Department learned that six aircraft plants were falling behind schedule on the West Coast. At the same time thirteen of thirty-eight shipyards were also behind schedule. The Boeing Plant in Seattle, producing vital B-17 bombers, had serious problems.[31]

The president of the company had warned Roosevelt in January 1943 that a labor shortage would lead to production failures by the summer. Temporary measures had failed to solve the problem. Some 20,000 workers in aircraft plants were leaving their jobs each month. Almost half of the women and 40 percent of the men failed to finish out the year in these plants. Rather than blame the workers, the WMC charged management with inefficient labor practices. Boeing in particular was "a rat hole" for manpower. McNutt explained that this company had to hire 150,000 workers to maintain a labor force of only 30,000 over a twelve-month period. Pay scales at aircraft plants were less than at shipyards; foremen harrassed workers. The government had assigned too many contracts to the West Coast. Neither the WPB nor the War Department cooperated with the WMC in establishing production priority ratings. Hence, the shortages continued.[32]

By early September the complaints from the War Department finally forced Roosevelt to ask Byrnes to investigate. Byrnes knew that McNutt and the War Department disagreed over the cause of the problem. Seeking a fresh view, Byrnes decided to call in Bernard Baruch, the master mobilizer of World War I, to review the problem. Baruch and John Hancock received full cooperation from McNutt in the study. After looking over the problem Baruch concluded that the key to the difficulty was improved coordination among the WPB, the War Department, and the WMC, something McNutt had known for months. Baruch's report to Byrnes called for decentralizing the administration of manpower and for a resurvey of the entire production program in light of available manpower. The report also called for increased draft deferments on the

West Coast. In sum, Baruch and Hancock agreed with McNutt's assessment. They did not think a national service act was required. As the report "largely expressed the position taken by WMC," McNutt felt vindicated.[33]

Officially established on September 15, 1943, the West Coast Plan (WCP) went into effect slowly. In many ways it resembled the controlled referral system adopted earlier in Buffalo, but was more elaborate and involved the cooperation of more agencies. For success the plan depended upon the work of two new committees: an Area Production Urgency Committee and an Area Manpower Priorities Committee. The Production Urgency Committee (PUC) consisted of representatives from procurement agencies such as the WPB and the War Department. Following the initial recommendation of the WPB in Washington, the Area PUC decided which plant or factory was most important to the war effort. The Area Manpower Priorities Committee (MPC) consisted of the same membership as the PUC with the addition of the area manpower director. This MPC determined the priorities and allocation of manpower on the basis of recommendations by the PUC. The administrators of the West Coast Plan were local leaders and the entire administration complemented McNutt's gospel of decentralization. Even the Selective Service cooperated by providing sixty-day extensions of deferments for workers at the request of employers.[34]

McNutt's ideas seemed justified in the West Coast Plan: it was voluntary, it was local, and it required the cooperation of production, military, and manpower officials. The cooperation, however, seemed halfhearted. The WPB objected to using its control over material allocation as a bludgeon to enforce WMC regulations. Gustav Peck of the WPB thought that the West Coast Plan was just a worthless rehash of old ideas. A few residents of the West Coast disliked the plan because it favored young, upstart war industry over older firms in allocating men and material. General Lewis Hershey disliked interfering with the autonomy of local boards in granting deferments. The War Department detested the additional power granted to McNutt and the WMC.[35]

Undersecretary Patterson especially resented McNutt's intrusion into manpower utilization in plants. As for military deferments, Patterson and Ralph Bard of the navy wrote Hershey urging that such dispensations be granted sparingly. Within the WMC itself labor and management representatives feared that the West Coast Plan was merely a disguised national service. Labor advisors disliked James Byrnes entering the manpower question because he was considered unfriendly to unions. Some of this opposition melted when John Hancock explained to labor officials at the WMC that both he and Baruch had totally opposed national service in their report.[36]

If obstruction by Patterson was not enough, McNutt also faced problems with Nelson of the WPB over the plan. Nelson failed to carry out his responsibility under the Baruch scheme. The WPB refused to cut back on material for less-essential industry because Nelson feared such a step would provoke public resentment. William K. Hopkins, the regional director for the WMC, told a Senate subcommittee in April 1944 that neither the army nor the navy procurement agencies bothered to cooperate with the West Coast Plan. Procurement agencies continued to place millions of dollars in contracts in labor-short areas without consulting local committees.[37]

Given such opposition, it seems remarkable that the West Coast Plan accomplished anything. But by November 15, 1943, both PUCs and MPCs were functioning in San Diego, Los Angeles, San Francisco, Portland, and Seattle. Production urgency lists, manpower priority lists, and employment ceilings were established in each area. The Selective Service postponed the induction of essential workers. The WPB soon admitted to Byrnes that in two months the West Coast Plan had stimulated several community efforts to increase local labor supply. Labor ceilings had led to a reduction of labor requirements in numerous plants, especially navy shipyards. Although "differences of opinion" among the WMC, the army, and the WPB limited progress in Oregon and Washington, the War Department finally admitted that McNutt had been right about the problems at Boeing in Seattle. Faulty utilization rather than labor shortages had caused the problem. No doubt the West Coast Plan did ease labor recruitment problems at key plants, did lead to more realistic estimates of labor needs by management, did force procurement agencies to note the importance of labor supply in assigning contracts, and did provide experience in cooperation on the local level. By May 15, 1944, the West Coast Plan had been extended

to ten additional areas in the nation. By August 1944 the program
became national.[38]

VII

Throughout all of 1944 McNutt expanded the role played by employment stabilization programs. In January the WMC announced
that physicians, dentists, veterinarians, sanitary engineers, and
nurses who were working as employees in essential or locally needed
activities would be stabilized. These professionals would now need
certificates of availability before they could take new jobs. By February the controlled referral program was in effect in seventy-eight
different areas involving some 4,600,000 workers. The WMC also
became more aggressive in challenging the estimates of labor needs
by management. Utilization studies became more frequent. In
April 1944 McNutt reported to the AFL that in thirty-eight industrial areas across the nation manpower priority committees, similar
to the ones on the West Coast, were functioning. These committees
continued to establish employment ceilings on the basis of the minimum number of men needed to meet production schedules. Labor
ceilings had been created in twenty-nine labor-short areas. Controlled
referral existed for all workers in eighteen areas, for males only in
twelve areas, and for all workers in essential activity in seventy-two
areas. The WMC now conducted utilization studies at the rate of
500 per month. McNutt concluded: "This program is working."[39]

His confidence seemed justified as the North African campaign
against Rommel's Afrika Korps concluded successfully and as Allied
troops swept over Sicily and invaded Italy. By the spring of 1944
rumors of a major invasion of the European continent floated
around English pubs and American bars. An increasing number of
Americans expected the war to end by December. In February
Bernard Baruch offered a plan for the efficient reconversion of the
economy from war to peace. McNutt did not dispute this optimism
despite persistent problems in such cities as Detroit, which still suffered from a deficit of 30,000 workers.[40]

Yet as General Eisenhower gathered and trained his forces before
launching them against Hitler's Fortress Europa, another type of
danger threatened those managing the home front. Roosevelt saw
it. Patterson and Stimson had seen it even earlier. McNutt now saw

it. Overconfidence about the war was leading to increased separation from war industry by workers seeking a job with a civilian future. To combat this, McNutt launched his own offensive to coincide with the military invasion of Europe. He announced in early June that by July 1 the entire nation would be under a priority referral system. McNutt explained to the press that war industry now needed an additional 350,000 men in sixty days. While men were fighting in Europe and Asia some civilians were leaving their war jobs. During an interview conducted by CBS radio, McNutt stressed the importance of avoiding overconfidence. He explained that his new plan was not radical and had been in effect in several local areas. Under this system the worker was offered as much freedom of choice as a war economy could afford. Everyone had to do his part, he insisted, as he stressed the voluntary and democratic dimensions of the plan. Even Patterson at the War Department, no supporter of McNutt's voluntary approach, contributed a public statement endorsing national priority referral. Although he expected severe labor shortages shortly, Patterson admitted that the "situation would be far worse if priority referral and other programs had not been applied."[41]

In mid-June McNutt directed that manpower priority committees be established by July 1 in all Group 1 and Group 2 labor market areas. After July 1 all male labor had to be hired through either the USES or other approved agencies. Employment ceilings had to be established by a priority committee. McNutt called this system democratic and voluntary because the worker was not compelled to take a job at lower pay. The worker would be offered successive job opportunities. Under such circumstances McNutt could not understand charges that his plan was dictatorial.[42]

Privately, McNutt hoped this plan would help avoid the need for a labor draft. If the WMC plan failed, he felt sure that national service would be inevitable. As finally implemented on July 1, 1944, McNutt's scheme consisted of several different programs: employment ceilings were fixed in specific establishments in 184 areas covered by manpower priority committees, these same committees would decide which industries should get workers, the recruiting of workers by USES would be intensified on an interregional basis, a national manpower priorities committee was established to review employer labor orders requiring interregional recruitment, and the priority referral system requiring that employers hire all male workers through the USES was extended to the entire nation.[43]

Interregional recruitment appeared a good idea on paper but problems had already developed in the field. Three different industries presented WMC with opportunities to test the concept: foundry work, nonferrous mining, and the lumber industry in the Northwest. New military weapons required a gross expansion of forge and foundry work. Such work was sweaty, backbreaking, and underpaid. Not surprisingly, efforts at interregional recruitment met scant success. By July 1944 McNutt was pleading over the radio for 20,000 men to work for ninety days at forgings and castings for ships, planes, tanks, and heavy trucks. Production had dropped below schedule in 300 critical plants in Buffalo, Chicago, Boston, Detroit, Milwaukee, and other cities.[44]

The lumber industry had the same need for physically fit young men. Shortages had developed in the Northwest because men had moved into the higher-paying and less-demanding war work in the cities of Seattle and Portland. In April 1944 McNutt announced that 60,000 lumber and pulpwood workers had to be found before autumn. The importation of 5,000 Canadian woodsmen provided some relief in New England but not in the Northwest. Shortages continued even after the War Department pledged full cooperation to McNutt.[45]

Miners also saw economic mobilization as a splendid opportunity to leave their dangerous and arduous vocation for something more pleasant. They left at a time when copper and other nonferrous metals were desperately needed by the war machine. The Roosevelt administration tried various expedients to cope with this crisis. The WPB shut down gold mining in 1942, but the hope that these miners would move into the copper pits was unrealized. By midsummer of 1942, the army had furloughed more than 4,000 ex-miners back to their jobs. Still production lagged. Miners moved to farms where they had immunity from the draft. In 1943 McNutt sought help from the War Department. He explained that despite interregional recruitment, paying transportation costs, deferring miners, importing 4,000 Mexicans, and adjusting wages, the mines could not meet their production schedules without "the immediate furloughing of several thousand soldiers with mining experience.'' Secretary Stimson and Undersecretary Patterson disliked the proposal, which amounted to rescuing McNutt from his own inefficiency. Also, mine unions bitterly resented the use of soldiers. Reid Robinson, president of the International Union of Mine, Mill and Smelter Workers, wrote to Patterson that men in uniform should fight the war ''rather than making up for the unfortunate mistakes that have occurred in the treatment of the manpower problem.'' Patterson finally told McNutt in June 1943 that the War Department thought it would be ''unwise to release soldiers on inactive duty to work in non-ferrous mines.''[46]

Manpower problems in lumbering, foundry work, and mining continued into 1944. Now, with the invasion of Europe on June 6 and the departure of workers suffering from peace fever, the situation appeared out of control. The army, now on the attack, began using material at an unprecedented rated. New production schedules were imposed on war industries where just months before cutbacks had occurred. At this point James Byrnes, as Director of War Mobilization, supported McNutt by extending the provisions of the West Coast Plan to the entire nation by a directive of August 4, 1944. The directive also announced that ''upon application of the chairman of the WMC, all interested government agencies will apply any and all sanctions lawfully available to the Government, including allocation of materials, fuel, power and services to ensure compliance. . . .'' Once again the WPB, the War Department, and the Selective Service were told clearly that they must cooperate with McNutt in solving the manpower problem.[47]

On August 7 the WMC issued regulations ordering all regional manpower directors to put into effect an employment ceiling program. Employment ceilings were directed particularly against plants producing civilian goods in areas where war plants were short of labor. Not surprisingly, both organized labor and management considered this move a disguised labor draft. The WMC now asserted the authority to keep workers at a plant through controlled referral, to release workers from a nonessential plant through ceilings, and to determine where the released workers could find new jobs. Yet McNutt kept calling his plan voluntary and democratic. McNutt felt certain the plan would succeed because ''the average American is willing to take work most needed in the war effort.'' The new program drew 400,000 new workers into war plants. Yet, at the same time, at least 300,000 other war workers went looking for civilian jobs.[48] So much for the willingness of American workers.

The effectiveness of the new manpower plan was hampered by the same problems that worked against mobilization from the very beginning. McNutt lacked statutory power and congressional support. Also, he and President Roosevelt tried to accommodate too many special interests in the mobilization process. Under the new ceiling program, for example, workers with reemployment rights under the terms of a union contract had to be referred, if they requested it, to a job which also had such rights. Reinstatement rights defined by the National Labor Relations Board had to be recognized. The entire program of manpower control had to accommodate the labor-management precedents. Employers in essential or locally needed activities could employ apprentices in excess of the employment ceiling. As for priority referral, a plant's priority in receiving workers was affected by whether or not management practiced racial or sexual discrimination in hiring, and whether there was compliance with existing WMC programs. While McNutt spoke of forced release in November and December 1944, other officials spoke of borrowing workers. Anna Rosenberg in New York began a policy of borrowing key workers from nonessential industry for critical jobs in radar production. Regional manpower directors across the country adopted the same policy.[49]

As McNutt struggled to find workers for munitions plants in the United States, American soldiers in Europe continued to expend material at an unprecedented rate. Officers explained that excessive bombardments and high firing rates served to save the lives of combat troops. American firepower rather than American men would take German positions. In addition, the rapid advance of the Allied armies across France reduced the life expectancy of equipment. Eisenhower continued to demand more material. The administration responded on December 9, 1944, when Byrnes issued another work-or-fight order. He directed General Hershey to order local draft boards to induct all men from eighteen to thirty-seven who were not in essential war industry or who had left war work for civilian jobs. The order did produce a considerable transfer of workers. Byrnes had acted only a few days before German troops launched a massive counter-attack in the Ardennes Forest, demolishing the hope for an early end to the war.[50]

Although Byrnes had taken the play away from McNutt by 1945, the latter remained a busy man. The reversals in Europe led to a new campaign for national service legislation. At the same time pressure continued to build for the reconversion of manpower and plants to peacetime use. On the operational level McNutt's attempts to impose a voluntary system of manpower mobilization reached an ambiguous conclusion. From 1942 to 1945 McNutt and his agency had moved from voluntary referrals to controlled referrals to labor ceilings. All during this time the WPB and the Selective Service were supposed to help enforce the WMC program. Work-or-fight orders had been issued in 1942, 1943, and 1944. One executive order after another had given McNutt more power. Now, for the first three months of 1945, President Roosevelt requested from Congress a national service law, a law which would affect McNutt's operation.

Notes

1. Roosevelt to governors, December 19, 1941, box 20-139, RG 211, National Archives; Southern Governors' Conference to Roosevelt, May 20, 1942, official file 15-H, Franklin Roosevelt Papers, Hyde Park, N.Y.; files for October 13, 1941, July 16, 1942, May 20, 1942, quotes from June 26, 1943, June 18, 1942, in McNutt Papers, The Lilly Library, Indiana University, Bloomington, Ind.; *New York Times*, March 13, 1942, p. 12.

2. McNutt address to New England Conference, November 19, 1942, McNutt Papers; minutes of meeting between McNutt and Byrnes, March 10, 1943, box 20-139, RG 211; *New York Times*, November 3, 1942, p. 12.

3. Leonard P. Adams, *Wartime Manpower Mobilization* (Ithaca, N.Y.: Cornell University Press, 1951), p. 41; *New York Times*, January 5, 1943, p. 12, April 11, 1943, sec. 3, p. 14, August 7, 1943, p. 24, September 26, 1943, p. 42, June 28, 1944, p. 7, August 30, 1944, p. 19, and March 29, 1945, p. 24; *Monthly Labor Review*, July 1944, p. 89; manuscript for radio show "Steel Horizons," April 8, 1945, McNutt Papers.

4. *Monthly Labor Review*, September 1942, p. 482, May 1943, p. 1033, June 1943, p. 1118, September 1944, p. 661, and February 1945, p. 291.

5. *Ibid.*, May 1944, p. 996; *New York Times*, June 24, 1944, p. 26.

6. *Monthly Labor Review*, April 1945, p. 911; files for August 29, 1945, and October 1, 1945, McNutt Papers.

7. Speech file of April 29, 1942, McNutt Papers.

8. McNutt to McSherry, March 21, 1941, box 1B-manpower administration 117, RG 211; speech files of October 13, 1941, and December 11, 1941, McNutt Papers.

9. McNutt testimony before House Committee, January 14, 1942, McNutt Papers; speech file of May 6, 1942, McNutt Papers.

10. Speech files of April 29, 1942, November 1942, December 14, 1942, and December 23, 1942, McNutt Papers; Clara Beyer to Secretary Perkins, February 10, 1942, complained: "If the Labor Department is to have *any* functions at all during the war period the in-plant training function definitely belongs here." See A 159, folder 111, Clara Beyer Papers, Schlesinger Library, Radcliffe College, Cambridge, Mass.

11. *Monthly Labor Review*, May 1943, p. 1029; *New York Times*, January 31, 1943, Sec. 3, p. 11; entry of March 25, 1943, presidential diary of Harold Smith, Roosevelt Library, Hyde Park, N.Y.

12. Speech files of January 31, 1943, and September 17, 1943, McNutt Papers. By 1943 some 281 public and private colleges had been approved for use by the military in specialized training. See *Monthly Labor Review*, May 1943, p. 1029.

13. J. S. Studebaker to state directors, May 5, 1945, box 20-73, RG 211; *Monthly Labor Review*, April 1945, p. 914.

14. *Business Week*, March 27, 1943, p. 100; *ibid.*, November 6, 1943, p. 94; McNutt interview by Ernest Lindley, November 7, 1943, McNutt Papers; *New York Times*, August 31, 1944, p. 21, and March 22, 1945, p. 38.

15. *New York Times*, May 29, 1942, p. 34.

16. Grenville Clark and Arthur L. Williston, *The Effort for a National Service Law in World War II, 1942-1945* (Dedham, Mass.: privately published, 1947), pp. 48-51; *Business Week*, October 3, 1942, pp. 17-18; *Monthly Labor Review*, August 1943, p. 406; see Lester V. Chandler and Donald H. Wallace, eds., *Economic Mobilization and Stabilization* (New York: Holt, Rinehart, Winston, 1951), p. 141, for a critical estimate of the ESP's effectiveness.

17. Joel Seidman, *American Labor from Defense to Reconversion* (Chicago: University of Chicago Press, 1953), p. 159; *New York Times*, December 11, 1942, p.1.

18. Seidman, *American Labor*, p. 159; *Monthly Labor Review*, October 1942, pp. 714-15; Chandler and Wallace, *Economic Mobilization*, p. 141; McNutt interview, September 10, 1942, McNutt Papers; McNutt quoted from file of October 21, 1942, McNutt Papers; *New York Times*, December 11, 1942, p. 1, and December 15, 1942, p. 25.

19. Minutes of WMC, May 20, 1942, box 5-100, RG 211; *New York Times*, February 5, 1943, p. 1; *Monthly Labor Review*, June 1944, p. 1337; *New York Times*, February 6, 1943, p. 12; Herman M. Somers, *Presidential Agency: OWMR, The Office of War Mobilization and Reconversion* (Cambridge: Harvard University Press, 1950), pp. 167-69.

20. McNutt to Hon. Wendell Berge, Assistant Attorney General, October 29, 1943, box 1-1, RG 211.

21. *New York Times*, November 4, 1943, p. 33; *Monthly Labor Review*, February 1944, p. 464; McNutt to Fairchild Publications, December 7, 1943, McNutt Papers; *Monthly Labor Review*, November 1943, p. 932; speech file of January 12, 1944, McNutt Papers.

22. Correspondence file of Collis Stocking, box 20-92, 1945, RG 211.

23. Julius Applebaum to McNutt, February 4, 1943, box 1-1, RG 211; Roosevelt official file 4905 for March-April 1943, Roosevelt Papers; *New York Times*, January 14, 1943, p. 35; Colonel Gow to CG, February 7, 1945, box 185, Robert Patterson Papers, Library of Congress, Washington, D.C.

24. Adams, *Wartime Manpower*, p. 44, says McNutt's order had little effect. For another view see Somers, *Presidential Agency*, p. 169; *New York Times*, August 18, 1943, p. 40, and January 9, 1945, p. 14.

25. Samuel I. Rosenman, ed., *The Public Papers and Addresses of Franklin D. Roosevelt*, 13 vols. (New York: Harper and Row, 1938-1950), 12: 152-53.

26. L. H. Baum to McNutt, April 19, 1943, box 20-74, RG 211; speech file of April 27, 1943, McNutt Papers; Clark and Williston, *Effort for National Service*, p. 54; Adams, *Wartime Manpower*, p. 49.

27. McNutt article for *Manchester Guardian*, April 14, 1943, and speech file of April 27, 1943, McNutt Papers; regulations quoted from Carol Riegelman, *Labour-Management Co-operation in United States War Production* (Montreal: International Labour Office, 1948), pp. 42-43; *New York Times*, April 18, 1943, pp. 1, 40-41.

28. Chandler and Wallace, *Economic Mobilization*, p. 143; Adams, *Wartime Manpower*, pp. 50-51; speech file of January 13, 1944, McNutt Papers. See also entry for August 16, 1943, Henry Morgenthau Presidential Diary, 656: 61, Roosevelt Library, Hyde Park, N.Y.

29. *New York Times*, May 16, 1943, p. 12; McNutt to Austin, July 12, 1943, box 1-1, RG 211.

30. Radio broadcasts, May 23, 1943, May 30, 1943, and August 25, 1943, McNutt Papers.

31. Polenberg, *War and Society*, p. 22; Chandler and Wallace, *Economic Mobilization*, p. 145; John D. Hertz to Patterson, August 30, 1943, box 324, Harry Hopkins Papers, Roosevelt Library; John Dos Passos, *State of the Nation* (Boston: Houghton Mifflin, 1943), pp. 314-15; *Business Week*, August 28, 1943, p. 13; Byron Fairchild and Jonathan Grossman, *The Army and Industrial Manpower* (Washington, D.C.: U.S. Department of the Army, 1959), pp. 129-135; Somers, *Presidential Agency*, p. 144.

32. *New York Times*, August 11, 1943, p. 18; Fairchild and Grossman, *Army and Manpower*, pp. 30, 130, 139-145; speech file of October 21, 1943, McNutt Papers; *Monthly Labor Review*, February 1943, p. 415; *New York Times*, February 11, 1943, p. 14.

33. *New York Times*, September 4, 1943, p. 26, and September 12, 1943, p. 4; minutes of Management-Labor Policy Committee, September 14, 1943, box 5-98, RG 211; quote from Somers, *Presidential Agency*, pp. 146-47, see also pp. 61, 148-152.

34. See Chandler and Wallace, *Economic Mobilization*, pp. 144-45 for a good description of the plan; speech file of October 21, 1943, February 1, 1944, "Why You Must Take a War Job," by McNutt in McNutt Papers; digest of WPB minutes, September 21, 1943, box 12, Nelson Papers; for the role of the Selective Service see Hershey to Byrnes, September 15, 1943, White House file 41-43, Hershey Papers, Military History Research Collection, Carlisle Barracks, Pa.; *New York Times*, September 10, 1943, p. 18, and September 19, 1943, p. 16.

35. Somers, *Presidential Agency*, pp. 148-152; Hershey to state directors, October 23, 1943, office file, WW II, Hershey Papers; Lt. Col. Ben R. Howell to Lt. Col. William S. Iliff, September 24, 1943, index file, *ibid.*; Lt. Col. K. D. Pulcipher to George H. Baker, September 27, 1943, index file, *ibid.*

36. Fairchild and Grossman, *Army and Manpower*, p. 146; Albert A. Blum, "Sailor or Worker: A Manpower Dilemma during the Second World War," *Labor History* 6 (Fall 1965), p. 236; minutes of Management-Labor Policy Committee, October 19, 1943, box 5-98, RG 211; Somers, *Presidential Agency*, p. 152n.

37. Chandler and Wallace, *Economic Mobilization*, pp. 147-48; *New York Times*, April 6, 1944, p. 11.

38. Chandler and Wallace, *Economic Mobilization*, pp. 146, 148-49; Lt. Col. K. D. Pulcipher to Col. George H. Baker, October 14, 1943, index file, Hershey Papers; Fairchild and Grossman, *Army and Manpower*, p. 137; minutes of WMC, December 2, 1943, and December 16, 1943, RG 211; *Monthly Labor Review*, February 1944, p. 463.

39. *Monthly Labor Review*, February 1944, p. 317, and June 1944, p. 1337; speech file of April 13, 1944, McNutt Papers; *New York Times*, March 9, 1944, p. 12, and April 26, 1944, p. 38.

40. *Business Week*, May 13, 1944, p. 100; *New York Times*, May 20, 1944, p. 17, and May 28, 1944, p. 24.

41. *New York Times*, June 2, 1944, p. 1, and June 3, 1944, p. 1; McNutt interview on CBS, June 4, 1944, McNutt Papers; Patterson press release, June 5, 1944, box 184, Patterson Papers; speech file of June 6, 1944, McNutt Papers.

42. Speech file of June 9, 1944, McNutt Papers; *New York Times*, June 13, 1944, p. 22, June 28, 1944, p. 25, and June 29, 1944, p. 36.

43. *Monthly Labor Review*, July 1944, pp. 87-88; McNutt article, August 23, 1944, and testimony to House Subcommittee on Appropriations, April 26, 1945, McNutt Papers.

44. Digest of War Production Board minutes, May 2, 1944, box 12, Don Nelson Papers, Huntington Library, San Marino, Calif.; McNutt quoted in *New York Times*, July 5, 1944, p. 1; *New York Times*, July 10, 1944, p. 17; radio speech, July 9, 1944, McNutt Papers.

45. Hershey to Patterson, March [n.d.], 1943, box 184, Patterson Papers; Patterson to McNutt, April 30, 1943, *ibid.*; *New York Times*, April 27, 1944, p. 13; radio speech by McNutt, May 13, 1945, McNutt Papers; A. A. Hoehling, *Home Front, U.S.A.* (New York: Crowell, 1966), p. 69.

46. Donald Nelson, *Arsenal of Democracy* (New York: Harcourt, Brace, 1946), p. 171; digest of War Production Board minutes, September 1, 1942, box 12, Nelson

Papers; Lubin to Hopkins, November 4, 1942, file 324, Hopkins Papers; F. R. Denton to James Boyd, May 21, 1943, box 184-5, Patterson Papers; McNutt to Patterson, May 22, 1943, *ibid.*; Reid Robinson to Patterson, August 19, 1943, *ibid.*; Patterson to McNutt, June 10, 1943, *ibid.*

47. *Monthly Labor Review*, December 1944, p. 1319; quoted in Somers, *Presidential Agency*, p. 154; Riegelman, *Labour-Management Co-operation*, p. 47.

48. Byrnes quoted in *Monthly Labor Review*, October 1944, p. 749; *Monthly Labor Review*, August 1944, p. 303; *New York Times*, August 11, 1944, p. 28; McNutt quoted in file of August 21, 1944, McNutt Papers; Fairchild and Grossman, *Army and Manpower*, p. 203.

49. *New York Times*, November 23, 1944, p. 33, and December 30, 1944, p. 24; *Monthly Labor Review*: September 1944, p. 519, February 1945, p. 295, April 1945, p. 916.

50. Byrnes to Roosevelt, December 20, 1944, James Byrnes Papers, Clemson University Library, Clemson, S.C.; Fairchild and Grossman, *Army and Manpower*, p. 202.

CHAPTER 4

The National Service Alternative

Roosevelt's decision to establish the War Manpower Commission did not mean he was ignorant of the advantages of a national service law. As early as 1942 the President was bombarded with arguments in favor of a labor draft. The two men most eager for such an alternative were Grenville Clark and Henry Stimson. Clark, an old friend who had clerked in the same law firm as Roosevelt, played a major role in marshaling public support for the Selective Service bill of 1940. Both Clark and Stimson were charter members in that elite corps of eastern lawyers who believed fervently in internationalism. No sooner had the United States declared war than they began advocating the expansion of the military draft to cover civilian labor.[1]

I

Before the War Manpower Commission started Clark felt voluntarism was bankrupt as a solution to the mobilization of labor. He preferred national service because such a step would do much "to pull the whole country together and keep it united. . . ." On a practical level he argued that volunteer labor was unreliable during war.[2] As Roosevelt groped for a direction to manpower mobilization he welcomed Clark's suggestions. On April 14, 1942, Clark urged the President to register all men and women from ages eighteen to sixty-five and push through Congress a bill giving the administration the power to force the registrants to serve in any capacity the government desired. Four days later Roosevelt issued an executive order establishing the WMC under McNutt with his commitment to a voluntary plan, but instructed him to begin a study of the national service alternative. The new manpower czar created a subcommittee within the WMC to draft a proposal.[3]

Roosevelt thought it best to go slowly on such a radical step. As no serious labor shortages had occurred, the administration felt there was time to experiment. Before congressional committees McNutt announced that national service "might never be necessary," but he would have a bill ready if the President wanted to act. As for Grenville Clark, he was dismayed by Roosevelt's decision to give McNutt responsibility for national service. Clark thought McNutt a political hack with presidential ambitions.[4]

National service might have been popular in the War Department but both McNutt and Donald Nelson of the WPB disliked what they thought was an attempt to militarize the entire mobilization question. Secretary of War Stimson, in contrast, supported national service but worried about giving too much power to a civilian such as McNutt. Stimson also feared that pushing a national service bill in the fall might delay congressional approval for the drafting of eighteen-year-olds. In fact, McNutt would have accepted national service if it meant increased power for the WMC, but he did have reservations about Clark's proposal which seemed to be a pro-employer measure.[5]

Opposition to national service also came from other sources. Frances Perkins, the Secretary of Labor, felt that such a step was much too drastic.[6] Organized labor felt the same way. After receiving McNutt's request for an opinion, the MLPC of the WMC issued a statement in October 1942 which recognized the "supreme moral obligation to render personal service in the war effort," but doubted that converting such a moral obligation into a legal one would solve the manpower problem.[7] McNutt informed Roosevelt that the presidents of various unions had been consulted and that they had refused to even discuss national service. "Under no circumstances," wrote McNutt, "could labor accept such a law."[8]

In the Senate, Harry Truman's special committee to investigate the national defense program considered the national service idea.

Truman reported confidentially to Roosevelt that it would be a mistake to "even consider" such compulsory legislation. Voluntary methods had not been given a fair test. Similar opinions reached the President from the House where John H. Tolan's special committee investigating labor migration reported that the average American was confused by the lack of coordination among government agencies dealing with manpower.[9]

Such opposition led Roosevelt to decide, as an alternative to national service, to reorganize the WMC and give McNutt more power. Clark tried desperately to prevent McNutt's expansion of power. But Roosevelt, instead of firing McNutt, placed the Selective Service under the WMC. This executive order of December 1942 reflected the opinions of organized labor and Congress, but it also represented continued faith in McNutt and a voluntary approach.[10]

II

Such faith was soon tested. Despite increased activity by McNutt and the WMC, a severe manpower shortage developed during 1943. National service thus received a new lease on life. Clark and Stimson became optimistic and even Congress seemed receptive to a new approach to manpower mobilization. In January, a subcommittee of the Senate's committee on appropriations began extensive hearings on manpower. The hearings were mainly concerned with the shortage of agricultural labor and eventually led to an amendment to the Selective Service law providing occupational deferments for farm workers.[11] But the testimony also revealed drawbacks in McNutt's work. Despite various new devices for recruiting labor, shortages continued, especially on the West Coast.

With little encouragement or direction from the President, but a great deal from Clark, Congressman James Wadsworth and Senator Warren Austin introduced a national service bill in Congress on February 8, 1943 (S. 666; H. 1742). This congressional initiative finally forced Roosevelt to attend to the problem. At a cabinet meeting on February 19, the President asked McNutt and Stimson to consider again the feasibility of national service despite the disagreement within the administration over the Austin-Wadsworth bill.[12] At the same time Roosevelt turned to Sam Rosenman, an old friend and troubleshooter, to conduct a fresh investigation of the entire manpower problem. Rosenman began his task in February by turning for advice to Oscar Cox of the Justice Department. Cox, a confirmed New Dealer, recommended that Roosevelt try to amend the Austin-Wadsworth bill and make it an administration measure, despite its Republican origins. Rosenman admitted that the President's intentions remained a mystery, but national service did not seem to have priority. Cox warned that if national service failed to pass in Congress it would create political problems for Roosevelt, even though he had not sponsored the bill. Rosenman explained that "someone around here is drawing a bill for us," but he was ignorant of the earlier drafts made by Clark and McNutt.[13]

Roosevelt created confusion over lines of authority and responsibility for leadership in the debate over national service. At a cabinet meeting on March 4 McNutt explained to the President that within days Stimson, Knox, and Patterson would join him [McNutt] in testifying before Congress on the Austin-Wadsworth bill. McNutt urged Roosevelt to spell out the administration's position on national service to prevent cabinet members from contradicting each other. Roosevelt could only reply vaguely that he favored the idea of national service but that Rosenman had not completed his study. The President wanted to delay taking a position until he read Rosenman's report.[14]

Rosenman, in carrying out Roosevelt's orders, established a special review board to investigate manpower. The board included, in addition to Rosenman, James Byrnes, Bernard Baruch, Admiral William Leahy, and Harry Hopkins. The men heard testimony from the various agencies interested in manpower. As part of his testimony McNutt submitted the draft of a national service bill which Roosevelt had commissioned in 1942. This draft imposed a national service obligation on everyone sixteen and over, male and female. As a concession to congressional sensibilities, the WMC draft provided that national service would end 180 days after a peace treaty was signed or upon passage of either a presidential proclamation or a concurrent resolution.[15] The key provision obligated workers to render service and employers to accept workers as the government required.

Here was a national service system which McNutt felt could pass Congress and also take advantage of the skills developed by the WMC, which would administer the act if Roosevelt desired such a system. At the same time McNutt argued against national service to the Rosenman board. A new system would take months to put into operation and there was no pressing need for it. Rosenman's report to Roosevelt agreed. None of the witnesses who appeared before the review board felt national service had to be passed immediately. Most decisive to the political minds of men such as Hopkins and Byrnes was the simple fact that such a law had little chance of passing Congress until the American people had been "conditioned" to such a radical step by Roosevelt.[16]

At the War Department Stimson and Patterson were disappointed at the lack of enthusiasm for national service. Although he had drafted a bill, McNutt now felt no urgency. He sensed Roosevelt's own reluctance and hung back. But Patterson rushed to Capitol Hill to testify in favor of Austin-Wadsworth. Stimson, after reflecting on the issue, decided to remain silent. He turned down Clark's appeal to join a public campaign but did write two forceful memos to Roosevelt urging support of the bill.[17] As the war effort expanded Stimson felt sure national service would become inevitable. Already on April 8, 1943, Roosevelt was forced to freeze wages and prices. In early May John L. Lewis took his United Mine Workers out of the pits, a move which threatened all war industry.[18]

Stimson and Secretary Knox of the navy thought to capitalize on the public irritation to Lewis's strike to push through national service. Congress began debating the Smith-Connally bill, which would give the President power to draft strikers. Congressman Wadsworth quickly wrote Knox and Stimson that the national service bill, still stalled in committee, might be amended to complement Smith-Connally. Both military leaders approved the idea and urged Roosevelt to support an amendment providing that national service would go into effect only to prevent a serious work stoppage in certain production areas. But now opposition arose from an unexpected source. Undersecretary Patterson objected to tying national service to Smith-Connally. The latter was an antistrike bill while national service was a mobilization measure. He feared if the military became involved in labor-management disputes everyone would be offended. Roosevelt agreed and also vetoed the Smith-Connally bill on June 25. Congress quickly overrode the presidential veto and passed the War Labor Disputes Act (Smith-Connally), but the national service bill remained in committee.[19]

Within the next few weeks McNutt accelerated his program. He came out for drafting fathers rather than essential workers. In September James Byrnes established a manpower program for the West Coast. Clark denounced such actions as too little and stressed that public opinion wanted more. For example, a Gallup poll of August 29, 1943, asked "if there is a shortage of men and women workers for war industries this fall should the Government draft persons to fill these jobs?" Some 79 percent said yes and only 14 percent said no. Stimson continued to argue to Roosevelt that national service would be valuable as a sign of the common obligation of all citizens to support the war. Roosevelt tried to placate Stimson and Clark by once again instructing Rosenman to study the feasibility of national service.[20]

Ironically, Rosenman turned to the WMC for advice because Roosevelt had originally assigned the drafting of a national service bill to this agency. William Haber, McNutt's assistant, responded by rushing forward with the draft bill which had been floating around the agency for six months. In the War Department Patterson and Stimson repeated the old arguments for national service.[21]

Other members of the administration, however, still opposed the idea. Byrnes and Baruch had worked hard to set up the West Coast Plan. They thought it inconsistent to turn to national service before their plan had been given a fair trial. Baruch wrote Roosevelt urging delay on compulsory legislation. Baruch felt it was unfair to draft labor without some tighter control over industrial profits. He bluntly warned that he would testify against national service if called before a congressional committee.[22]

Roosevelt could not ignore such a threat even though it left him in a quandary. After some six months of hearings Congress had not acted on the Austin-Wadsworth bill. Left without clear presidential guidance, Congress appeared increasingly unenthusiastic on national service. Within the administration, disagreement continued over the idea. McNutt was willing to draft another bill but he felt the WMC was doing an adequate job with voluntary controls. Nelson of the War Production Board shared McNutt's opinion. Gustav Peck of WPB, in a year-end summary, wrote that the worst was over in manpower. He expected needs and supplies to be balanced in early 1944.[23]

At the War Department national service remained highly desirable. Stimson spent considerable time with Wadsworth and Austin, trying to help promote their bill. After much badgering, the Secretary obtained from Roosevelt a promise that national service would receive attention in early 1944. The President had visited combat zones in North Africa during his trip to Teheran. This firsthand experience with the problems of war led him to reconsider national service. On December 28, 1943, Stimson, Knox, Patterson, Forrestal, Emory S. Land, and H. L. Vickery cosigned a letter to Roosevelt in which they urged passage of national service because the life of the nation and civilization was at stake. "In such a time," they wrote, "there can be no discrimination between the men and women who are assigned by the government to its defense at the battlefront and the men and women assigned to producing the vital materials. . . ."[24]

III

As Roosevelt drafted his State of the Union address for January 11, 1944, several pressing issues in addition to national service confronted him. On the home front he sought some means of stabilizing the economy and preventing a recurrence of the labor disputes of 1943. After having visited the fighting front, he realized more than ever the importance of domestic support for the military. He also wanted tax reform and price controls. Despite his noble intentions, Roosevelt now blundered badly. He recommended a program to Congress which he knew had support from only one element in the administration, a program that lacked majority support on Capitol Hill.

National service still seemed a mistake to several of Roosevelt's advisors. Harold Smith, the Director of the Budget, personally argued that the time was past for such a measure. He came away from a conference with the feeling that "probably he [FDR] was being sold a bill of goods." Byrnes and Baruch wanted more time for their West Coast program. Nelson believed the manpower crisis was over. McNutt, after an extensive field trip, submitted that the WMC was doing a fine job. Not only did Roosevelt ignore this opinion, he also failed to offer Congress specific guidelines on the type of national service bill he desired and he linked it to such sensitive topics as tax reform and price control. James Wadsworth called this strategy "muddying the waters."[25]

Whatever Roosevelt's motives, the War Department rejoiced at the State of the Union message. Stimson had anticipated the presidential call by promising James Wadsworth that Patterson and Howard Petersen in the War Department would aid in pushing the bill through Congress. Wadsworth counted on this support for statistics and personal testimony. He was not disappointed.[26] Military men paraded before congressional hearings.

Yet a month later the national service bill remained as far from passage as in 1943. Indeed, the prospects seemed even less promising because of a deterioration in relations between the White House and Capitol Hill. Roosevelt's program, as expressed in the State of the Union address, was floundering due to a lack of coordination with party leaders. One result of this breakdown was the rejection of Roosevelt's tax reform bill. Instead, Congress passed a substitute bill which evoked from Roosevelt a stinging veto message. In turn, the veto prompted the resignation of Senate Majority Leader Alben Barkley. In the midst of this controversy, Roosevelt had little time for national service.

By late March both Stimson and Clark agreed that the President needed prompting if national service was to be saved. In Congress an amendment appeared to substitute a draft of those classified 4-F for true national service. Making matters even worse, administration dissension over national service became public. On March 23 Donald Nelson announced his support for the 4-F amendment and told the House Military Affairs subcommittee that a general labor draft was no longer needed. A few days later McNutt appeared before the same committee and announced his opposition to national service. The press began to play up the disagreement between Roosevelt's civilian and military advisors.[27]

To add to the President's woes, confusion reigned within the camp of supporters of the bill over how to respond to the 4-F amendment. Ironically, military testimony before Congress hurt rather than helped the cause. Patterson and General Brehon Somerville both exaggerated the problems of material shortage and were frequently forced to revise their comments. Howard Petersen and Patterson, whom Clark counted on for passage of the bill, now felt it essential to reject the 4-F compromise. Privately, Petersen admitted that nothing short of a military disaster would save the national service bill from amendment. Upon hearing this estimate,

Stimson decided to compromise. He informed Byrnes that the 4-F amendment would be acceptable if it could be made part of a civilian draft rather than being placed under Selective Service. Byrnes agreed with Stimson on the compromise, but now Patterson refused to give up on the original bill. Byrnes concluded that the entire national service enterprise was a mess. Senator Austin agreed. Both men were confused and irritated.[28]

In the midst of this confusion the White House remained silent. When, in April, the War Department sought to save national service by urging Roosevelt to apply pressure on Congress, the President asked Rosenman for guidance. The judge recommended that Roosevelt issue a new message to Congress, stressing the increasingly urgent need for national service and withdrawing his demand for tax reform. Rosenman also counseled the President to stress the unfortunate departure of thousands of men and women from war industry and to admit that "it is not necessary to have a universal act imposing compulsion . . . over the entire population." Roosevelt's only hope was to request a bill which would enable the administration to deal with specific shortages in local areas, to establish maximum labor ceilings, and to prohibit rehiring by channeling all labor through the USES. In fact, Rosenman called for legislative sanctions for the existing WMC program, especially the West Coast Plan. The administration had come full circle. But Rosenman offered a concession to the military by recommending that Roosevelt inform Congress that a new manpower czar would be appointed and that the Selective Service would not be used to implement the act.[29]

While Roosevelt mulled this proposal, Stimson and Patterson gave up on national service and were reduced to testifying in favor of a new bill sponsored by Senator Ralph O. Brewster which gave legislative authority to McNutt's work-or-fight orders.[30] A year which had begun with such bright prospects for national service was now running its course with McNutt still running a voluntary manpower program.

IV

The Allied invasion of Europe took place on June 6, 1944. By July 31, 1944, General George Patton's Third Army had launched a massive breakthrough and the collapse of the German army in

France began. If a stalemate had occurred on the beaches of Normandy the hopes for national service might have been revived. But with military success McNutt seemed a more realistic prophet about manpower than the War Department. On September 8, McNutt testified before the Truman committee of the Senate that although some shortages still existed he contemplated an early end to manpower controls. As for national service, he testified that "for us to say that a shortage of 200,000 men calls for such legislation at a time when we have 66,600,000 in industry and the armed forces would be foolish."[31]

Manpower mobilization seemed to be doing nicely but the winds of war blew in strange patterns. What the thrust of Patton's tanks lost for Stimson in July, the lunge of German panzer divisions helped him recover in December. On December 16, 1944, Hitler launched a last desperate gamble on the western front. A massive spearhead of 1,000 tanks and assault guns broke through the American lines in the Ardennes Forest. The Battle of the Bulge was finished for Germany by December 26, although the final American offensive did not begin until March 1945. Yet, while it lasted, the German counterattack frightened the American public. The War Department saw the battle as an opportunity to push through a national service bill.[32]

Stimson laid it on the line for Roosevelt following a cabinet meeting of December 22, 1944, a few days before the collapse of the German offensive. He told the President that manpower shortages were so critical that without national service he would have "to use the Selective Service Act as a substitute . . . and draft men who were not physically fit for combat duty and use them for industry for production." Such a procedure was inefficient because it did not touch women while the armed forces desperately needed more nurses. Roosevelt agreed with Stimson and told him to draft a message to Congress calling for national service to cover men and women between ages eighteen and forty-five. Stimson returned to his desk and told Patterson to get busy writing a bill.[33]

Grenville Clark, always in tune with the War Department, also planned to begin a massive lobbying campaign on December 30, but Patterson restrained him. The Undersecretary knew Stimson was making progress in enlisting Roosevelt's full support. The President would not want to follow like a cockboat in Clark's wake.

But Clark remained suspicious and warned that "trying to guess the mental processes of the Great White Father is a risky business." The campaign should not be delayed too long. Patterson agreed and hoped that Stimson could persuade the Joint Chiefs to join with the President in an appeal to Congress for national service. General George Marshall, Admiral Ernest King, and Stimson took their case to the White House.[34]

January 1945 was a crucial month for Roosevelt and for the United States. Events crowded in from the fighting front and the diplomatic front. The German salient still existed. The Russians had recognized the Lublin government instead of the Polish government in England. Within a few weeks Roosevelt would fly to meet Stalin and Churchill at Yalta in the Crimea. An inauguration had to be held as the President began his fourth term. In the midst of these problems and pressures, the War Department wanted national service.

As eyes focused on the White House, the national service issue reemerged on Capitol Hill. On January 5 a new bill (May-Bailey) was introduced. In keeping with the recommendation of Byrnes, the new bill provided for a draft of registered workers from eighteen to forty-five who held 4-F classification and who refused to accept war jobs. Ironically, McNutt was touring European battlefields when this new proposal arose. The message which Roosevelt finally sent to Congress on manpower reflected a compromise between the Byrnes and Stimson views. Stimson was disappointed at the age range and at the use of the draft as punishment. Rosenman explained to the Secretary that while the President agreed in theory with the need for true national service Congress would never pass such a law.[35]

As hearings began on the May-Bailey bill, Stimson and Byrnes continued to disagree over what the administration should expect from Congress. Stimson wanted national service; Byrnes preferred just a 4-F draft. Congressman John Sparkman soon asked if the hearings by the House Committee on Military Affairs would be limited to a 4-F draft or cover national service. Congressman Andrew J. May, a cosponsor of the bill, replied that passage of a 4-F draft might make national service unnecessary. But the War Department emphatically disagreed with this reasoning. Stimson continued to urge Roosevelt to endorse true national service because a 4-F law would be "wholly inadequate," as labor battalions were useless. In response Roosevelt continued to explain to Stimson the realities of legislative politics. The President was sympathetic to the calls from his military advisors and even offered to warn Congress that the army was at the end of its divisional strength. He promised to meet with congressional leaders within a few days.[36]

The next day, Friday, January 12, the President left for Hyde Park. Stimson continued to badger him and even sent a special courier plane up the Hudson River with a draft message calling on Congress to pass national service. Although not sharing Stimson's sense of urgency, Roosevelt did ask his secretary, William Hassett, to draft a new message to Congress on the issue. The final product failed to please Stimson and he asked Roosevelt to drop the message and just pen a private note to Chairman May, a note which Marshall and King could cosign. On January 16, Marshall and King arrived at the White House for the meeting with leaders of the House and Senate Military Affairs Committees. The comments at this meeting convinced Roosevelt, as Byrnes had predicted, that a 4-F draft was the most he could expect from Congress, despite Stimson's pleas. But to please the Secretary of War, Roosevelt also wrote a letter to Chairman May announcing that the May-Bailey bill would "go far to secure the effective employment in the war effort of all registrants under the Selective Service law." As prompt action was more important than details, Roosevelt asked Congress to pass the May-Bailey bill to show American fighting men that the nation stood behind them. Attached to this note were letters from Marshall and King expressing the urgency of the military's needs. Marshall announced that personnel losses over the last two months had taxed the replacement system to the "breaking point."[37]

Proof of the unpopularity of national service emerged during congressional hearings. On January 10, 1945, representatives of the army and navy appeared before the House Committee on Military Affairs. Undersecretary Patterson opened the War Department's case by explaining that he supported HR 1119 (May-Bailey) only as the first step toward a general national service law. The current bill would affect only 4-F types from ages eighteen to forty-five, requiring them to work in war industry or be drafted into labor battalions.

As he had in 1944, Patterson once again requested that the military not be burdened with work battalions. He recommended an amendment to the bill providing for civil penalties rather than drafting those who refused to take war jobs.[38]

Both Patterson and Ralph Bard of the navy made a strong case for national service but the committee reacted with hostility. Several congressmen, especially Dewey J. Short and Ivor D. Fenton, emphasized that the real problem was not a shortage of men but faulty administration. When Congressman Short asked for evidence of weapon shortages on the battlefront, Patterson admitted "there is none." He also admitted that the German breakthrough in December had not been due to a lack of weapons or men.[39]

Julius Krug, who had recently replaced Nelson as head of the War Production Board, appeared next before the committee. He parroted the military line about endorsing HR 1119 but hoping for more. While impressive in his command of production statistics, Krug stumbled badly when he spoke of the method to be used to administer the bill. When Clare Boothe Luce inquired about the role of McNutt and the WMC under the bill, Krug became confused and admitted that General Hershey could entirely ignore McNutt in determining manpower shortages.[40] Under May-Bailey, it appeared, Selective Service rather than the WMC would administer any labor draft.

Congresswoman Luce had uncovered a sticky problem, a problem which was already creating dissension within the Roosevelt administration. As originally drafted, the May-Bailey bill gave the Selective Service System (SSS) control over administering the limited 4-F labor draft. But McNutt rightly felt such a procedure would waste the talents of the WMC. When James Byrnes met with his advisory board at the Office of War Mobilization and Reconversion on January 9, McNutt's supporters stressed the need for an amendment to May-Bailey which would put the WMC rather than the SSS in charge of allocating civilian manpower. This argument won strong support from organized labor and management. The War Department, however, disagreed. Patterson felt that no one in the country had confidence in McNutt and that Hershey would be more sympathetic to War Department guidance.[41]

The WMC officials began to worry about their future. While McNutt toured battlefields in Europe, his deputy, Judge Charles M. Hay, tried to defend WMC in testimony on the May-Bailey bill before the House committee. Hay stressed such achievements of WMC as stabilization, priority referral, and labor ceilings. He refused to support the bill in its present form. Instead, he argued that the WMC could do the job and called for legislation to strengthen McNutt's position.[42] His testimony launched a flood of opposition to May-Bailey. In rapid succession a series of opponents to any military-controlled labor draft appeared.

Lewis G. Hines, representing the AFL, testified in a way which demolished much of the publicity given out by the military. The overriding theme of Hines's testimony, as well as that of Phillip Murray of the Congress of Industrial Organizations, was that no labor shortage existed which would justify national service. Hines explained how he had sat down with General Somerville and received a list of eighty-five factories supposedly short of labor. Upon checking with local labor officials, Hines found that "in every instance . . . these needs were exaggerated for some reason or other." Consistently, labor found that the figures of the WMC were more realistic than those of the War Department. Indeed, both Hines and Murray applauded the good job which McNutt was doing and endorsed legislation to support him. These labor leaders saw HR 1119 as a foot in the door for national service and rejected it.[43]

Somewhat surprisingly, considering traditional labor-management hostility, leaders of American business supported the testimony of the unions in opposition to May-Bailey. Frederick C. Crawford, representing the National Association of Manufacturers, testified in opposition to national service and HR 1119. He joined other management leaders such as Michael J. Hickey of New Jersey and Forrest E. McGuire of Syracuse in calling for legislation providing more authority to McNutt's existing programs of employment ceilings, controlled referrals, and compulsory releases.[44]

Indecision over whether shortages were serious and over how the May-Bailey 4-F draft would be administered added to the confusion. Congressman Short hinted that Chairman Andrew May was not "too hot about" the bill, something May vigorously denied. Colonel Francis V. Keesling of the SSS complimented the hedging testimony of General Hershey by admitting that of the 3,500,000 4-F types in the nation no one could tell how many were already working in war industry. Keesling also drew attention to the autonomy of local draft boards which would presumably administer the proposed 4-F draft.[45] Such words only contributed to the second thoughts of many congressmen.

At the White House the President remained busy with foreign policy problems. After his endorsement of January 16, Roosevelt allowed James Byrnes to monitor the bill. Soon, both Byrnes and Roosevelt departed for Yalta to meet with Stalin and Churchill. No wonder Undersecretary Patterson returned from his appearance before the House committee deeply pessimistic about national service. In his mind the discarded Austin-Wadsworth bill was infinitely superior to the May-Bailey bill. But the War Department had to be satisfied with what it could get and on January 24 it got May-Bailey. The House Military Affairs Committee approved HR 1119 by a vote of twenty to five. The bill dealt only with 4-F types and provided for supervision by the SSS. This second feature would hurt chances of passage in the Senate and the bill appeared doomed unless Byrnes and his aide, General Lucius Clay, could reconcile the rivalry of McNutt and Hershey. As Byrnes left for Yalta, Clay decided to call a meeting of all interested parties. He wanted to promote a united front and he was worried over some recent articles "apparently inspired by the WMC," which hinted that labor applications were increasing so rapidly that May-Bailey would not be needed. In this hostile atmosphere Patterson, Krug, Bard, and McNutt met on January 27 with Clay to discuss the May-Bailey bill. The meeting was friendly and all participants agreed to support the bill in the Senate. Most importantly, they all agreed to support an amendment to the bill which would allow Byrnes to designate McNutt as the operating head of the 4-F draft rather than Hershey. This amendment was the price paid for McNutt's support of the bill, but Byrnes had favored such a procedure even earlier.[46]

Eyes focused on the Senate after the House finally passed the May-Bailey bill on February 1, 1945, by a vote of 246 to 165. Before debate began in the Senate the administration, in keeping with the Clay compromise, sought to introduce the amendment giving power to the WMC. Such a move provoked controversy. An earlier attempt by Congressman Jerry Voorhis to substitute for May-Bailey a bill giving power to the existing WMC program had lost on a teller vote in the House by 205 to seventy-one. Mrs. Luce had announced that a vote for the Voorhis bill would be a vote of confidence in McNutt. "I would not challenge the honesty or fairness of any man in government," she declared, "but the judgment of the War Manpower Commissioner is open to question."[47]

His judgment was open to question in the Senate as well. Given the War Department's distrust of McNutt and the House's suspicions of his ability, no one should have been surprised when opposition arose to the Byrnes amendment to May-Bailey. On February 5, 1945, Clay wrote to Byrnes that "the existing situation with respect to the May Bill is rather uncertain." When Byrnes left the country he believed that a united front had been created by the various members of the administration, including the War Department. This agreement called for endorsing an amendment to May-Bailey giving Byrnes the power to designate McNutt to administer the 4-F labor draft. Accordingly, the Senate Military Affairs Committee began considering a revision of May-Bailey which would provide Byrnes with directorship and strengthen the WMC at the expense of the SSS.[48]

Now, at this critical stage, with both Roosevelt and Byrnes out of the country and the hearings under way, Clay felt "the War Department lost its nerve." In fact, loss of nerve had little to do with what ensued. The War Department began to renege on the Byrnes compromise because Stimson and Patterson now saw good prospects for passage of May-Bailey without having to accept the distasteful pill of control by McNutt. The House-passed May-Bailey bill gave power to Hershey who was controlled by the War Department. Stimson and Patterson and others at the War Department used phone calls and personal visits to members of the Senate committee to pass the word that the new Byrnes amendments were not needed; Stimson preferred they be withdrawn.[49]

This War Department lobbying only confused the issue. Several members of the Senate committee were in favor of giving Byrnes and McNutt control. They resented the reversal of the War Department. Senator Edwin C. Johnson publicly charged that the War Department was trying to sabotage the bill by saying one thing publicly but another privately. Publicly the military endorsed Byrnes's amendment but privately the military argued for the original bill passed by the House. Clay, acting for the absent Byrnes, refused to draw back from the original agreement on the amendments, an agreement which the War Department had endorsed. To make matters worse, General Hershey, who had also agreed to support Byrnes's amendments, was now reneging on his commitment. According to Clay, Hershey's agents had passed the word to senators that the general preferred to assume the role outlined for him in the bill passed by the House. In the midst of this quibbling Byrnes's advisory board released to the Senate committee a resolution adopted earlier endorsing the agreement to assign the WMC a major role in the new manpower bill. As Senate hearings began, the administration's delicate compromise had come unstuck. Clay blamed the War Department and Hershey for the problem.[50]

Senate committee hearings began on February 6 and lasted until February 15. In many ways the testimony was a rehash of what had been said to the House committee. Stimson appeared with a ringing endorsement of national service. Patterson came next and reiterated his presentation to the House. Before stepping down Patterson could not resist dismissing as worthless the work of the WMC. He, like Stimson, stated unequivocally that the psychological factor was probably the most important reason for passing the bill. Secretary of the Navy James Forrestal also agreed that the moral sanction of the law was infinitely more important than its legal sanctions.[51]

In the afternoon the committee heard a series of witnesses who were, to varying degrees, opponents of any civilian draft. McNutt, recently returned from Europe, testified that he favored the bill as amended, not because the WMC program had failed, but because he could use more statutory power. He also challenged Patterson's attack on the WMC, insisting that the various programs had worked effectively. He warned that if Congress passed the May-Bailey bill without the Byrnes amendments, the entire program built by WMC would be destroyed. "In all candor," McNutt testified, "our war effort will be hurt rather than helped" by an unamended May-Bailey bill. Specifically, he warned against giving Hershey power over civilian manpower. The Selective Service operated under the influence of the military in McNutt's opinion.[52]

On the next day, when Krug of the WPB and Hershey appeared, they met a series of embarrassing questions. Krug endorsed the amended May-Bailey bill, but had hardly concluded his statement when he was attacked by Senator Joseph O'Mahoney. The senator forced Krug to admit that American workers had responded enthusiastically to openings in war work over the last few months. Krug also admitted that he favored using the existing WMC arrangements, which seemed to be working well. Having disposed of Krug, the senators turned to General Hershey. The Director of Selective Service was in no mood to risk his neck for the military or for the House version of May-Bailey, which gave him control of the labor draft. Too often he had acted at Stimson's urgings, only to be left alone to take the ensuing criticism. Hershey finally admitted he favored an amended May-Bailey bill. Despite, or perhaps because of, such testimony, the new bill (HR 1752) was in trouble.[53]

Testimony from several hostile witnesses united with existing reservations by senators to create momentum for redrafting the entire May-Bailey bill rather than just amending it. Ironically, the original bill passed by the House (HR 1119), which the War Department had planned to use as a springboard to true national service and the displacement of McNutt by Hershey, was slowly being transformed into a legislative endorsement of the WMC. Once again in the Senate hearings, representatives of organized labor appeared or wrote to denounce the May-Bailey bill even with the Byrnes amendments. These critics saw both HR 1119 and HR 1752 as disguised national service. Labor leaders documented case after case of the War Department exaggerating labor shortages and of layoffs occurring in areas where the military insisted more workers were needed. While downgrading the military with one hand, these witnesses upgraded McNutt with the other. They recommended statutory power for the WMC. Ira Mosher, president of the National Association of Manufacturers (NAM), recommended a law putting teeth into local WMC stabilization programs. The three major segments of the labor market—management, unions, farm groups—agreed that McNutt's approach was working, that labor shortages were purely local, and that if a law had to be passed it would be best to give power to McNutt and the WMC.[54]

V

The War Department now entered the fray and sought to reverse the tide of battle. Undersecretary Patterson sent telegrams to all editors of *Stars and Stripes*, the GI newspaper, requesting soldier opinion polls and editorials which could be used to convince senators to pass the May-Bailey bill. Secretary Stimson launched a personal campaign to cultivate members of the Senate Military Affairs Committee. Over to Woodley, Stimson's Washington estate, came Senator Thomas, the chairman, for a fireside chat. Thomas admitted to Stimson that Roosevelt would probably get some kind of bill. Thomas personally opposed a labor draft but would do his best to satisfy Stimson and Roosevelt. Next, Stimson sought out Senator Johnson and tried to convert him. After his conferences Stimson realized that the bill had a "thorny road" before it. He fumed at the absence of both Byrnes and Roosevelt during this critical period in Congress. Thousands of miles away in the Crimea the President finally acceded to a request from Clay and sent a personal message on February 11 to Senator Barkley expressing hope that "legislation embracing the principle of the May bill can be speedily enacted," as it would "greatly contribute to the success of our arms." Such statements were fine, but in Stimson's mind, they were little cure for the problem of "absentee leadership."[55]

Byrnes returned from Yalta on February 13. Stimson called for an immediate conference to save May-Bailey and to put an end to public confusion. With conflicting statements and alternate bills floating around, Stimson argued to Byrnes that the time had arrived for an appeal over the head of Congress to the American people. Byrnes agreed that the Senate committee was out of control. He gave Stimson permission for a public appeal to save an amended May-Bailey.[56]

Few men were better prepared for such an appeal than Stimson. He was universally admired and had served four presidents with distinction. If any man besides Roosevelt could turn the tide it was the bipartisan Secretary of War. He arranged with the Blue Network for an address to the nation and took the air on February 18 with confidence. He denounced the Senate committee for stalling the May-Bailey bill and hinted that special-interest groups with "trivial" goals had captured control of the senators. These delays cost lives and indicated a failure of democracy, he concluded. Stimson was proud of the speech, despite the curious reaction it produced.[57]

Two days later the Senate committee voted twelve to six to reject the May-Bailey bill. The committee took up as a substitute the O'Mahoney-Kilgore bill, supported by a mixed coalition which included Johnson, Downey, Chandler, Kilgore, Murray, O'Mahoney, Wagner, Burton, Thomas, Wilson, Revercomb, and Bridges. This bill provided for control of all workers by the WMC which would have power to set employment ceilings and regulate hiring and firing of workers. Employers who disobeyed WMC regulations were liable to a $10,000 fine and one year's jail sentence plus loss of tax shelters and government contracts. Employees were also subject to fines and jail sentences. There were additional provisions to insure control of farm workers and to protect seniority and other labor rights.[58]

Despite the committee vote, Stimson still felt he had done some good. His speech had at least forced the committee to get off the fence and offer the substitute O'Mahoney-Kilgore bill. Now the War Department worked to defeat the substitute. Patterson explained to Byrnes that the bill simply legitimized McNutt's procedures which had already failed. To legalize employment ceilings would not affect millions of workers in small enterprises. After hearing these objections Byrnes decided to call another meeting of all officials involved in manpower mobilization. Although the antipathy between McNutt and the War Department was now obvious, Byrnes managed to hammer out an agreement on strategy. The administration would strive to reverse the decision of the Senate committee on the floor of the Senate. Byrnes still had hopes of saving the amended May-Bailey bill which would insure the principle of compulsion while also guaranteeing civilian control. McNutt agreed to this course because he saw no hope of the O'Mahoney-Kilgore bill being accepted by the House. But Byrnes underestimated his task. On March 8, 1945, the O'Mahoney-Kilgore bill passed the entire Senate by a vote of sixty-three to sixteen. The joint House-Senate Conference Committee now remained the only opportunity to salvage something of Roosevelt's original proposal.[59]

Stimson had gone along with Byrnes's compromise because he hoped that with Roosevelt's return it might be possible to change the tide of congressional sentiment. The Secretary made this strategy clear to the President at a private meeting on March 3. Without Roosevelt's personal involvement Stimson feared the worst. The President, however, hesitated to repeat constantly futile calls for a labor draft because such an exercise would diminish his prestige. More and more politicians were asserting that Roosevelt did not really want national service in any form. Critics pointed to the opposition role of such Democratic stalwarts as Kilgore and Wagner. To satisfy Stimson, however, Roosevelt promised to meet privately with congressional leaders.[60]

As the joint Senate-House conference began, Roosevelt met with Senators Truman and Barkley and Congressmen Rayburn and McCormack. The President urged them to pass a manpower bill as soon as possible. He still hoped for May-Bailey but he was not optimistic. After the congressmen left he complained at the tendency of these politicians to waste time on the rules of Congress. The President sensed that congressional leaders hoped Germany would soon collapse and make the bill unnecessary. To prevent such a delaying tactic he decided to make one more public appeal. On March 9, he told the press that the voluntary manpower system was inadequate and that he wanted the May-Bailey bill passed rather than the Senate version. As the Senate-House conference dragged on Roosevelt grew more irritated. He refused to send any new messages to Congress until it acted on manpower. Privately, the President complained that while Congress kicked manpower around almost every battle of the war could have been won more decisively with more men and material.[61]

On March 21, Roosevelt told the press it would not be appropriate for him to comment further while the committee was still deliberating. His patience appeared to pay off when the conference committee reported out a compromise manpower bill similar to the original May-Bailey with the Byrnes amendments. Now Roosevelt made his fourth public appeal since the first of the year. In a telegram to Senator Elbert D. Thomas, Roosevelt urged the Senate to accept the compromise. Although the bill did not contain all that Marshall,

King, and Roosevelt had originally recommended, the President
still felt that the compromise proposal merited approval. Echoing
Stimson, Roosevelt wrote that passage of the bill would boost the
morale of American fighting men. As Roosevelt pleaded for passage of the compromise bill, Paul McNutt issued a manpower report in which he saw a "positive betterment in the employment
situation." James Byrnes issued a report promising a speedy return
to the free enterprise system. Byrnes wanted the May-Bailey bill,
not to fight the war, but to help with reconversion. No wonder
congressmen remained dubious.[62]

The confusion and doubts came to an end on April 3. A few days
earlier, buoyed by Roosevelt's message, Senator Barkley had reported growing sentiment for the amended May-Bailey bill. But by
April 2 even Roosevelt knew he lacked the votes. The next day the
Senate voted forty-six to twenty-nine against the Senate-House
conference bill. To add insult to injury, the Senate, by a voice vote,
next insisted on endorsing the O'Mahoney-Kilgore bill and called
for a new conference with the House. No new conference was held.
In the War Department the corpse of national service quivered a
few times before expiring. Goldthwaite Dorr suggested to Stimson
that they accept the O'Mahoney-Kilgore bill. The Secretary seemed
sympathetic but agreed to give Patterson a hearing. Now bitter in
defeat, the Undersecretary admitted that without some bill labor
and management could avoid all controls. He also felt that Byrnes's
replacement, Fred Vinson, could control McNutt. But Patterson
preferred to take nothing rather than a worthless bill that continued
McNutt's silly ceilings and manpower referrals.[63]

After three and half years the national service issue ended in
defeat for the administration. Despite the united support of the
President and his leading military advisors, the Senate rejected what
was defined as an essential war power. The bill would not have met
defeat if a workable alternative to national service had not existed.
That alternative, McNutt's War Manpower Commission, provided
enough evidence to critics that voluntarism rather than coercion
was the best solution to manpower mobilization. If McNutt had
fallen on his face early in the war, national service would have become a more likely solution. But during the early years of mobilization, as McNutt struggled with powerful interest groups within the

economy, few observers could predict that he would survive until 1945.

Notes

1. Grenville Clark and Arthur L. Williston, *The Effort for a National Service Law in World War II, 1942–1945* (Dedham, Mass.: privately published, 1947), pp. 2-4; Clark to Stimson, April 17, 1942, box 139, Henry L. Stimson Papers, Yale University Library, New Haven, Conn. For another view of this same issue see George T. Mazuzan, "The National War Service Controversy, 1942–1945," *Mid-America: An Historical Review* 57 (October 1975), pp. 246-58.

2. G. Clark, "Memorandum as to a National Service Act," April 14, 1942, box 139, Stimson Papers.

3. Roosevelt to Clark, June 13, 1942, box 140, Stimson Papers; memo for McNutt from Roosevelt, May 4, 1942, official file 4905, Franklin D. Roosevelt Papers, Roosevelt Library, Hyde Park, N.Y.; Mazuzan, "War Service," pp. 247-48.

4. Clark to Roosevelt, July 3, 1942, box 140, Stimson Papers; Clark to Stimson, May 20, 1942, and July 6, 1942, *ibid.*; Mazuzan, "War Service," p. 249; Stimson to Roosevelt, July 10, 1942, box 140, Stimson Papers; Henry Stimson Diary (July 10, 1942), 39: 155, Yale University Library.

5. Stimson Diary (September 17, 1942), 40: 80-87; Patterson to Dorr, August 3, 1942, box 147, Robert Patterson Papers, Library of Congress, Washington, D.C.; Clark to Stimson, October 21, 1942, box 141, folder 1, Stimson Papers; McNutt to Byrnes, October 16, 1942, pack. 5, pt. 2, James Byrnes Papers, Clemson University Library, Clemson, S.C.; Clark and Williston, National Service Law, pp. 52-53; Clark to Stimson, October 27, 1942, box 141, Stimson Papers; Stimson to Clark, November 2, 1942, box 141, *ibid.*

6. Perkins to Grace Tully, July 31, 1942, OF 4905, folder 1413-F, Roosevelt Papers.

7. Interim report to the chairman of the WMC submitted by the MLPC, October 31, 1942, box 5, Samuel Rosenman Papers, Roosevelt Library.

8. McNutt to Roosevelt, October 28, 1942, OF 4905, Roosevelt Papers.

9. Harry Truman to Roosevelt, October 23, 1942, pack. 5, pt. 2, Byrnes Papers; U.S., Congress, House of Representatives, Fifth Interim Report by Select Committee Investigating National Defense Migration, pursuant to HR 113, hearings on *Changes Needed for Effective Mobilization of Manpower*, 77th Cong., 2d sess., 1942, pp. 1-6 (hereafter cited as *Tolan Committee Hearings*).

10. Clark to Roosevelt, November 4, 1942, copy in box 183, Patterson Papers; Clark to Stimson, November 9, 1942, box 141, Stimson Papers; Clark to Stimson, December 2, 1942, *ibid.*; Stimson to Roosevelt, November 18, 1942, *ibid.*; *Tolan Committee Hearings*, pp. 14-16.

11. U.S., Congress, Senate, Committee on Appropriations, hearings on *Investigation of Manpower*, 78th Cong., 1st sess., 1943, 3 pts.; Albert A. Blum, "The Farmer, the Army and the Draft," *Agricultural History* 38 (January 1964), pp. 34-42.

12. Stimson Diary (February 19, 1943), 42: 66; minutes of Women's Advisory Committee, February 11, 1943, p. 4; record group 211, National Archives, Washington, D.C.

13. Daily Calendar of Oscar Cox, February 27, 1943, p. 2, Oscar Cox Papers, Roosevelt Library.

14. Patterson to Stimson, March 4, 1943, box 171, Stimson Papers; Milton Handler to Oscar Cox, March 4, 1943, box 9, manpower file, Rosenman Papers.

15. Fowler V. Harper to Byrnes, March 9, 1943, pack. 5, pt. 2, Byrnes Papers; Samuel I. Rosenman, *Working with Roosevelt* (New York: Harper and Row, 1952), pp. 419-22.

16. Statement by William Haber to Presidential Board, March 10, 1943, pack. 59, pt. 1, Byrnes Papers; Byrnes to Roosevelt, March 14, 1943, *ibid.*

17. Virginia Price to McNutt, April 3, 1943, box 168, series 36, RG 211; Clark to Stimson, April 19, 1943, box 142, folder 2, Stimson Papers; Stimson to Clark, May 1, 1943, *ibid.*; Lt. Col. Ralph F. Gow to H. C. Petersen, March 31, 1943, box 183, Patterson Papers; Rosenman, *Working with Roosevelt*, p. 420.

18. J. D. Brown to Patterson, June 3, 1943, box 184, Patterson Papers.

19. Frank Knox to Roosevelt, June 8, 1943, and Patterson to Knox, June 11, 1943, box 183, Patterson Papers; notes by Stimson, June 8, 1943, box 171, Stimson Papers; Clark to Stimson, June 25, 1943, folder 17, box 142, *ibid.*

20. Stimson notes on conference with Roosevelt, June 29, 1943, box 171, Stimson Papers; digest of War Production Board minutes, August 31, 1943, box 12, Donald Nelson Papers, Huntington Library, San Marino, Calif.; Stimson memo for Roosevelt, July 1, 1943, box 47, Rosenman Papers; Clark and Williston, *National Service Law*, p. 75.

21. G. H. Dorr memo for Patterson, September 14, 1943, box 184-5, Patterson Papers; Patterson to McNutt, September 14, 1943, *ibid.*; Haber to Rosenman, September 4, 1943, box 47, Rosenman Papers; Stimson to Roosevelt, September 16, 1943, folder 33, box 142, Stimson Papers.

22. B. Baruch to Roosevelt, September 8, 1943, box 47, Rosenman Papers; diary of Harold L. Ickes (September 17, 1943), 11: 8180-1, Library of Congress, Washington, D. C.

23. James P. Mitchell to Patterson, November 18, 1943, box 184, Patterson Papers; Gustav Peck to Nelson, December 20, 1943, box 13, Nelson Papers.

24. Memo of telephone conversations, Stimson and Wadsworth, December 23, 1943, Stimson and Austin, December 23 and 30, 1943, folder 31, box 171, Stimson Papers; Stimson, Knox, Patterson, et al., to Roosevelt, December 28, 1943, box 151, Patterson Papers; Mazuzan, "War Service," p. 254. See Rosenman, *Working with Roosevelt*, p. 423, on Roosevelt's continued hesitation.

25. Richard Polenberg, *War and Society: The United States, 1941-1945* (Philadelphia: J. B. Lippincott, 1972), p. 178; presidential conference no. 14, January 7,

1944, Harold Smith Papers, Roosevelt Library; Harold Ickes Diary (January 16, 1944), 11: 8543; Lt. Col. John K. Collins to Patterson, January 27, 1944, box 184, Patterson Papers; Colonel Collins attended a meeting of the War Manpower Commission at which McNutt and Nelson both opposed national service. Wadsworth quoted in Polenberg, *War and Society*, p. 178.

26. Telephone memorandum, Stimson and Wadsworth, January 14, 1944, box 172, Stimson Papers; Clark to Patterson, January 14, 1944, box 151, Patterson Papers.

27. *New York Times*, March 25, 1944, p. 9, and March 29, 1944, pp. 1, 20; telephone memorandum, Clark and Stimson, March 13, 1944, box 172, Stimson Papers; Mazuzan, "War Service," p. 257.

28. Col. John P. Dinsmore to Patterson, February 3, 1944, relayed word that Congresswoman Edith Rogers of Massachusetts had challenged Patterson's testimony on the labor problems in Lowell, box 151, Patterson Papers; Petersen to Patterson, March 25, 1944, box 151, *ibid*.; Stimson to Byrnes, telephone memorandum, March 29, 1944, box 172, Stimson Papers; Patterson to Stimson, March 31, 1944, box 284-5, Patterson Papers; Stimson to Costello, telephone memorandum, April 12, 1944, file 2, box 172, Stimson Papers.

29. Rosenman memorandum to Roosevelt [n.d.], box 47, Rosenman Papers; *New York Times*, April 21, 1944, p. 1.

30. *New York Times*, May 4, 1944, p. 18, and June 3, 1944, p. 8. The Bailey-Brewster bill provided that men of draft age in war jobs must obtain permission from local draft boards before quitting jobs. If they failed to obtain permission, they were subject to the draft. A Gallup poll of June 2, 1944, found that 56 percent of the public favored such a law while 32 percent opposed it. Stimson Diary (May 4, 1944), 47: 16.

31. *New York Times*, September 9, 1944, p. 13.

32. B. H. Lidell Hart, *History of the Second World War*, 2 vols. (New York: Capricorn Edition, 1972), 2: 639-59.

33. Stimson Diary (December 22, 1944), 49: 116-17; Patterson to Stimson, December 27, 1944, box 151, Patterson Papers.

34. Clark to Stimson, January 2, 1945, box 147, Stimson Papers.

35. *New York Times*, January 7, 1945, p. 1; Stimson Diary (January 10, 1945), 50:31-32.

36. U. S., Congress, House Committee on Military Affairs, hearings on *Mobilization of Civilian Manpower* (HR 1119), 79th Cong., 1st sess., 1945, pp. 2-5; memorandum of Stimson conversation with Roosevelt, January 11, 1945, box 172, Stimson Papers.

37. William D. Hassett, *Off the Record with F.D.R., 1942–1945* (New Brunswick, N.J.: Rutgers University Press, 1958), p. 311; Stimson to Roosevelt, January 13, 1945, file 18, box 147, Stimson Papers; Stimson to Roosevelt, January 15, 1945, OF 4905, Roosevelt Papers; *New York Times*, January 17, 1945, p. 1, and January 18, 1945, p. 13.

38. Hearings on *Mobilization of Civilian Manpower*, pp. 21-34. Congressman Elston pointed out to Patterson that McNutt had testified on March 28, 1944, that

national service was not needed and that he would return to Congress if such a need arose. "We have not heard from him," Elston added.

39. *Ibid.*

40. *Ibid.*, pp. 37-54.

41. *New York Times*, January 10, 1945, p. 14, and January 12, 1945, p. 1; Patterson to Stimson, January 11, 1945, file 17, box 147, Stimson Papers.

42. Hearings on *Mobilization of Civilian Manpower*, pp. 57-64; *New York Times*, January 11, 1945, p. 1.

43. Hearings on *Mobilization of Civilian Manpower*, pp. 188-287, 353-62. George Addes of the United Auto, Aircraft Workers testified that labor shorts were due to "gross manpower waste, poor production planning . . . refusal to use women and minorities and poor wages." Addes to Patterson, box 185, Patterson Papers.

44. Hearings on *Mobilization of Civilian Manpower*, pp. 353-62; *New York Times*, January 17, 1945, p. 14.

45. Hearings on *Mobilization of Civilian Manpower*, pp. 227, 256, 444-60.

46. Patterson to Stimson, January 11, 1945, file 17, box 147, Stimson Papers; Patterson to Rosenman, January 11, 1945, box 151, Patterson Papers; *New York Times*, January 12, 1945, p. 1, where Sidney Shalet reported that Byrnes had agreed to allow McNutt to administer the bill; Clay to Byrnes, January 27, 1945, Byrnes Papers; *New York Times*, January 25, 1945, p. 1. Hershey felt that May-Bailey would have passed if Byrnes had not gone to Yalta. Interview with General Lewis B. Hershey, May 26, 1975.

47. *New York Times*, January 31, 1945, p. 12, and February 2, 1945, pp. 1, 12.

48. Clay to Byrnes, February 5, 1945, pack 178, Byrnes Papers; *New York Times*, February 3, 1945, pp. 1, 20.

49. Clay to Byrnes, February 5, 1945, pack 178, Byrnes Papers.

50. *Ibid.*

51. U.S., Congress, Senate Committee on Military Affairs, hearings on *Mobilization of Civilian Manpower* (S. 36, HR1752), 79th Cong., 1st sess., 1945, pp. 12-24, 23-26, 26-51, 62-65, 67-85 (hereafter cited as *Senate Manpower Hearings, 1945*).

52. *Ibid.*, pp. 95-106, 108-124; *New York Times*, February 8, 1945, p. 1.

53. *Senate Manpower Hearings, 1945*, pp. 126-51, 152-71; memorandum of conversation between Col. Robert Cutler and General Hershey, February 10, 1945, box 184-5, Patterson Papers; Hershey interview, May 26, 1975. To demonstrate the confusion, as Krug testified on the urgency of national service, a deputy regional director of the War Production Board, Eugene S. Pleasonton, announced that no such law would be needed if war plants used manpower more efficiently. *New York Times*, February 14, 1945, p. 9.

54. *Senate Manpower Hearings, 1945*, pp. 125-26, 171-98, 207-36, 237-52, 312-29. Testimony by farm representatives was split. James Patton of the National Farmers Union opposed HR 1752 and called for a "unified and strengthened WMC." W. R. Ogg of the American Farm Bureau Federation favored HR 1752 but spent most of his time complaining that the Selective Service was ignoring farm deferments. See pp. 262-78. A Gallup poll of February 9, 1945, asked if Congress should

pass a law allowing local draft boards to draft civilians for war work, if government and military officials said it was essential. Some 56 percent said yes and 36 percent said no. See *Senate Manpower Hearings, 1945*, pp. 337-38.

55. Patterson to editors of *Stars and Stripes*, telegram, February 2, 1945, box 185, Patterson Papers; Stimson Diary (February 4, 1945), 50: 82; *ibid.* (February 13, 1945), 50: 108; Robert Cutler, memorandum of talk with Hershey, February 10, 1945, box 184-5, Patterson Papers; Roosevelt to Barkley, telegram, February 11, 1945, folder 69 (1), Byrnes Papers; *New York Times*, February 13, 1945, p. 14.

56. *New York Times*, February 13, 1945, p. 25; *Senate Manpower Hearings, 1945*, pp. 254-55; Stimson Diary (February 15, 1945), 50: 113.

57. *New York Times*, February 17, 1945, p. 1, February 19, 1945, p. 1, and February 20, 1945, p. 1; memorandum of telephone conversation, Stimson to Meyer, February 16, 1945, box 172, Stimson Papers.

58. *New York Times*, February 15, 1945, p. 14, February 21, 1945, p. 1, February 25, 1945, sec. 4, p. 2, and March 9, 1945, p. 1; *Senate Manpower Hearings, 1945*, pp. 65-66, 86, 304.

59. Patterson to Byrnes, February 21, 1945, box 184-5, Patterson Papers; Stimson Diary (February 22, 1945), 50; 132.

60. Stimson notes of conference with Roosevelt, March 3, 1945, folder 15, box 172, Stimson Papers.

61. Hassett, *Off the Record*, p. 321; *New York Times*, March 10, 1945, p. 13; Harold Smith Presidential Diary 14 (March 12, 1945), Roosevelt Library.

62. *New York Times*, March 15, 1945, p. 12, March 21, 1945, p. 1, March 29, 1945, p. 1, and April 1, 1945, pp. 1, 28; Stimson Diary (March 17, 1945), 50: 198; Roosevelt to Thomas, March 28, 1945, Byrnes Papers.

63. Dorr to Stimson, April 5, 1945, box 185, Patterson Papers; Patterson to Stimson, April 6, 1945, *ibid.*; *New York Times*, March 31, 1945, p. 15, April 3, 1945, p. 1, and April 4, 1945, p. 1.

In the Factory

Throughout the elaboration of McNutt's manpower strategy he faced a continuous struggle with special-interest groups. Organized labor, for one, pressed vigorously and continuously for more control of manpower policy. With the exception of the Selective Service System, no other agency offended as many people as the War Manpower Commission. McNutt could retain his manpower consensus only by being realistic about interest group politics in Roosevelt's broker state. He had to find a role for organized labor in his system of mobilization.

I

Organized labor played an important role in economic mobilization during World War II, touching on virtually every aspect of manpower plans. Neither Roosevelt nor McNutt could ignore the attitudes and actions of labor leaders. Labor entered World War II in a position strengthened by such New Deal legislation as the Wagner Act and the Fair Labor Standards Act controlling minimum wages and hours. Although union leaders lacked the impact on mobilization policy exhibited by the leaders of big business, the war was good to labor. Union membership grew from 10.5 million in December 1941 to 14.75 million by V-J Day. Throughout the war both Roosevelt and McNutt strove to insure that mobilization would not be used as an excuse for stripping unions of rights won in the 1930s. Labor itself resisted any attempt at retreat or at regimentation.[1]

Organized labor remained loyal to several principles throughout mobilization. Determined to maintain the advances made in wages and in collective bargaining status, labor leaders felt it essential to gain representation on all government boards affecting economic mobilization. During the period of preparedness labor made headway. Although both William Green of the AFL and John L. Lewis of the CIO opposed American involvement in war in 1939, fearing the effect of mobilization on labor rights, by 1940 several changes had occurred. After the passage of lend-lease to England, Green pledged cooperation in preparedness. Phillip Murray replaced Lewis as head of the CIO and in December 1940 offered Roosevelt an "Industry Council's Plan" to give labor an equal share in decision-making on economic mobilization. During the period from September 1939 to December 1941 some 1.5 million additional Americans joined unions. Free-shop bastions such as Little Steel and the Ford Motor Company signed collective bargaining agreements.[2]

In Washington President Roosevelt insisted that Sidney Hillman of the Amalgamated Clothing Workers Union play a role in the National Defense Advisory Commission and subsequent mobilization agencies. Hillman had Roosevelt's support to insure that defense contracts did not go to industries which flaunted New Deal labor laws. Despite being outnumbered by businessmen and ignored by the military, Hillman did his best to promote unionism in the midst of mobilization. His efforts, however, went unrewarded among the leaders of both the AFL and CIO. Green distrusted Hillman because of his role in the creation of the CIO. Phillip Murray remained dissatisfied because Hillman held office due to his personal friendship with Roosevelt. Murray wanted a more formal, institutionalized acknowledgment of labor's role.[3]

In addition to dissatisfaction with Hillman, both the labor leaders and Roosevelt recognized by early 1941 that the increased level of mobilization was placing strains on existing mechanisms for government supervision of labor relations. Neither the National Labor Relations Board nor the conciliation service of the Department of Labor could handle the increase in labor unrest. The unrest in turn led to a growing antilabor sentiment in Congress and among state

CHAPTER 5

governors. To confront these problems, on March 19, 1941, Roosevelt created a National Defense Mediation Board (NDMB) with representation from the public, management, and labor. The NDMB would conduct hearings and studies leading to recommendations for settlement of labor disputes.[4]

Roosevelt hoped the NDMB would help achieve his goals of rapid mobilization, an end to strikes, and continued protection of labor from exploitation. Despite a personal feud with John L. Lewis, which intensified during the 1940 election, Roosevelt had the firm support of both Green and Murray. These two men had given a no-strike pledge for defense industry as early as November 1940. On the eve of Pearl Harbor, the President sent a message to both the AFL and CIO calling for an end to dual unions as a step toward national unity. In a fireside chat he stressed that "we must make sure in all that we do that there be no breakdown or cancellation of any of the great social gains which we have made in these past years." Roosevelt remained sympathetic to unions despite the problems caused in 1941 by strikes in defense plants and in the mines. He remained sympathetic but he would not use the power of the government to enforce a closed shop on certain coal mines and would occasionally use troops to occupy important defense plants suffering from strikes. He met with labor leaders again on December 17, 1941, and announced agreement on a no-strike and no-lockout pact for the duration of the war. A few weeks later, in January 1942, the NDMB was reorganized as the War Labor Board (WLB) to deal with wage disputes and a Victory Committee of union representatives was set up to consult with the President when needed.[5]

Through these actions and others Roosevelt sought to reassure labor throughout the war that he was acting in its best interest. He consistently reaffirmed his commitment to the preservation of all labor rights, including seniority and reemployment rights for men drafted into the military or shifted to new jobs. Although the Victory Committee did not meet formally, he tried to keep in touch with Bill Green and Phillip Murray to solicit labor's opinion on anything affecting manpower mobilization. It was no surprise that Roosevelt should be receptive to labor's support for the establishment of a War Manpower Commission and to the recommendation that McNutt be appointed chairman in the spring of 1942.[6]

II

By 1942 Paul Voorhis McNutt had come a long way in his relationship with American labor. As a product of Indiana politics, he had few contacts with strong labor groups except in the northwest regions of the state. While governor of Indiana in 1935 he earned the epithet "Hoosier Hitler" because he called out the National Guard to put down a general strike in Terre Haute. He soon redeemed himself by promoting workmen's compensation insurance and antiinjunction laws for the state. As head of the Federal Security Agency he demonstrated a typical New Dealer's enthusiasm for the virtues of collective bargaining and for the role of organized labor in the economy. By 1940, while seeking status as a national political figure, he realized the need to capture the labor coalition enlisted under Roosevelt. With mobilization under way, McNutt supported a continuation of labor rights and privileges. In 1941 he denounced critics who insisted that the administration had to choose between production for defense and a closed shop. Developing the theme he would cling to throughout the war, McNutt insisted that free labor could always outproduce slave labor. In his mind, "the only government policy which is compatible with a democratic society is to insure to both labor and management complete protection of their rights under the law. . . ." Here was a man after labor's own heart.[7]

When Franklin Roosevelt prepared to create the WMC in April 1942, organized labor insisted upon control over the head of the new agency. As the AFL and the CIO joined for a patriotic rally in Pittsburgh, Paul McNutt conveniently appeared and cemented his reputation as a friend of labor. McNutt warned that conservatives hoped to use the occasion of war to attack and destroy independent unionism. He promised to fight against such an attack and began by defending the work-record of labor. Sixty million workers had stayed on the job while critics focused on a few who had left. He urged an increase in wages and dismissed fears that a forty-hour week would hurt production. Critics who wanted to conscript labor were only helping Hitler and Mussolini. Free labor was an essential part of the democratic ideology providing a philosophical foundation and justification for the war. The audience cheered and in Washington Roosevelt appointed McNutt as the new manpower czar.[8]

McNutt received his appointment on April 18, 1942, and never wavered in his commitment to the cause of free labor winning the war. When reporters asked him what would be the role of unions in the War Manpower Commission, McNutt replied that labor would have a leading role. Expressing disappointment that no labor representative was seated on the WMC itself, he vowed to remedy this defect by immediately establishing an advisory committee of both management and labor. When reporters tried to bait him into admitting that his duties, such as assigning new workers to closed-shop industry, might have the effect of forcing union membership upon individuals, McNutt agreed. But he insisted that closed-shop rules would not be ignored. At the same time McNutt continued to emphasize the importance of voluntary cooperation, of free labor, and of a role for union leaders in the WMC. His ideas would soon be tested.[9]

As manpower shortages grew in 1942, McNutt promised again and again that the WMC would not draft labor. As labor piracy reared its ugly head across the nation, McNutt reassured labor that neither a freeze nor a work-or-fight order was imminent. Although he admitted that normality was "out for the duration," in his Labor Day address of August 14, 1942, he continued to stress the vital connection between free labor and the war aims of the Allies. He promised that no major action would be taken without first consulting labor representatives. McNutt proudly boasted at the end of 1942 that the administration's manpower program had been conceived and executed with the full cooperation of labor leaders.[10] The honeymoon, however, was about to end.

In early 1943 General Hershey wrote that "the Manpower Commission, whether they [sic] will or not, in the minds of not a little of the public is the champion of industrial labor." McNutt, as Hershey saw, continued to do his best to protect the workers' rights. He supported full, paid vacations for labor even during wartime as a means of improving efficiency. When called upon to execute what amounted to a limited labor freeze because of Roosevelt's "Hold the Line" order of April 8, 1943, McNutt seemed sympathetic to labor's criticism and sought a larger role for Phillip Murray and William Green in any stabilization plan. When McNutt applied a forty-eight-hour work rule to the steel industry in June, he consulted with union representatives and provided exemptions, despite objections from management. On June 15, McNutt named Clinton S. Golden, a Murray crony, as vice chairman of the WMC and special advisor on labor problems. In speech after speech McNutt praised the cooperation of labor, even as he imposed greater regimentation. Because labor advisors sat in on all manpower decisions at the WMC, McNutt felt democracy was working in manpower management. Appearing on a radio program alongside of Green and Murray, McNutt paid tribute to the cooperation of labor. He concluded, "we all believe in voluntarism." Interpreting the Atlantic Charter in a way which may have shocked Winston Churchill, McNutt affirmed that the Allied cause involved the right of collective bargaining for the world.[11]

To McNutt's embarrassment, however, President Roosevelt began 1944 by calling for a national service law. In 1944 McNutt spoke less of voluntary cooperation and more of the need for labor to meet the production crisis generated by the invasion of Europe. As his program became more coercive, including the West Coast Plan and labor ceilings, McNutt tried to focus labor's attention on the prospects after the war. He suggested that labor concern itself with "the next problem on labor's agenda and democracy's agenda: jobs for all Americans, for war workers, for soldiers, for women, for the handicapped, for the minority groups, for all Americans who want jobs." Despite the new controls imposed on labor, McNutt continued to enjoy support. In December 1944 rumors circulated in Washington that he would soon replace Frances Perkins at the Department of Labor.[12] The shift did not take place, but by 1945 McNutt had established himself as the leading spokesman in the Roosevelt administration for a new age of labor-management cooperation.

III

McNutt made his reputation in labor circles by a combination of attractive rhetoric and concrete deeds. Throughout the war he preached industrial partnership with an end to class divisions. As one instrument for implementing such utopian notions, McNutt focused on labor-management committees on both the local and national level. Reflecting the thinking of both Phillip Murray and

Donald Nelson, local committees had been established in war plants as a means of solving manpower problems before the creation of the WMC. They proved to be channels of communication, enabling workers to understand the overall mission of the plant and informing managers of particular reasons for absenteeism and turnover. By the end of 1942 some 2,000 such committees existed, representing more than four million workers. At the peak of the war effort 5,000 committees existed involving seven million workers. Both the AFL and CIO consistently supported the formation of such committees.[13]

Just as important in providing labor input to mobilization and even more visible was the National Management Labor Policy Committee (MLPC) of the WMC. On May 25, 1942, less than six weeks after being appointed manpower czar, McNutt fulfilled his promise to labor supporters who had complained about the absence of a representative on the WMC. McNutt decided to sidestep entirely the WMC and create another agency with representatives from management, labor, and agriculture. The creation of the MLPC changed the entire structure of manpower mobilization for McNutt. Within months the MLPC had effectively displaced the original WMC as the major advisory body to McNutt. The chairman contributed to this coup because "of a deep conviction that only through the cooperation of labor and management could a manpower policy be formulated that would have roots in the practical necessities of American wartime industry." Like Roosevelt, McNutt practiced consensus politics. If he expected to make a voluntary manpower program work, he had to insure that the policies adopted had the support of all constituents affected. McNutt issued the order creating the MLPC in May 1942, but the first meeting did not take place until June 9.[14]

To advance further the prestige of the MLPC McNutt had President Roosevelt amend his original executive order to provide for this new advisory agency. Surprisingly, considering his sensitivity to consensus politics, Roosevelt hesitated to oblige McNutt by enhancing the status of the MLPC. McNutt explained that the MLPC sought the same status as the formal WMC and he supported the idea. Phillip Murray of the CIO continuously complained that labor was being "hoodwinked" in the mobilization administration. Re-

fusing this modest request to recognize the MLPC would only pre-
cipitate problems.[15]

Roosevelt, who had originally resented the multiplying of executive
orders and agencies, now gave in and on December 5, 1942, issued
Executive Order no. 9279 giving the MLPC official status. Organized
labor sent Frank Fenton, Clint Golden, and Walter Reuther to look
after its interest. From management came R. E. Gillmore, Randall
R. Irwin, and C. J. Whipple. McNutt bade them welcome and announced that the MLPC was "co-equal with the Commission
[WMC] and that no action would be taken without consulting it."[16]

McNutt spent much of his time trying to keep the members of the
MLPC happy about the course of manpower mobilization, a her-
culean task. The original members had fought the labor-management
wars of the 1930s and remained suspicious of each other. At a
meeting on February 26, 1943, Walter Reuther urged the committee
to endorse a guaranteed minimum wage. His suggestion stunned
management members who resented any attempt to use wartime
mobilization for social reform. The committee voted to take no
action on the proposal and McNutt decided the next month to reorganize. He appointed the presidents of the AFL, the CIO, the Order of Railway Conductors, the National Farmer's Union, the
American Farm Bureau, the United States Chamber of Commerce,
and the National Association of Manufacturers. The new committee gave equal representation to labor, agriculture, and management. As all groups opposed national service legislation, they would
hopefully support McNutt's voluntary program and help make it
work.[17]

In reality, McNutt had created a rival power which would threaten
his own position. The new MLPC wasted little time in asserting its
independence. Margaret Hickey of the Women's Advisory Committee (WAC) in the WMC requested that she be given full membership on the MLPC. Hickey and the other women on the WAC
recognized the growing power of the MLPC. However, despite the
request of McNutt, the MLPC rejected Hickey's membership application. At a meeting of the WAC on May 12, 1943, McNutt tried
to explain that he had supported Hickey's request but had been re-
buffed. The women had difficulty understanding how the manpower czar could be overruled by an advisory committee. The

answer was that McNutt had fallen victim to his own conception of the MLPC as an interest-group senate. The MLPC argued that if Hickey obtained membership the committee would no longer represent functional economic elements in mobilization. McNutt feared that Hickey's presence might "disturb the balance of the Committee."[18]

As McNutt adopted more coercive manpower tactics such as stabilization plans, he became more strident in his enthusiasm for the MLPC. He insisted in April 1943 that "every policy stated by the WMC in its first six months of life received the unanimous approval of the MLPC." Every Tuesday afternoon the MLPC met in WMC headquarters, with Frank P. Fenton replacing Green and Michael Ross sitting in for Murray. McNutt admitted that differences of opinion existed, but insisted a consensus always emerged.[19]

McNutt exaggerated the spirit of cooperation exhibited by organized labor through the MLPC. When McNutt attempted to stabilize workers on April 16, 1943, labor rose in wrath. Businessmen also protested what they called a dictatorial approach. Opposition mounted as the controlled referral plan went into effect in Buffalo, New York. The plan itself was mild and did not give the USES power to transfer men against their will. Local manpower priority committees, staffed by the military and the War Production Board, presented the USES with a daily list of companies which should receive priority in the referral of men. Despite safeguards, businessmen objected to any interference with their hiring. Labor felt that all wage differentials in local plants should be eliminated before prohibiting a worker from shifting jobs. The CIO held a special meeting to discuss what it called the "arbitrary freezing of men to jobs without reference to the needs of war production." Because McNutt's order ignored different wage scales in different plants, the CIO called it antilabor. Green of the AFL denounced McNutt's attempt to penalize labor with such an unneeded action.[20] Labor representatives on area manpower commissions across the country walked out.

This uproar had an effect. Both McNutt and Roosevelt were still committed to a voluntary mobilization program. Without the support of labor and management the entire edifice of controls would collapse. Within days of the initial regulation, an amendment was prepared by the WMC which allowed local USES offices to permit the transfer of workers in essential industry at higher pay if the worker would be effectively utilized in the war economy. By April 28 the WMC had approved a plan to extend the new controlled referral plan to all areas covered by existing stabilization agreements. But this new controlled referral plan allowed workers in thirty-five essential industries to move for higher wages. McNutt capitulated to the opposition of labor and a new consensus manpower program emerged.[21]

IV

McNutt was right when he argued that the MLPC would defuse the opposition of labor and management to mobilization regulations. But this support could only be gained by allowing interest groups to play a role in formulating manpower policy. If this concession insured that the program would stress voluntary methods, it mattered little because McNutt himself had no faith in coercion. Never fully integrated with the WMC staff, the MLPC primarily served the practical purpose of insuring some consensus on manpower mobilization. The harmony between McNutt and MLPC survived until 1945, not because either labor or management controlled policy, but because both McNutt and Roosevelt believed in a voluntary and decentralized approach to manpower mobilization. If a centralized and dictatorial mobilization plan had been adopted, there would have been no MLPC.[22]

At the same time, without the cooperation of the MLPC, McNutt's work with labor mobilization, already difficult, would have become impossible. Through the MLPC McNutt established favorable relations with local unions who helped recruit labor. To fill shortages of certain skills the WMC would sign an agreement with unions which would act as a surrogate for the USES in recruiting, placing, and referring workers. The building and construction trade unions proved very useful in this way. In December 1944 McNutt announced that "as a result of proposals of labor members of the MLPC . . . wider use of facilities of organized labor will be made . . . to recruit workers for war industries."[23]

This rapport and cooperation would end if labor at any time suspected that McNutt's recruiting policies threatened existing employee rights. Union members of the MLPC consistently resisted attempts by the WMC to promote the use of alien labor. When the Roosevelt administration, through the WMC and the State Department, began importing Mexican and Caribbean labor, labor leaders on the MLPC complained bitterly. They also objected to any attempt to use prisoners of war for labor. By October 1943 a total of 164,000 such prisoners were in the country. McNutt sought the approval of the MLPC for an agreement between the WMC and the War Department which would allow prisoners to take nonwar jobs. Frank Fenton of the AFL denounced the idea. He feared that such workers (aliens and prisoners) would be competition for American workers. McNutt responded by giving verbal assurances to union leaders that he would balance the need to use prisoners productively with the problem of unfair competition for American labor. On December 24, 1943, he announced the following guidelines: (1) prisoners would be used only when free labor was not available; (2) prisoners would not be used in any way to depress wages, working conditions, or job opportunities for free labor; (3) prisoner wage rates would not be less than prevailing rates for the same type of work in the same area; and (4) working conditions would be equal to the conditions for free labor. Despite these promises the AFL remained opposed and McNutt went ahead without a consensus. William Green proceeded to denounce McNutt for using prisoners in an indiscriminate way in the lumber and pulp industry.[24]

In this dispute, as in many other disputes which arose between the administration and labor during the war, the underlying problem revolved around conflicting estimates of manpower shortages. Throughout the entire war, labor evaluated McNutt's work on the basis of two absolutes: mobilization should be voluntary and the key to effective mobilization was proper utilization. As McNutt's program became more and more coercive, labor gave more emphasis to voluntarism.

As early as December 1942 Phillip Murray sent McNutt a plan for mobilization which called for better coordination between procurement and the WMC, an end to discrimination against hiring women and blacks, and an expansion of the USES. McNutt agreed with all of these points. He agreed again in March 1943, when Green and Murray reported that the gross need of labor up to December 1943 was 10,940,000, a figure within reach of a voluntary program.

All manpower needs in 1943, according to Green, Murray, and McNutt, could be met without resorting to compulsion. Green and Murray felt the key to the problem remained proper utilization and administration. They thought that the "functional consolidation of the work of WPB and of the WMC" and shifts within the labor force itself could solve all problems. Labor also supported McNutt's call for additional power. In October 1943 the AFL presented a six-point program which required coordinating production and procurement with the WMC, better utilization of workers, an end to discrimination in hiring, and the creation of labor-management committees to supervise utilization. Walter Reuther announced that "there is no manpower shortage in America. There is bad manpower utilization in America."[25] Here was the root of much labor unrest.

Fortunately, McNutt had little to do with the problem of strikes. Roosevelt created the National War Labor Board (WLB) in January 1942 and this agency, rather than the WMC, took the heat created by wage disputes during the war. When Roosevelt moved against a strike-bound plant, the problem involved the military and the Selective Service. McNutt stood on the sidelines. In June 1943, irate over strikes by the United Mine Workers, Congress passed and sent to Roosevelt the Smith-Connally or War Labor Disputes Act, to curtail labor rights. McNutt endeared himself to unions by opposing the bill. He wrote congressmen that the bill would "retard rather than advance the Nation's productive efforts." He recommended that Roosevelt veto the bill. When confronted with strikes, McNutt proved just as sympathetic. He instructed local USES offices to make no referrals, except in rare cases, which would aid directly or indirectly in filling jobs vacated because of a strike or lockout or where the job was involved in a labor dispute. McNutt would not have the WMC involved in recruiting scab labor.[26]

V

Although wage controls were outside of McNutt's direct responsibility, he could not avoid some involvement. During the period 1942 to 1945 the War Labor Board handled some 17,807 labor disputes and granted wage adjustments in 353,749 instances involving twenty-three million workers. Such wage adjustments had an impact on manpower recruitment and McNutt recognized the relationship early in his career. At a meeting of the WMC in May 1942 he explained to his colleagues that the fixing of wage rates by the WLB directly affected the WMC's ability to recruit labor. Secretary of Labor Perkins, ever suspicious of McNutt's thirst for power, denied that the wage problem had any connection with manpower shortages. McNutt patiently explained that labor pirating was directly connected to wage control, but he argued in vain. Perkins warned him that if he became involved in wage disputes and the working of the WLB, he would make many enemies for the WMC. But more than overweening ambition drove him on. In his mind the manpower problem could never be solved unless the federal government developed a national wage policy.[27]

McNutt never did convert Perkins but he had better luck with James Byrnes, appointed as Director of Economic Stabilization in October 1942. Shortly after assuming his duties he received a lengthy memo from McNutt's assistant, William Haber. Haber argued that in a free market relative wage rates did affect workers' decisions to transfer to new jobs. Only "if wage stabilization is approximately achieved, can the adjustments in wage differential necessary for proper allocation of manpower be brought about," he wrote. Yet there was "no evidence that the [WLB] distinguished between transfers that would promote and those that would impede war production." Neither McNutt nor Haber called for equality of wages for comparable jobs in different companies and areas. They knew such a proposal would be unrealistic, but they did think the adjusting of wage rates should take into consideration manpower needs.[28]

Byrnes appreciated the relationship between wages and manpower much better than Secretary Perkins and took immediate steps to promote coordination between the WMC and the WLB. Eventually, these steps led to Roosevelt's decision to issue a "Hold the Line" order on April 8, 1943, freezing prices and wages. Before that final step, however, Byrnes worked with McNutt who established liaison with the WLB and supplied it with data on the effect of turnovers and labor migration in certain wage cases. By May 1944 McNutt had reached an agreement with the WLB which provided that before an employer could certify a case to the WLB asking for a wage increase to promote recruitment the plant needed certification from McNutt that no other device could solve the manpower shortage.[29]

McNutt also earned distinction with labor groups by his resistance to military attempts to impose more discipline on workers. Secretary Stimson and Undersecretary Patterson of the War Department had little sympathy for protecting labor rights during wartime. They felt that military needs should dictate all manpower decisions and, if these needs led to the curtailment of freedom, that was the price of war. Although he later changed his mind, Stimson originally supported the Smith-Connally Act. From 1943 to July 1945 the army seized more than twenty-five strike-bound plants. Patterson saw such strikes as close to treason.[30]

Such attitudes made labor leaders suspicious of any sign that the military might gain control over manpower mobilization. In January 1943, according to Phillip Murray, Lieutenant General Brehon Somervell had total control over the economic life of American workers. In March 1943 William Green publicly opposed the plan to raise the army manpower level to 8.2 million in 1943. This tension between the military and labor continued despite propaganda efforts by Patterson in 1944. He arranged to have several union leaders tour the European battlefield in hopes that "if they can get overseas and come back with first-hand reports of what the boys at the front are doing, it will not only help production and morale but will help them suppress radical elements." The trip might also erode opposition to national service.[31]

It would take more than a quick tour of the front to eliminate the tension between the military's desire for total mobilization and labor's insistence on a voluntary program. The MLPC remained especially vigilant. On August 4, 1944, James Byrnes issued an order creating a national employment ceiling program. General Somervell had won Byrnes over by arguing that the Allied advance in Europe was being delayed because of production failures due to manpower shortages. The MLPC and McNutt both disputed such an interpretation and Byrnes promised that the WMC would maintain control over all labor recruitment. In November 1944 McNutt emphasized that free American labor had far outproduced the slave labor of Europe. In his opinion, neither national conscription nor tighter sanctions was the answer to shortages.[32]

VI

McNutt had little trouble defending labor against the ambitions of the military. But he had much more difficulty in convincing labor that despite an ever-tightening WMC program he still respected labor rights and believed in voluntarism. He made sure that the MLPC played a role in all major decisions by the WMC. He insisted that seniority rights and other labor rights be respected within the stabilization plans.[33]

Occasionally, McNutt failed to hold his consensus together, as in the case of his labor freeze of April 1943, which led Victor Reuther and other labor leaders to resign from manpower committees. But within a few weeks McNutt won labor back by moving cautiously to implement the new plan and consulting labor at each step. He promised to allow exceptions in the ceiling when it conflicted with contractual seniority rights. When, in July 1944, McNutt instituted another national priority referral system, labor did not protest. William Green called upon his followers to cooperate with McNutt's voluntary method. Even when McNutt moved to forced labor referrals in late 1944 and early 1945, he managed to localize labor resistance.[34]

McNutt always preached a voluntary program because of his own liberal bias, but also because he expected trouble if anyone threatened the American workers' hard-won rights. When pressure from Roosevelt and the military finally made him adopt his most rigorous program of forced transfer of workers, he could not have been surprised at the resistance he met. The problem began when he tried to impose forced transfer on workers in New Bedford, Massachusetts, in an industry producing tires for the military. As early as July 1944 McNutt reported a severe shortage of some 6,000 workers in the tire industry. The shortages continued and began to threaten production schedules for planes and trucks. The military furloughed some 150 ex-tire workers to the Fisk and Firestone companies in New Bedford, but McNutt estimated that another 1,300 would be needed. No more soldiers were available and national service was stalled in Congress.[35]

For the next several weeks McNutt tried every device in his arsenal to man the plants. The Area Management-Labor Committee met on December 27 and confessed its failure. The antiunion reputation of the tire plants made it difficult to recruit workers. Fisk and Firestone had no insurance systems, no union contacts, and no childcare facilities. On February 13, 1945, just as Congress debated the desirability of a national service law, McNutt instituted a forced-release program for New Bedford. This program amounted to the strongest action possible under current WMC regulations. It had worked in Allentown, Pennsylvania, and Dayton, Ohio, but the New Bedford scene was more complex because of union-management tension. As the problem in New Bedford unfolded, union leaders in Washington testified against the new national service bill. Dennis Leary and James Kennedy, leaders of the Textile Workers Union in New Bedford, wrote President Roosevelt protesting any forced staffing of the Firestone and Fisk mills. Arthur M. Harriman, the mayor of New Bedford, wired his objections to forced release. Roosevelt passed these protests on to McNutt.[36]

The forced-release plan, which had the support of all the area manpower people except labor, called for ten New Bedford textile mills to furnish a minimum of 500 workers for the critical tire plants. The textile mills began by furnishing the USES with a list of skilled workers who could do the work required at Fisk and Firestone. The wages offered at the tire plants were equal or higher than those at the textile plants, but the work was heavier, night shifts were frequent, and union rights few. Union leaders encouraged the textile workers to resist McNutt's order. Of the 118 workers initially scheduled for transfer, only twelve agreed to take new jobs after their interviews with the USES. About half of the initial group refused to appear for interviews. Some eighty-five workers appealed to the MLPC in Washington. The Textile Workers of America, CIO, sought an injunction from the United States District Court in Boston. On February 20, 1945, Judge Charles E. Wyzanski rejected the petition but his opinion did not encourage McNutt. Judge Wyzanski rejected the Textile Workers request on the grounds that McNutt's forced-release order was a mere recommendation, not an enforceable command. Such a recommendation could not impinge upon constitutional rights. The cul-de-sac for McNutt, however, was that if he did seek to enforce the transfers by prohibiting the hiring of noncooperative workers, his action might well be unconstitutional. Such a prohibition, in the eyes of labor, appeared tantamount to a lockout to which they would respond with a general textile strike. New Bedford presented a united front against the WMC plan. McNutt, enough of a politician to know when to retreat, wired Mayor Harriman and offered to recall the transfer order if the mayor could find 250 volunteers to work for Fisk and Firestone. In New Bedford, the USES continued its interviews. Paul M. Devine, area director for the WMC, announced on March 8 that out of thirty-seven workers the USES had found only three willing to transfer.[37]

On March 16, 1945, the MLPC held a special meeting in Washington to consider the New Bedford problem. Local officials testified. S. R. Jason of the Teamsters protested the forced-release program as a denial of democratic rights. As he saw it, the WMC threatened labor with taking work at Fisk or Firestone or not working at all. Jason urged the government to take over the factories and enforce union rights. Fred W. Steele, representing the Cotton Manufacturers Association of New Bedford, disputed Jason's charges of antiunion management at the tire plants, but agreed with labor in opposition to forced release. For McNutt the key question was not the need of tire-cord fabric, nor the antiunion attitude of management, but whether or not the WMC had followed correct procedure and exhausted all alternatives before adopting forced release. The history of the problem demonstrated that area manpower committees had tried voluntary tactics to staff the plants, including ceilings, priority referral, utilization studies, house-to-house canvasses, and publicity campaigns. The results had been meager. According to McNutt, forced release was the only remaining option. If the WMC allowed local groups to repudiate forced release it would have a domino effect on other manpower programs across the nation. Despite this argument, the labor representatives of the MLPC remained unconverted. Joyce O'Hara and Frank Fenton denied that local authorities had been consulted before forced release was adopted. Fenton urged McNutt to admit that he had made a mistake. Without the free cooperation of labor and management, no WMC program could work. Fenton echoed the voluntary philosophy McNutt had been selling throughout the war. The MLPC concluded its special session by passing a resolution rejecting forced release and supporting voluntary methods.[38]

The next day, a Saturday, a special delegation from MLPC met with McNutt and urged him to retreat. He refused to budge, argu-

ing that he had given local authorities every opportunity to solve
the problem. Why should he withdraw his forced-release order
without tangible evidence that local management and labor could
solve the problem. McNutt admitted that he distrusted these local
officials who, he felt, had tried to deceive him earlier. The delegation left McNutt's office empty-handed. Two days later, on March
20, the entire MLPC met again, with the threat of national service
legislation looming in Congress. Using rather devious reasoning,
Fenton and others argued that McNutt had issued his order deliberately to provoke opposition, thereby demonstrating to congressmen
the impossibility of a voluntary program and the need for national
service legislation. McNutt, stung by such sophistry, stormed into
the meeting to defend his actions. He had made a career preaching
voluntarism and decentralization in manpower mobilization. In
testimony before Congress on the pending national service bill he
had called for legalizing the WMC's program rather than a more
coercive new system. McNutt resented Fenton's attempt to destroy
this reputation. Neither side backed down and the labor representatives of the MLPC warned McNutt to either revoke his forced-
release order or face the immediate withdrawal of all union officials
from all WMC programs. McNutt stood firm but pleaded with
Fenton and others to consult with William Green and Phillip Murray
before acting.[39]

Fenton and O'Hara refused to be put off, although they had
misinterpreted McNutt's motives. From the point of view of local
workers in New Bedford, there seemed little practical difference
between forced release and national service. Fenton and O'Hara
carried the MLPC with them. Although regretting the break in
friendly relations with McNutt, the MLPC announced to the press
that the forced-release program was being used "for the purpose of
lobbying the Congress in support of compulsory service legislation."
According to the MLPC, McNutt had attempted to create a situation where the voluntary method would appear to fail. Forced release went into effect without coordination with area officials.
Since the order was illegal, no further appeals would be held on the
transfer of workers. The citizens of New Bedford could solve their
own problems through a voluntary, community program as soon as
the "threat of bureaucratic coercion [is] removed. . . ." Fenton and
Ted Silvey representing labor and Joyce O'Hara, S. Duncan Black,

and H. H. Parmelee representing management signed the statement.[40]

Much of the statement was patent nonsense. McNutt's decision to issue forced release was not connected to the lobby for national service. The evidence points in the opposite direction. The national service bill being considered by Congress might well put McNutt out of business. Also, the failure of an existing WMC program could only help men such as Henry Stimson and Grenville Clark who urged the stronger approach of national service. McNutt's entire career had been predicated on voluntarism. He had no reason to give it up now, when the end of the war was in sight. The New Bedford case, however, did reveal clearly the limits of McNutt's voluntarism. The key to the uproar was union rights. If Fisk and Firestone had been unionized, the transfers probably would have occurred without such resistance. McNutt was correct when he told the WMC meeting of March 22 that labor-management trouble in New Bedford went back several years. When McNutt entered the scene after repeated attempts at a local solution had failed, he entered a simmering union-management dispute. Despite the war, despite critical material shortages, traditional American factionalism had to be served. New Bedford factionalism generated enough power to help destroy McNutt's consensus. What had worked in Allentown, Philadelphia, and Newark would not work in New Bedford because a different labor-management climate prevailed. Without the cooperation of the MLPC, McNutt simply marked time with his program. Within weeks the issue became academic because new military priorities eliminated the dire need for Fisk and Firestone products.[41]

VII

With the exception of the New Bedford blowup, McNutt had managed to maintain good relations with labor throughout the war. The WMC program of priority referrals and stabilization had been supported by labor. The level of cooperation was surprising, given the great changes of war. By the summer of 1945, the American labor force was quite different from what it had been before the war. In 1940 one-quarter of the civilian labor force had been in the manufacturing industry. By 1945 this figure had jumped to one-third. The average age of the American worker had increased from thirty-seven to forty. The total labor force had increased from fifty-four million to sixty-four million. The female workers in industry had doubled while the male work force had increased by 37 percent. Union membership had grown from 8.5 million to 14.5 million. Men disagreed over the impact of these changes and their meaning. Some insisted that labor achieved its position of power in the American economy only as a result of World War II. Others pointed out that big business benefited more than any segment of the economy from the war. But labor did play an important role through the WMC. Granted that labor officials lacked the power of management officials in the War Department and the WPB, still, the MLPC indicated that labor had come a long way from the 1930s. McNutt was proud of how his work with the WMC helped promote industrial democracy.[42]

McNutt was elated when, on March 28, 1945, the members of the MLPC collaborated for a "New Charter for Labor and Management." The charter members of the MLPC, including Eric Johnston of the Chamber of Commerce, William Green, and Phillip Murray, signed the document proposing a new code to govern relations in the marketplace, a code which seemed an affirmation of what McNutt had worked for during the war. The code advocated: "(1) the highest degree of production and employment, (2) private competitive capitalism, (3) no unnecessary burdensome restrictions on management, (4) free collective labor bargaining, (5) security of the individual against the hazards of unemployment, incapacity and old age, (6) stimulation of untrammeled foreign trade, and (7) the establishment of an international security organization." For McNutt, the apostle of voluntary, decentralized manpower mobilization, the pronouncement seemed a benediction on his wartime service.[43]

Notes

1. The best general study of labor during the war is Joel Seidman, *American Labor from Defense to Reconversion* (Chicago: University of Chicago Press, 1953). Scholars disagree on the impact of the war on the labor movement. Recently, Paul A. C. Koistinen, "Mobilizing the World War II Economy: Labor and the Industrial-Military Alliance," *Pacific Historical Review* 42 (November 1973), pp. 443-78, argues that labor played only a minor role in the wartime economic mobilization and that the experience had little effect in changing the basic power structure in American society. David Brody, "The Emergence of Mass-Production Unionism,"

in *Change and Continuity in Twentieth-Century America*, John Braeman, Robert H. Bremmer, and Everett Walters, eds. (Columbus, Ohio: State University Press, 1964), pp. 243-62, places emphasis on the realization of labor rights during the war. Robert K. Murray, "Government and Labor during World War II," *Current History* 37 (September 1959), p. 148; Seidman, *American Labor*, pp. 107, 195, says the proportion of workers under collective-bargaining contracts rose from 30 percent of all eligible in 1941 to 48 percent in 1945.

2. Seidman, *American Labor*, pp. 18, 21-22, 23, 27, 53; Bruno Stein, "Labor's Role in Government Agencies during World War II," *Journal of Economic History* 17 (September 1957), p. 398.

3. Koistinen, "Mobilizing the World War II Economy," pp. 444, 471; Seidman, *American Labor*, pp. 26, 28; Eliot Janeway, *Struggle for Survival* (New Haven: Yale University Press, 1951), p. 160; Stein, "Labor's Role," p. 389; Donald Nelson, *Arsenal of Democracy: The Story of American War Production* (New York: Harcourt, Brace, 1946), p. 314.

4. Seidman, *American Labor*, pp. 45, 55, 56, 57, 69.

5. *Ibid.*, pp. 25, 38, 43, 44-45, 65-67, 80, 88-89; *Monthly Labor Review*, April 1942, p. 867.

6. Isador Lubin and David Niles to Hopkins, June 25, 1942, box 324, Harry Hopkins Papers, Roosevelt Library; Watson to Roosevelt, May 3, 1943, OF 4025, Franklin D. Roosevelt Papers, Hyde Park, N.Y.; *Complete Presidential Press Conferences of Franklin D. Roosevelt, 1941-1945*, 25 vols. in 12 books (New York: Da Capo Press, 1972), 24: 137-38 (September 29, 1944), hereafter cited as *PPC*; *New York Times*, December 9, 1942, p. 1, and November 2, 1943, p. 16. Anna Rosenberg, area director of New York manpower, acted as a liaison agent between Roosevelt and the leaders of labor. For a comprehensive study which concludes that unions sold out to Roosevelt and capitalism see Nelson N. Lichenstein, "Industrial Unionism under the No-Strike Pledge" (Ph.D. dissertation, University of California, Berkeley, 1974), 2 vols.

7. Files for November-December, 1940, Paul McNutt Papers, The Lilly Library, Indiana University, Bloomington, Ind.; *Business Week*, April 25, 1942, p. 7; quoted in speech file of April 19, 1941, McNutt Papers; George I. Blake, *Paul McNutt: Portrait of a Hoosier Statesman* (Indianapolis: Central Publishing, 1966), pp. 160-62.

8. Memorandum for Roosevelt from General Watson, January 29, 1942, OF 4025, and memorandum for Roosevelt from MEF, March 27, 1942, OF 2025, Roosevelt Papers; speech file of April 7, 1942, McNutt Papers.

9. Press conference, April 20, 1942, McNutt Papers.

10. Speech files of April 29, 1942, June 18, 1942, and December 3, 1942, McNutt Papers; McNutt to Central Labor Union of Pennsylvania, August 14, 1942, and McNutt, "Work or Fight" manuscript, December 31, 1942, McNutt Papers. Koistinen, "Mobilizing the World War II Economy," p. 451, admits that the WMC was the one agency over which labor had some influence.

11. Hershey memorandum for Executive Director, WMC, February 22, 1943, staybacks, 1942-1943, General Lewis B. Hershey Papers, Military History Research Collection, Carlisle Barracks, Pa.; press release, April 12, 1943, McNutt Papers; Seidman, *American Labor*, pp. 160-61; J. D. Brown to Patterson, June 3, 1943, box

184, Robert Patterson Papers, Library of Congress, Washington, D.C.; *New York Times*, June 16, 1943, p. 31; files for June 25, 1943, August 1, 1943, and August 16, 1943, radio address, September 6, 1943, file for September 11, 1943, speech, October 11, 1943, "Labor Goes to War" manuscript, October 1, 1943, all in McNutt Papers.

12. Quote in file of July 29, 1944, see also files of August 16, 1944, August 26, 1944, and biennial report, December 1944, McNutt Papers; *New York Times*, December 11, 1944, p. 1.

13. Nelson, *Arsenal of Democracy*, p. 318; Stein, "Labor's Role," p. 401; Seidman, *American Labor*, p. 177; Carol Riegelman, *Labour-Management Co-operation in United States War Production* (Montreal: International Labour Office, 1948), p. 196.

14. Quoted in address to AFL, October 11, 1943, McNutt Papers.

15. Speech file of October 11, 1943, McNutt Papers; Roosevelt to Director of the Budget, October 29, 1942, OF 4905D, Roosevelt Papers; Byron Mitchell to Garber, October 30, 1942, box 5, manpower file, Samuel I. Rosenman Papers, Roosevelt Library.

16. Stein, "Labor's Role," p. 402; Management Labor Policy Committee minutes, October 28, 1942, box 5-98, Record Group 211, National Archives, Washington, D.C.; Riegelman, *Labour-Management Co-operation*, p. 30.

17. Management Labor Policy Committee (MLPC) minutes, February 26, 1943, box 5-98, RG 211; Stein, "Labor's Role," p. 402; *Monthly Labor Review*, May 1943, p. 1033.

18. Minutes of Women's Advisory Committee, May 12, 1943, RG 211; quote in speech file of May 21, 1943, McNutt Papers.

19. Speech files of May 21, 1943, and October 11, 1943, and manuscript for *Pennsylvania Federationist*, October 1, 1943, McNutt Papers; MLPC minutes, November 2, 1943, box 5-98, RG 211.

20. Leonard P. Adams, *Wartime Manpower Mobilization* (Ithaca, N.Y.: Cornell University Press, 1951), pp. 45-46, 48; CIO quoted in *New York Times*, April 29, 1943, p. 11; *New York Times*, April 21, 1943, p. 17, and April 18, 1943, p. 1.

21. Murray, "Government and Labor," p. 151; *New York Times*, April 20, 1943, p. 36, April 21, 1943, p. 17, April 27, 1943, p. 10, and April 29, 1943, p. 11.

22. For a rather idealistic view of management-labor cooperation see Nelson, *Arsenal*, p. 325; McNutt to Robert L. Dreifuss, March 31, 1945, McNutt Papers. For another view see R. J. Thomas, "What Labor Did," in *While You Were Gone*, Jack Goodman, ed. (New York: Simon and Schuster, 1946), pp. 189-212; John Dos Passos, *State of the Nation* (Boston: Houghton Mifflin, 1943), pp. 43, 48; Jeannette Fleisher to Mrs. Nash, November 16, 1944, box 20-142, E117, RG 211; also see Riegelman, *Labour-Management Co-operation*, pp. 35, 54, 88, 336.

23. *Monthly Labor Review*, February 1944, p. 466, and April 1945, p. 916; U.S., Congress, House, Committee on Military Affairs, hearings on *Mobilization of Civilian Manpower*, HR 1119, 69th Cong., 1st sess., 1945, p. 219.

24. MLPC minutes, August 7, 1942, July 27, 1943, August 10, 1943, October 5, 1943, and December 5, 1944, box 5-98, RG 211; McNutt quoted in McNutt to

Claude Ballard, December 14, 1943, box 1-1, RG 211; *New York Times*, January 19, 1944, p. 13. See also Byron Fairchild and Jonathan Grossman, *The Army and Industrial Manpower* (Washington, D.C.: U.S. Department of the Army, 1959), pp. 189-196 for a discussion of the use of prisoners and the War Department. See also John H. Moore, "Italian POW's in America," *Prologue* 8 (Fall 1976), pp. 141-51.

25. Seidman, *American Labor,* p. 78; *New York Times*, August 25, 1944, p. 9, and December 21, 1942, p. 17; Green and Murray to Byrnes, Baruch, Leahy, Hopkins, and Rosenman, March 23, 1943, box 5, manpower file, Rosenman Papers; *New York Times*, October 6, 1943, p. 30.

26. McNutt to F. J. Bailey, June 1943, OF 407B, Roosevelt Papers; *Monthly Labor Review*, December, 1943, p. 1124. Hershey also opposed this bill; see Hershey to Congressman Andrew May, April 22, 1943, file of 78th Cong., Hershey Papers.

27. Murray, "Government and Labor," p. 150; WMC minutes, May 6, 1942, box 5-100, RG 211; speech file of June 18, 1942, and testimony before Senate Military Affairs Committee, October 21, 1942, McNutt Papers.

28. Haber to Fleming, October 9, 1942, pack. 5, pt. 2, James Byrnes Papers, Clemson University Library, Clemson, S.C.

29. McNutt to Byrnes, October 16, 1942, pack. 5, pt. 2, Byrnes Papers; Byrnes to McNutt, October 22, 1942, *ibid.*; W. R. Start to Byrnes, October 29, 1942, *ibid.*; *Monthly Labor Review*, June 1944, p. 1197.

30. Fairchild and Grossman, *Army and Manpower*, pp. 34, 57, 79.

31. Murray's interpretation of a growing military-industrial complex finds support from Koistinen, "Mobilizing the World War II Economy," pp. 464-78 *passim*. *New York Times*, January 25, 1943, p. 27, and March 1, 1943, p. 1; Patterson to Roosevelt, July 18, 1944, OF 4025, Roosevelt Papers.

32. MLPC minutes, August 8, 1944, box 5-98, RG 211; *New York Times*, October 12, 1943, p. 39, and November 22, 1944, p. 15.

33. *New York Times*, December 31, 1942, and April 16, 1943, p. 1; *Monthly Labor Review*, February 1944, p. 467.

34. *New York Times*, April 22, 1943, p. 26, April 23, 1943, p. 11, June 6, 1944, p. 10, and January 6, 1945, p. 7; *Business Week*, July 8, 1944, p. 102, January 13, 1945, p. 107, October 14, 1944, p. 100, and February 3, 1945, p. 92.

35. *New York Times*, July 28, 1944, p. 12, and January 7, 1945, p. 31; Byrnes to Roosevelt, December 20, 1944, Byrnes Papers.

36. Riegelman, *Labour-Management Co-operation*, pp. 94-96; Leary and Kennedy to Roosevelt, March 9, 1945, OF 4905, and Harriman to Roosevelt, February 17, 1945, *ibid.*, Roosevelt Papers.

37. *New York Times*, February 21, 1945, p. 12, March 3, 1945, p. 9, and March 9, 1945, p. 32; *Business Week*, March 3, 1945, p. 98, and March 10, 1945, p. 103.

38. MLPC minutes, March 16, 1945, box 5-98, RG 211.

39. *Ibid.*, March 20, 1945, box 5-98, RG 211.

40. News release, March 20, 1945, McNutt Papers.

41. Minutes of Women's Advisory Committee, March 21, 1945, series 32, RG 211; WMC minutes, March 22, 1945, box 5-100, RG 211; MLPC minutes, March

27, 1945, box 5-98, RG 211; speech file of April 5, 1945, McNutt Papers; Riegelman, *Labour-Management Co-operation*, p. 96.

42. Koistinen, "Mobilizing the World War II Economy," admits that labor played an active role in the WMC but argues that this agency lost power in 1943. For a more optimistic view of labor's role during the war see Brody, "Emergence of Unionism" and Siedman, *American Labor*.

43. *New York Times*, January 2, 1945, p. 12; Murray, "Government and Labor," pp. 151-52; Thomas, "What Labor Did?" p. 209; Stein, "Labor's Role," p. 406; Riegelman, *Labour-Management Co-operation*, p. 347; quote in *Monthly Labor Review*, June 1945, p. 1342.

CHAPTER 6

On the Farm

Farm labor represented another major interest group with which McNutt had to struggle during the war. Like organized labor, the farm lobby worked day and night to protect its interest in the midst of mobilization. This work led to congressional discrimination in favor of farm labor through special deferment status. In the words of General Hershey, "the farm labor problem has been the worst that we have had to face."[1] Throughout the war McNutt's attempt to provide adequate labor for American farms pulled him into a political thicket in which the barbs of Congress, the farm lobby, the War Department, and the President all took their toll.

I

The farm problem had been around long before mobilization for war. Despite the various New Deal agricultural laws, which provided subsidy payments for farming, by the end of the decade it was clear that too many farmers were remaining on the land. The Bureau of Agricultural Economics estimated that in 1940 there were 2,500,000 people in excess of actual labor needs in agriculture. The total farm population had grown by 980,000 during the 1930s. W. L. Clayton, a farm economist, announced that there was a surplus of two million farm families as the decade began. In November 1940 Chester Davis, director of the Agricultural Adjustment Administration, proposed that five million low-income, single-crop farmers leave the land and go into defense industry. Industrial labor shortages, rather than farm shortages, worried the administration. Acting on such advice and on the imperatives of market mechanics, farmers migrated to the factories with a vengeance in 1941 and 1942. From 1939 to 1942 the average earnings of a factory worker increased anywhere from 95 to 157 percent. Farm wages in July 1942 were 61 percent higher than in July 1939, but the daily wage of $2.45 in July 1942 compared poorly with the entering wage rate of $5.08 for an eight-hour day earned by a common male laborer in industry. No wonder farmers headed for factory personnel offices.[2]

At this early stage the migration of farmers appeared a healthy development. No one worried about a failure of food production and departing farmers were quickly replaced by the existing surplus of farm labor. Neither McNutt nor Roosevelt gave much thought to a potential farm labor shortage. During the National Defense Migration Hearings in the House of Representatives in 1941 extensive reports appeared on the general manpower problem, but few reliable statistics were presented on farm labor.

By the summer of 1942, however, less optimistic reports appeared. Governor John Moses of North Dakota soon wrote the President asking for a ninety-day military deferment for all young men in his state because of the shortage of farm labor. From Omaha, Nebraska, reports arrived that a record crop of corn had been planted but the labor for harvest was unavailable. Senator James E. Murray of Montana also wrote of the desperate need for farm labor in his state. Edward A. O'Neal, the powerful president of the American Farm Bureau Federation, called on James Byrnes to urge Roosevelt to recognize that agriculture was a war industry. According to O'Neal, agriculture had lost some 1,500,000 workers in the last two years. He urged that the Selective Service extend an occupational deferment to all "necessary men" in agriculture. Here was the first expression of the need for a blanket deferment for farmers, an idea which would wreak havoc with McNutt's manpower plans.[3]

McNutt, by the summer of 1942, knew of the growing farm problem, but he did not think labor shortages would become acute until 1943. He established close liaison with Claude Wickard, the Secretary of Agriculture and an old political crony from Indiana. The issue of farm labor came up during a meeting of the WMC in May 1942. Wickard and General Hershey both supported O'Neil's idea of protecting farm labor. Hershey, who was raised in a farming community, insisted that no one could really replace a drafted farm boy but another farm boy, as one had to grow up on the farm to be effective in the field. Wickard agreed with this gloss on the agrarian myth but it met opposition from city-bred types. Franklin Roosevelt consistently argued in 1942 that farmers could do the job if they used their ingenuity and overcame a defeatist attitude. Despite demurrals from Vice President Henry Wallace, Roosevelt insisted that farmers were not working as hard as they had thirty years before. McNutt and Frances Perkins agreed. Everyone recognized that young, single boys were leaving the farms in legions to take higher-paying jobs in industry. But at this stage not even Wickard thought the drain would be critical.[4]

McNutt and Roosevelt believed the farm labor problem could be easily solved. Roosevelt wanted farmers to work harder and also suggested that schoolchildren could work in the afternoons. McNutt agreed that there were many untapped labor sources and advocated a volunteer program of young students who would spend their summers on the farm. Getting back to nature would do wonders for city boys. These ideas, reminiscent of the Civilian Conservation Corps during the 1930s, were attractive but there were many problems in their execution. Farm workers in the summer of 1942 received an average of less than thirty cents an hour, which was far below the industrial rate. The entire wage structure in agriculture was chaotic. There was no collective bargaining and no minimum wage. In the South black agricultural workers remained in a state of semi-serfdom. As one farmer complained: "Who ever heard of payin' a nigger more than a dollar a day? It's running 'em plum crazy." Ignoring such attitudes and to relieve some of the pressure forcing a migration to the factory, McNutt told a House Agricultural Committee in September that farm wages should be brought in line with industrial wages. In October, while testifying before the Senate Military Affairs Committee, he admitted that although two years ago a surplus existed in farm labor the 1943 crop might be hurt by labor shortages. He urged a raise in wages and promised to help transport farm workers to where they were needed.[5]

Nice words, but farm lobbyists had already begun to lobby Congress for protection from the draft. Beginning in the 1920s farmers had become accustomed to bringing their problems to Congress. This strategy had paid off in the past and would pay off now. By World War II the farm lobby in Congress was a powerful and close-knit unit. The lobby paid attention when dairy farmers began to complain. A survey in Los Angeles county revealed a labor turnover in dairy farming of more than 100 percent of the hired labor force in the first half of 1942. Senator Joseph Ball and fourteen other senators wrote Roosevelt on October 8, 1942, of the need for man-power action in this area. Governor Dwight H. Green of Illinois added his plea. The President continued to equivocate. He assured everyone of his awareness of the critical role of farm labor in the war effort, but he hoped that McNutt might solve the problem with his newly expanded WMC. McNutt, although still as skeptical as Roosevelt, realized that some action was needed because several congressmen had begun to lobby for special legislation giving a blanket deferment to farmers.[6]

Such a blanket deferment was prohibited by the Selective Service law, but this drawback did not prevent Congressman Stephen Pace and Senator Millard Tydings from asking Hershey about the feasi-bility of such an action. Hershey recommended against it. He did not think "that agriculture would care to have the stigma attached that might occur under a blanket deferment." The congressional lobby disagreed. Tydings asked Hershey to draft just such a bill, which would not violate the Selective Service law, in October 1942. Hershey and McNutt now both realized that unless they could come up with some sort of alternate proposal, Congress would draft its own bill and tie the administration's hands in dealing with farm labor. A special deferment of dairy workers might satisfy Congress. But this proposal ran into strong opposition from the War Depart-ment. Stimson, Goldthwaite Dorr, and General George Marshall argued to McNutt that such a deferment would hurt the war effort. Authorized divisions were already seriously under strength. McNutt accepted their arguments but patiently explained political realities. Unless the WMC threw a bone to Congress in the form of a dairy worker deferment, a more extensive and mandatory deferment of agricultural workers would be forthcoming. McNutt failed to con-vince the military, but decided to stand firm. On November 6, 1942, the WMC issued a "Directive to Promote Employment Stabilization on Dairy, Livestock, and Poultry Farms."[7]

Under this order the Secretary of Agriculture and the USES were to assist in recruiting additional farm workers. The military would refuse to accept voluntary enlistments from such workers. War contractors were not to hire dairy farmers, and draft boards were not to draft them. Dorr accused McNutt of panicking. Yet McNutt knew that the directive would not solve the farm labor problem because the drain would continue as long as wages remained low. But if his move could delay a blanket deferment of agricultural labor from being imposed by Congress, it was worthwhile. Unfortunately, the partial deferment did no such thing.

In Congress the debate continued over providing a deferment for all necessary agricultural workers. Tydings felt it was foolish to continue to draft farm boys and expect the farmers to feed both the United States and its Allies. At the White House McNutt brought the issue up at a cabinet meeting on October 10, 1942, asking Harold Ickes if Indian labor could help with the cotton crop in Arizona. The President, however, decided to approach the problem in what Ickes called a "romanticized" way. Roosevelt hoped that young volunteers could do the job after they left school each day. In California schoolchildren had just helped bring in the prune crop, according to the President. But these ideas of a youth corps appeared unrealistic when dealing with the planting and harvesting of a major wheat crop. Wallace and Wickard defended the record of the farmers, but Roosevelt still believed they could do more. He rejected out of hand any idea of a blanket deferment for farmers, telling reporters at a news conference on October 20, 1942, "I don't think limiting amendments by groups, jobs, trades is the sound way of approaching it [shortages]." As a last resort, on November 12 he suggested to Stimson that the military enlist farmers and then furlough them at once into the enlisted reserve with the stipulation that they would not be called to active duty if they stayed on the farm. Neither Stimson nor Patterson liked this idea which discriminated against the young soldier who willingly served his country at a mere $50 per month.[8]

In the meantime McNutt continued to press for a raise in farm wages and an expanded use of women on the farm as the solution. The number of women working on farms did rise from some 500,000 in December 1941 to about 800,000 in December 1943. But McNutt's control over this problem was severely curtailed by Congress which,

on November 13, 1942, passed the Tydings amendment to the Selective Service law. The amendment provided deferments to essential
men working in agriculture and gave ample proof of the power of
the farm lobby. The final form of the bill protected the farmer from
both draft calls and raids by industry. Although the Selective Service did eventually draft some two million farmers during the war,
Stimson and Hershey both felt in retrospect that this group had beat
the draft. McNutt brought the issue before a November 28 meeting
of the WMC. Everyone agreed that the Tydings amendment amounted
to a freeze of agricultural labor. But most of the members of the
WMC agreed with McNutt that they would just have to live with
the amendment. Later, an elaborate work-credit plan was devised
to guide local draft boards on the essentiality of each farm worker.[9]

The War Department continued to insist that no shortage of farm
labor existed, but McNutt now agreed with farm experts Wallace
and Wickard. By the end of 1942 the WMC estimated that some
700,000 farm workers would be lost to the military even with the
Tydings amendment. Some 200,000 men and 300,000 women were
available as replacements. To make matters worse, an additional
3.5 million workers would be needed during the peak harvest season
in 1943, up from the 11,700,000 who had worked the 1942 harvest.
The USES had recruited three million farm workers for harvest
time in 1942 and, according to the Department of Agriculture, all
food production goals for the year had been met or exceeded. To
meet future needs McNutt planned mobile farm work groups with
the cooperation of the Farm Security Administration. He worked
with Secretary Wickard to promote the transfer of farmers from
substandard lands to more productive areas as a means of expanding production and continued to press for higher wages for farm
labor. During peak harvest work, McNutt used the USES to train
and mobilize local nonfarmers to take to the fields. These efforts,
however, could not be fully executed without the cooperation of
the farm lobby and Congress. But prospects for such cooperation
seemed dim. In December 1942 the Executive Council of the National Farmers Union (NFU) passed a resolution calling for the
immediate reorganization of the entire War Manpower Commission.
Farmers disliked McNutt's work-credit scheme which, according
to critics, led to three out of every four farmers being classified as
"non-essential."[10]

Such criticism over the implementation of the Tydings amendment led McNutt to suspect that he was best rid of the entire problem of farm labor. On three separate occasions McNutt requested
additional funds to finance the Farm Placement Service of the
WMC. Each time Congress turned him down but also complained
over the shortage of farm labor. To make matters worse, the President was growing weary over these constant complaints. When
McNutt and Wickard whined about the farm labor shortages at a
cabinet meeting, Roosevelt objected: "You are always complaining
about shortages and difficulty but have no plan." This was unfair
because McNutt had attempted to placate the farm lobby in Congress by revising downward the number of work-credits needed for
deferment. General Hershey, in contrast, had informed local boards
that they could use their own judgment in evaluating farmers.[11]

In late January 1943 McNutt decided to stop whining and cut the
Gordian knot. If Congress refused to provide funds for recruiting
farm labor and if local draft boards refused to cooperate, he would
shift the entire responsibility to the Department of Agriculture.
Wickard already had field personnel working in this area of farm
labor and seemed happy to assume more responsibility. At a joint
press conference on January 25, 1943, McNutt and Wickard released
a WMC directive authorizing the Secretary of Agriculture to assume
"full operating responsibility for recruitment, placement, transfer
and utilization of agricultural workers." The two men also announced that some 3.5 million persons now working in nonessential
jobs would have to help harvest the year's crop. McNutt breathed a
sigh of relief after this transfer of authority, but he had not seen the
last of the farm problem.[12]

II

Unfortunately, Wickard was unprepared for his new duties.
According to James Byrnes, the Secretary of Agriculture was in
over his head. Farm protest over labor shortages continued to
mount. In New York C. C. Dumond, head of the State Farm Federation, predicted that many farmers would refuse to plant a crop
unless assured adequate help. A Gallup poll of February 14, 1943,
indicated that 39 percent of all farmers interviewed favored draft
deferments for farm labor and the furlough of soldiers to help

harvest the crop. Congressman Hampton P. Fulmer of South Carolina, chairman of the House Agriculture Committee, advocated furloughs in a visit to the White House. Roosevelt at first rejected such a scheme, but when farmers warned that the cotton crop in Arizona might be lost because of a shortage of labor, he changed his mind. Roosevelt knew that Congress was already drafting a new bill which would provide for such furloughs, despite War Department objections. Both Stimson and Patterson also knew of the dire need for cotton to make parachutes. McNutt, however, had serious reservations about using troops. He informed Stimson, through Fowler Harper, that the WMC had studied the problem in Arizona and discovered that no emergency existed. Civilian pickers were available to do the work but the growers refused to pay an attractive wage. Patterson and Stimson rejoiced that McNutt had relieved them from such a disagreeable assignment. Yet McNutt's pronouncement amounted to waving a red flag in front of the farm lobby in Congress.[13]

In late January the Senate Committee on Appropriations, under the control of the farm bloc, announced that a subcommittee would hold hearings on the subject of farm labor shortages. The Military Affairs Committee and the Senate Committee to Investigate the National Defense Program (Truman Committee) also announced plans to look into manpower. Congressman Hampton Fulmer and Senator John Bankhead proposed a bill calling for the automatic deferment of any man who worked on a farm in 1942. The bill also required that ex-farmers now in military service be released and returned to the farm. Senator Bankhead announced that one million men had to be released from military duty to prevent an acute food shortage. Another bill by Congressman Paul J. Kilday called for establishing the principle of "farm or fight." Kilday complained that McNutt's manpower plan for farmers threatened "the preservation of the family in American life." Congressmen Leroy Johnson and Charles Halleck also denounced McNutt. When the Senate Subcommittee on Appropriations began its special manpower hearings in early February 1943, McNutt appeared to be in serious trouble, despite his decision to dump the problem in Secretary Wickard's lap.[14]

Louis Stark, the manpower expert for the *New York Times*, predicted that McNutt would soon be kicked out of the WMC be-

cause of his problem with agricultural labor. Yet not only did
McNutt survive, but in an ironic twist these hearings helped him
retain his power. When he first appeared before the Senate subcommittee McNutt was optimistic about meeting all of the needs of
agricultural labor for the year. He had no sooner left the witness
chair when his optimism was challenged by none other than Secretary
Wickard, always in closer tune with the farm lobby. Wickard predicted that farmers would not be able to do the job with the same
amount of labor they had in 1942. Several senators, including Bankhead, rejoiced at this confirmation of their own pessimism. As
Wickard continued his testimony, however, he lost credibility. On
several occasions he appeared confused and unsure of his facts.
After his departure his statements were quickly shot to pieces by a
parade of officials from the Selective Service and the War Department. According to General Hershey some 85 percent of all farm
labor leaving the farm went into industry. The military received
only 15 percent. Wickard had testified that 60 percent went into the
military. Hershey also pointed out that some 216,000 men had already been reclassified under the Tydings amendment. A few senators decried McNutt's decision to shift responsibility to Wickard,
but Senator Carl Hayden admitted that such a shift was partially
the fault of Congress for failing to appropriate funds for the WMC.[15]

In a strange turnabout, the hearings strengthened McNutt's
position. His views on farm labor seemed consistent with the thinking of Hershey, Stimson, and Roosevelt. The President, despite
congressional opposition, continued to emphasize that the needs of
the military were paramount. When reporters asked him how the
country could staff an enlarged army and also care for spring
planting, he reminded them that in Russia some 300,000 schoolchildren from ages twelve to eighteen had helped perform that task.
The United States could do the same, as McNutt had been saying.
Although Roosevelt admitted that some troops might be used in an
emergency on the farms, he felt that the loss of one day by the
military would hurt training programs, as Stimson had been saying.
Privately, Roosevelt admitted that a few local draft boards might
make mistakes in taking farm labor but in many cases the young
men refused deferment, as Hershey had been saying.[16]

As Congress continued to debate various draft-exemption proposals, Roosevelt asked the cabinet on February 19 to consider

some solution. He wondered if it would be wise to draft young farmers and then furlough them to the farm for duty. McNutt joined Hershey and Stimson in opposing such a scheme. A bogus draft of farmers would fool no one. Although a few soldiers might be released in an emergency, Patterson predicted that the pending bills in Congress would force release of some 375,000 men from active duty. Furloughs would go on indefinitely. Hershey agreed. He had witnessed how the Bankhead bill was converted from a limited deferment program to an attempt to defer all farmers. As he wrote to McNutt, "these bills, if enacted, will consolidate all other groups . . . against the farmer." McNutt, Patterson, and Hershey all advised Roosevelt to fight such congressional proposals.[17]

The advice was appropriate but Roosevelt had to prevent an irate Congress from providing additional deferments for farm workers. Some sort of compromise seemed in order. The President worked with McNutt, Hershey, and Wickard to develop some plan to appease Congress while not offending the War Department. Although still filled with misgivings, McNutt finally supported a new agricultural labor plan announced to the press on March 7. Under this compromise plan, agents from the Department of Agriculture, serving on state and county war boards, were authorized to seek the deferment of all farm workers needed, even when the individual did not personally request a deferment. If the worker did not produce enough work units to warrant deferment under McNutt's rules and the Tydings Act, he would have thirty days to find a new job. Local draft boards could reclassify and defer men with agricultural experience who had left the farm but were willing to return. McNutt held a press conference to explain the virtues of the new plan to farmers. He argued that under this scheme he hoped to mobilize several million new farm workers. Women, schoolchildren, and civic groups would form volunteer farm armies. The Farm Security Administration would organize a mobile army of farm laborers to help. The administration also planned to recruit foreign farm workers. In his best pulpit style, McNutt exhorted farmers that the job could be done under this new scheme without any additional legislation.[18]

Despite McNutt's exhortations, the plan did not prevent congressional action. Two days after McNutt's announcement the Senate Military Affairs Committee reported out a bill calling for sweeping and mandatory draft deferments for all farm workers. On March 17, 1943, the Senate voted fifty to twenty-four for this Bankhead-Johnson bill. Before the bill could pass the House, however, a wave of public opposition developed. Public distaste for blanket deferments plus McNutt's alternative program helped defeat the measure in the House. Arthur Krock, a well-known journalist, wrote that several mailboxes in some farm areas had been painted yellow as a sign that a young man who had left the farm for war industry had returned upon hearing of the blanket deferment plan. Beyond the unfavorable public reaction and McNutt's new plan, the Bankhead-Johnson bill failed in the House partially because McNutt and Hershey made a secret deal with Congress not to draft young farmers and to interpret the Tydings amendment in a liberal spirit. Undersecretary Patterson began to suspect that such a deal had been made wnen he saw thousands of young farmers avoiding the draft. In December 1943, at a meeting of the WMC, Patterson began arguing with McNutt over whether or not the Tydings amendment prevented the drafting of some 440,000 young men on the farms. Patterson insisted that the language of the Tydings amendment was quite flexible. McNutt now admitted that this flexibility had been removed by a special agreement he and Hershey had made with congressional leaders to prevent passage of the Bankhead-Johnson bill. Hershey sat in confirming silence as Patterson fumed.[19]

III

McNutt had little trouble in justifying this deal given the attitude of Congress in 1943 and afterwards. He and Hershey always possessed a keener sense of political reality than the War Department. Still, even after this deal farm problems continued. Wickard seemed unable to cope. A special White House investigation of manpower in March 1943 concluded that Wickard's handling of farm labor had been "grossly inefficient." Both Wickard and his chief assistant seemed ill-informed and lacking in ability. The committee called for a new Secretary of Agriculture. The WMC admitted that the transfer of authority had not worked well. In fact, the WMC still did most farm labor recruiting through the USES.[20]

From the very beginning farm labor had been as much a political problem as a manpower management problem. Roosevelt kept assuring protesting congressmen that farmers were being deferred in large numbers. By March 1943 some 550,000 had been deferred. An additional three million would be deferred by the end of the year under the Tydings amendment. The War Department then began releasing men over age thirty-eight with farm experience. Eventually, these men were transferred to inactive status in the Enlisted Reserve Corps. As early as May 6, 1943, Chester C. Davis, War Food Administrator, announced that ample farm labor was available to produce and harvest all planned crops.[21]

Despite this testimony, Congress continued to harass McNutt. From farm lobbyists such as Congressman Fulmer of South Carolina McNutt received dire warnings about future legislation because local draft boards continued to induct key farm workers. On the other side, Undersecretary Patterson badgered McNutt about the thousands of young, able-bodied men who were using the Tydings amendment as a draft dodge. McNutt tried to explain that the problems of recruiting farm labor arose because of the refusal of Congress to appropriate money for that purpose. The USES worked with local farm officials in the Extension Service of the Agriculture Department, but more money was needed to finance the work. As for complaints about local draft boards, McNutt admitted to the White House that despite his directives some farmers were being drafted. Also, under the WMC employment stabilization program farm workers could accept a nonagricultural job for up to six weeks without bothering with a certificate of availability. As 1943 drew to an end McNutt still felt the barbs of farm critics in and out of Congress. Farm labor seemed to be a no-win proposition.[22]

After December 1943 the Selective Service became independent of McNutt's control and the focus of the farm labor dispute shifted from McNutt to Hershey. Individuals who complained that too few or too many farmers were being drafted had no reason to bother McNutt. These critics remained in Hershey's hair, however, until the end of the war. Several times before that date Hershey unsuccessfully attempted to tighten up farm deferments. He now seemed trapped by the Tydings amendment that he had helped compose. In April 1944, following a presidential order to crack down on all draft deferments, Hershey told the farmers that their first job was to fulfill their military obligation. At this time there were three farmers deferred for every industrial worker age twenty-six and under. Patterson kept prodding Hershey to draft more farmers throughout 1944. The debate continued into early 1945. In January, Hershey again asked local boards to review all deferments but also admitted that "there has been no change in the policy that essential agriculture must be protected and if necessary by the deferment of men ages 18 through 25 who cannot be replaced." In spite of criticism from the War Department, Hershey followed the farm lobby and protected agricultural labor.[23]

IV

During this period McNutt's farm problem was restricted to recruitment. The WMC had always been active in this area. During 1942 alone the WMC had used the USES to place more than three million workers on farms. Workers were recruited from Tennessee for shipment to the Southwest to help with the cotton crops. The Farm Security Administration worked closely with the USES to alleviate labor shortages for the sugar harvest in Louisiana and the citrus harvest in Florida. By late 1942 the WMC had established employment stabilization programs for the dairy, livestock, and poultry industries.[24]

President Roosevelt always felt the shortage in farm labor could be overcome by tapping voluntary labor from the community. McNutt did his best to promote this type of volunteering. He urged schoolteachers and their students to use their vacations working on farms. The USES and county agricultural agents acted as placement services for such volunteers. During the first year of the war more than one million 4-H boys and girls contributed to raising chickens, hogs, and cattle. The Office of Education supervised their selection and training and avoided taking children under fourteen away from school.[25]

McNutt also turned to women as a source of agricultural labor. In 1940 the Bureau of Agricultural Economics estimated that women made up about 5.8 percent of the nation's total farm labor population. By April 1, 1942, this figure had risen to 14 percent or a total of some 1,328,000 women farm workers in the United States. The formation of the Women's Land Army in 1943 to recruit volunteer workers helped relieve the crisis in key areas. Special uniforms and insignias promoted recruitment of college girls for summer work. These volunteer workers, under the direction of Florence Hall, were supervised by the Department of Agriculture. McNutt praised their work in helping save the 1944 crop of small fruits and vegetables. More than 90 percent of the girls attending Smith College pitched in on farms in New England.[26]

To supplement domestic volunteers McNutt also became involved in the importation of foreign agricultural laborers. At a meeting of the WMC on June 10, 1942, Secretary of Agriculture Wickard brought up the idea of using imported Mexican labor to help harvest crops in the South and Southwest. According to American farmers, without such aid many crops would perish. McNutt responded by supporting an importation program with the stipulation that aliens must return home at the end of a specified work period. Thus began the braceros program which would eventually lead to the employment of approximately 50,000 foreigners, mostly from Mexico, but also from Jamaica, the Bahamas, and Newfoundland. McNutt always insisted that this labor not be used in competition with domestic farm labor. Over the protest of the Immigration and Naturalization Service, he even promoted the idea of admitting these foreign workers without bond. The details of the importation of Mexican labor were worked out with the Department of Agriculture and the Department of State. In July 1943 the Mexican workers came under the control of the War Food Administration. McNutt had trouble satisfying the Management-Labor Policy Committee of the WMC that Mexican workers were not being used in competition with American labor. Union representatives at the WMC continued to fret that such foreign labor might migrate from farm to factory where they would depress wages.[27]

Because of this opposition within McNutt's organization, the recruitment of alien farm labor became more and more the responsibility of other agencies, such as the War Food Administration. McNutt, however, remained concerned with the treatment of these workers. If they met discrimination in wages, it was McNutt's job to check into the problem. He appointed a special committee to look into claims by Mexican workers that they were given only half of the wages paid to natives for the same work. After a few weeks of research, Will Alexander, McNutt's special assistant for alien labor, reported that discrimination against Spanish-American workers was widespread but there was little the WMC could do about the problem, given the paramount need for labor.[28]

V

During the manpower mobilization of World War II the American farmer enjoyed a privileged status. No other economic group received a blanket deferment from military duty and was immune to the indirect controls by the WMC. McNutt realized early in the game that farm labor was political dynamite. The farmer had too many friends in Congress. McNutt, in contrast, lacked the political muscle to impose a program on agricultural labor which would improve efficiency. Adopting stabilization plans or freezing labor might work in small areas such as dairy farming, but even here it merited quick criticism from the farm lobby. Congress refused to appropriate funds for McNutt to manage agricultural labor. The wisest and easiest solution seemed to be a delegation of the entire problem to Claude Wickard. The Secretary of Agriculture understood his role as protector of the farmer. Yet by giving power to Wickard, McNutt insured that his own efforts in industrial manpower mobilization would lack the integrity which came from approaching all of American manpower as a whole and seeing the economy, both farm and factory, as interrelated.

McNutt might be able to dump the farm problem on Wickard, but he faced other serious problems in mobilizing manpower which could not be so easily solved. In organized labor and in farm labor McNutt confronted groups which had considerable political influence. He also, however, had to deal with other segments of the working class which, in contrast, suffered from an absence of political power. Blacks and women faced discrimination.

Notes

1. Hershey to Brig. Gen. George H. Healey, November 16, 1942, staybacks, 1942-1943, General Lewis B. Hershey Papers, Military History Research Collection, Carlisle Barracks, Pa.

2. Lowry Nelson, "Farms and Farming Communities," in *American Society in Wartime*, William F. Ogburn, ed. (Chicago: University of Chicago Press, 1943), pp. 88-91; Eliot Janeway, *Struggle for Survival* (New Haven: Yale University Press, 1951), p. 153; *Monthly Labor Review*, December 1942, iii; David Hinshaw, *The Home Front* (New York: Putnam, 1943), p. 243. The following chapter draws heavily from the revealing article by Albert A. Blum, "The Farmer, the Army and the Draft," *Agricultural History* 38 (January 1964), pp. 34-42. Wage rates for agriculture did rise during the war. The weighted average farm wage rate for the nation as a whole more than doubled from October 1939 to October 1943. The increase was uneven across the country. The amount of wages per hired farm worker in 1943 was about 121 percent higher than in 1939, but one must compare this figure with the increase of 191 percent in net income for farm operators. The increase in output per farm worker from 1939 to 1943 was 26 percent. See *Monthly Labor Review*, January 1944, p. 15.

3. *Monthly Labor Review*, January 1942, p. 50; Flynn to Roosevelt, June 3, 1942, official file 1413, and Moses to Roosevelt, July 3, 1942, OF 1413, Franklin D. Roosevelt Papers, Roosevelt Library, Hyde Park, N.Y.; *New York Times*, September 20, 1942, sec. 4, p. 7; Murray to Roosevelt, OF 1913, Roosevelt Papers; O'Neal to Byrnes, October 26, 1942, James Byrnes Papers, Clemson University Library, Clemson, S.C.

4. Hershey to W. T. Phillip, March 26, 1942, staybacks, 1942, Hershey Papers; War Manpower Commission minutes, May 13, 1942, box 5-100, record group 211, National Archives, Washington, D.C.; Dean Albertson, *Roosevelt's Farmer: Claude R. Wickard in the New Deal* (New York: Columbia University Press, 1961), pp. 52-53, 287; *The Price of Vision: The Diary of Henry A. Wallace, 1942-1946*, John M. Blum, ed. (Boston: Houghton Mifflin, 1973), pp. 116-17. Wickard, an old farm boy from Indiana, had been a Democratic party crony of McNutt's.

5. McNutt to Mrs. A. J. Adair [*n.d.*], box 1-1, RG 211; McNutt speech, May 19, 1942, Paul V. McNutt Papers, The Lilly Library, Indiana University, Bloomington, Ind.; Haber to Fleming, October 9, 1942, pack 5, pt. 2, Byrnes Papers; report to Senate Military Affairs Committee, October 21, 1942, McNutt Papers; *New York Times*, September 29, 1942, p. 1; quote from John Dos Passos, *State of the Nation* (Boston: Houghton Mifflin, 1943), p. 69.

6. Senator Joseph Ball, et al., to Roosevelt, October 8, 1942, and Governor Green to Roosevelt, October 8, 1942, OF 1413, Roosevelt Papers.

7. Haber to Fleming, October 9, 1942, pack 5, pt. 2, Byrnes Papers; diary of Henry L. Stimson (October 22, 1942), 40: 171, and (October 23, 1942), 40: 175, Yale University Library, New Haven, Conn.; *Monthly Labor Review*, February 1943, p. 413; McNutt speech, November 20, 1942, McNutt Papers; Blum, "Farmer, Army and Draft," pp. 35-36; Hershey to Pace, September 3, 1942, staybacks, 1942, and Tydings to Hershey, October 15, 1942, White House file, 1941-1943, Hershey Papers.

8. Tydings to Hershey, October 15, 1942, White House file, 1941-1943, Hershey Papers; diary of Harold L. Ickes (October 10, 1942), 9: 7080, Library of Congress, Washington, D.C.; *Complete Presidential Press Conferences of Franklin D. Roosevelt, 1941-1945*, 25 vols. in 12 books (New York: Da Capo Press, 1972) 20: 157-59 (October 20, 1942), hereafter cited as *PPC*; Stimson Diary (November 12, 1942), 41: 40; Blum, *Price of Vision*, pp. 116-17.

9. McNutt speech, November 20, 1942, McNutt Papers; Hershey to Brig. Gen. George H. Healey, November 16, 1942, staybacks, 1942-1943, Hershey Papers; Blum, "Farmer, Army and Draft," p. 35; WMC minutes, November 28, 1942, box 5-100, RG 211; interview with General Lewis B. Hershey, Bethesda, Md., May 26, 1975.

10. K. S. Williams to Stark, December 21, 1942, Byrnes Papers; Nelson, "Farms and Farming Communities," p. 88; McNutt article, December 14, 1942, McNutt Papers; Gardner Jackson to Roosevelt, December 16, 1942, OF 1413, Roosevelt Papers.

11. Ickes Diary (January 2, 1943), 10: 7353; Roosevelt quoted in Albertson, *Roosevelt Farmer*, p. 36.

12. *Monthly Labor Review*, May 1943, p. 1025; *New York Times*, January 20, 1943, p. 33, and January 26, 1943, p. 11; Blum, "Farmer, Army and Draft," p. 36; memorandum by Presidential Screening Committee, March 10, 1943, box 20-139, RG 211.

13. *New York Times*, February 14, 1943, p. 40, February 14, 1943, p. 41, February 20, 1943, p. 1, February 25, 1943, p. 1, February 26, 1943, p. 17, February 28, 1943, sec 4, p. 2, and February 24, 1943, p. 1; Harper to Stimson, February 24, 1943, box 183, and Patterson to Roosevelt, March 1, 1943, box 183, Robert Patterson Papers, Library of Congress, Washington, D.C.

14. Blum, "Farmer, Army and Draft," p. 36; *New York Times*, January 26, 1943, p. 11, Kilday quoted in February 4, 1943, p. 1, February 15, 1943, p. 7, and February 26, 1943, p. 17; *Business Week*, February 27, 1943, p. 14.

15. *New York Times*, February 26, 1943, p. 17; U.S., Senate, Subcommittee on Appropriations, hearings on *Investigation of Manpower*, 78th Cong., 1st sess., 1943, pp. 54-92, 93, 116-20, 331-57, 143, 273-305, 324-30.

16. *PPC* (February 19, 1943), 21: 167-68.

17. *New York Times*, February 20, 1943, p. 1; Jonathan Daniels, *White House Witness, 1942–1945* (New York: Doubleday, 1975), p. 133; notes of cabinet meeting, February 19, 1943, box 171, Henry Stimson Papers, Yale University; Patterson to Hon. Robert R. Reynolds, March 1, 1943, *ibid.*; Patterson to Stimson, March 4, 1943, box 171, Stimson Papers; Hershey to Roosevelt, February 19, 1943, White House file, 1941-1943, Hershey Papers; Hershey to Executive Director, WMC, February 22, 1943, staybacks, 1942-1943, *ibid.*

18. Ickes Diary (March 6, 1943), 10: 7523; *Monthly Labor Review*, May 1943, p. 1030; *New York Times*, March 7, 1943, p. 1; McNutt statement for *Bangor Daily News*, March 8, 1943, McNutt Papers.

19. *New York Times*, March 10, 1943, p. 1, March 18, 1943, p. 1, March 19, 1943, p. 18, and April 8, 1943, p. 22; Blum, "Farmer, Army and Draft," p. 39; memorandum for record by Patterson, December 30, 1943, box 184, Patterson Papers.

20. Byrnes memorandum to Roosevelt, March 14, 1943, pack 59, pt. 1, Byrnes Papers.

21. *PPC* (March 26, 1943), 21: 230-31 (March 30, 1943), 21: 240-41; *New York Times*, March 27, 1943, p. 1, and May 7, 1943, p. 12.

22. *New York Times*, August 21, 1943, p. 5; Patterson to McNutt, September 22, 1943, box 184-5, Patterson Papers; McNutt to Harold Smith, September 30, 1943, box 20-140, RG 211; McNutt to James M. Barnes, September 18, 1943, box 1-1, RG

211; McNutt to W. H. Allen, October 29, 1943, box 1-1, RG 211; statement for *Rural Press*, October 1943, McNutt Papers.

23. Blum, "Farmer, Army and Draft," pp. 39-40; *New York Times*, April 16, 1944, p. 29; Patterson to Hershey, June 13, 1944, War Department correspondence, 1944-1945, Hershey Papers; Hershey to Patterson, June 23, 1944, box 184, Patterson Papers; quote in Hershey to state director of Alabama, January 23, 1945, staybacks, 1945, Hershey Papers; Hershey to Hon. Edwin L. Johnson, January 13, 1945, *ibid.*

24. Collis Stocking to General McSherry, December 9, 1942, box 20-145, RG 211; press statement by McNutt, December 23, 1942, and address of November 19, 1942, McNutt Papers; *New York Times*, January 3, 1943, sec. 9, p. 6. The WMC and the FSA paid the transportation for these workers to pick cotton.

25. McNutt radio notes, May 23, 1943, McNutt Papers; A. A. Hoehling, *Home Front, U.S.A.* (New York: Crowell, 1966), p. 71; memorandum by Clara Beyer of Children's Bureau, February 17, 1942, box 840, Eleanor Roosevelt Papers, Roosevelt Library, Hyde Park, N.Y.; J. W. Studebaker to Eleanor Roosevelt [n.d.], box 890, *ibid.*

26. Nelson, "Farms and Farming Communities," pp. 91-94; series 4, 1502, folder 10, Mary Anderson Papers, Radcliffe College, Cambridge, Mass.; minutes of Women's Advisory Committee, January 14, 1943, box 158, RG 211; *Monthly Labor Review*, February 1944, p. 455; WAC minutes, March 20, 1945, series 32, box 158, RG 211; *New York Times*, September 15, 1944, p. 22.

27. *Monthly Labor Review*, September 1944, p. 660; WMC minutes, June 10, 1942, box 5-100, RG 211; WMC minutes, June 24, 1942, *ibid.*; WMC minutes, July 22, 1942, *ibid.*; minutes of Management Labor Policy Committee, August 14, 1942, box 5-98, RG 211; Richard Polenberg, *War and Society: The United States, 1941-1945* (Philadelphia: J. B. Lippincott, 1972), pp. 85-86; Albertson, *Roosevelt Farmer*, p. 287. See also Robert C. Jones, *Mexican War Workers in the United States* (Washington, D.C.: U.S. Government Printing Office, 1945).

28. Memorandum by Employment Office Service Division of WMC, September 15, 1943, box 20-145, RG 211; WMC minutes, November 18, 1943, box 5-100, RG 211; Alexander to McNutt, December 22, 1943, box 1-1, RG 211.

CHAPTER 7

John Henry and War Work

McNutt had many problems to overcome in mobilizing manpower. Some were of his own creation, such as burdening himself with a decentralized and voluntaristic philosophy. Others, such as mediating between organized labor and other factions of government, or fighting the farm lobby, arose from the nature of American wartime politics. Another problem which came from historic forces beyond McNutt's control was prejudice against hiring blacks.

The war did modify traditional assumptions by white America about the inferiority of the black man, but only slightly. A few people wrote in the middle of the war that the Negro was making great strides because of "the growing spirit of tolerance and manpower needs." In 1944 a Supreme Court decision helped to end the white primary in Texas. The wartime emergency placed great strains on traditional social barriers. Such change should have benefited the black man, who had little place to go except upward on the social ladder. Robert Weaver made his move in the federal bureaucracy and William Hastie took a position as aide to Secretary of War Stimson. On June 25, 1941, under pressure from A. Philip Randolph's threatened march on Washington, President Roosevelt issued Executive Order no. 8802, prohibiting racial discrimination in defense work and creating the Fair Employment Practice Committee. Yet after the war James Baldwin, the black author, would

write that a certain hope had died. Despite Roosevelt's emphasis on
the Christian and democratic objectives of the war and upon mobilization rhetoric which stressed the importance of every man, woman,
and child for the war effort, blacks had been kept in their place.[1]

I

American society was segregated rigidly on the eve of World War
II. Some 75 percent of the nation's black population still lived in
the South and worked primarily in agriculture. Only one white in
ten in the South thought segregation should be abolished. In wartime Washington, blacks moved to the back of public buses as they
crossed into Virginia. They benefited only marginally from the
defense-related economic expansion before Pearl Harbor. Blacks
had been shoved even farther down by the depression and by the
willingness of unemployed whites to take lower-skilled jobs. The Social
Security Board revealed in the fall of 1941 that blacks had been
rejected as unsuitable for 51 percent of the 282,000 new jobs planned
before February 1942. While blacks made up about 10 percent of
the population, they held only about 3 percent of all the war jobs.
The National Defense Migration Hearings by the House of Representatives in 1941 concluded that massive discrimination existed in
defense industry against blacks, aliens, and second- and third-
generation Americans.[2]

As mobilization intensified so did racial animosity. In February
1942 race riots broke out in the Sojourner Truth housing project in
Detroit. Southern white residents reacted violently to the influx of
fourteen black families. In Mobile, Alabama, shipyards refused to
hire qualified blacks and instead asked the WMC to recruit white
workers from hundreds of miles away. In July 1942 a survey of
labor migration by the Works Progress Administration revealed
that unemployment rates for women and for blacks were three or
more times higher than the rate for white men. In Buffalo, New
York, employment was booming by the summer of 1942, with
54,000 workers added to defense plants since January, but employers continued to discriminate against blacks. Unions supported
such racism. Some managers argued that they would like to hire
blacks but that white workers would rebel at such a move. A rebel-

lion did occur in Mobile where the attempt by the Alabama Dry Dock and Shipbuilders Company to upgrade twelve black workers as welders led to a walkout by 20,000 whites. Similar strikes occurred in Baltimore at the Bethlehem Steel Company shipyard, at the Sun Shipbuilding Yard at Chester, Pennsylvania, and in Michigan, Ohio, and New York. The entire Philadelphia transit system went on strike when eight black motormen were hired. All male blacks in New Iberia, Louisiana, were driven out of town when they sought to set up a welders' training school.[3]

Problems were inevitable as vast numbers of new workers migrated to defense jobs. In cities such as Baltimore, Detroit, and Cleveland, southern whites by the hundreds of thousands and southern blacks by the tens of thousands moved in seeking employment and housing. When the government tried to provide emergency housing it had to consider local attitudes. In Dayton, Ohio, the McCall Corporation objected to the original site for public housing for blacks because it was too close to the plant in the event of rioting. In Indiana, at the Kingsbury Ordnance Plant, the government built segregated toilets and bomb shelters. Mayor LaGuardia of New York City regretted the scarcity of blacks on the police force, but they seemed unavailable, despite repeated recruitment campaigns. Only 155 blacks could pass the police examination in August 1943.[4]

Troubles boiled over in 1943. Working blacks, many born and raised in the North and now possessing well-paying jobs, were unwilling to accept docilely the type of Jim Crowism that their southern cousins had grown familiar with over the years. Two blacks were hired by the Youngstown Sheet and Tube Company in Cleveland in June 1943. They were told by their foreman to dress in the same locker with whites. When they met resistance from whites, the entire black labor force of more than fifty men walked out. In St. Louis, Missouri, some 3,700 black workers walked out to protest the failure to appoint a single black foreman. Then, on Sunday, June 20, 1943, at Belle Isle Amusement Park in Detroit, the explosion occurred. A race riot—thirty-four killed, 700 injured. Two months later, New York experienced a similar riot. Although these outbursts were soon brought under control by massive use of soldiers and police, such incidents demonstrated the powerful hold racism and discrimination still had on American society.[5]

II

In many ways Paul McNutt represented the very best of American liberalism in his approach to the race problem. His success and failure in dealing with the problem reveals the limitations of that liberalism. During World War I he had commanded some 2,000 black troops at Camp Jackson, South Carolina. While campaigning for governor of Indiana in 1932 he had often spoken out against the Ku Klux Klan. As governor he appointed one of the first blacks to a major state board. He opposed the poll tax. No doubt he agreed with President Roosevelt that wartime was no time to reform American social attitudes. Yet within the parameters established and controlled by the President, McNutt could at least speak out in defense of the black man's right to enjoy the benefits of manpower mobilization. Months before the war reached America and before McNutt assumed control of manpower, he made his position clear in an address at the seventy-fourth annual celebration of charter day at Howard University in Washington. He predicted a fine future for the blacks of America and a continuation of the progress made over the past several years. Despite the fatuous tone of these remarks, McNutt did make clear his opposition to racial discrimination. He pointed to the record of the National Youth Administration as evidence of his sincerity and promised that the USES would be fair in job placement. Black loyalty to America would be rewarded.[6]

In a press conference in Philadelphia in August 1941 he bluntly warned the city fathers of the need to end immediately racial discrimination. Philadelphia needed some 150,000 additional workers in the next few months to cope with war contracts. Such needs could not be met by importing white workers. The city should "let racial prejudice fly out of the window in tackling the job of building America's defenses." He urged Philadelphians to give the black man a chance to show what he could do. But attitudes changed slowly in the "City of Brotherly Love." One year later the entire urban transit system went on strike when eight black motormen were hired.[7]

Throughout 1942 McNutt waged a verbal battle with racial prejudice. As the new head of the WMC he insisted that prejudice was

unpatriotic. Highly qualified blacks were being denied jobs in aircraft plants, shipyards, and steel mills while these same plants complained about manpower shortages. Such actions only helped Hitler,
according to McNutt. His enthusiasm for black employment earned
him an invitation to address the Negro Labor Victory convocation
at the Golden Gate Ballroom on Lenox Avenue in Harlem, a long
way from Martinsville, Indiana. In his speech, carried nationwide
by the Blue Network, McNutt attempted to dispel vicious rumors
about the inability of black workers. These men were proving their
competence at the Newport News Shipbuilding and Drydock Company as machine operators, machinists, riggers, and bolters. Blacks
worked side by side with whites at Ford plants, at Lockheed, and at
the Denver Ordnance plants. As McNutt spoke, black soldiers were
guarding American cities. Prejudice and discrimination persisted,
but now it only helped the enemy. Later, in September 1942, he
called discrimination "our greatest waste." Some six million Negroes,
able workers all, were not being properly utilized. Movie-goers
heard McNutt via newsreels represent discrimination as "a threat
to the lives of American soldiers . . . something to be left to the
Nazis."[8]

These philippics had little effect on the rate of black employment
over the next several months. By May 5, 1943, McNutt admitted to
the American Legion that discrimination continued. Of all blacks
working in the shipbuilding industry, only 3 percent worked at a
skilled level. But when black newspaper editors asked McNutt to
comment on the problem, he chose to accentuate the positive. He
explained that in July 1942 blacks comprised 5.8 percent of the
twelve million workers in plants reporting to the USES. By March
1943 this figure had climbed to 6.7 percent, or 937,000 nonwhites in
16,000 establishments with 14,673,000 workers. McNutt concluded
that the USES and the WMC were "breaking down resistance to
the use of Negro workers." Breakthroughs had occurred in hiring
in Virginia and Georgia shipyards. McNutt assured his black readers
that their cause was on the rise and he was confident that "the advances made . . . during the war will not be lost in the post-war period." "It is the logic of history," he told members of the AFL,
"that we must abandon our own intolerance and prejudice in order
to win a war against them."[9]

Privately, McNutt admitted that minority groups were still discriminated against in upgrading. But it would be senseless and even dangerous to dwell on such negative facts. McNutt chose to remain a cheerleader. He wrote article after article for the black press extolling the virtues of the black soldier and black worker. Even before Norman Vincent Peale, such positive thinking had some power. Soon black leaders took up the theme. The black press had no wish to promote black radicalism. Julius A. Thomas of the National Urban League sent McNutt data showing that more blacks than ever were working in skilled and semiskilled jobs. McNutt played up this fact in an article for the *Chicago Defender* in December 1944. In 1941 blacks made up 3 percent of the war labor force. By September 1942 the figure had jumped to 5.7 percent. At the end of 1944 it stood at 8.4 percent. McNutt denounced those who engaged in hate strikes and promised that the Roosevelt administration would work to see that black gains were not lost during reconversion. "The color line in industry," he concluded, "is a line against democracy."[10]

III

Like most public figures, McNutt allowed his desires to distort his presentation of what was happening to the black man in the economy. More then most, however, he tried throughout the war to bring the actions of his agency into line with his rhetoric on race. McNutt went out of his way to accommodate black spokesmen from the beginning of his term as director of the WMC. Several black leaders, including D. J. E. Walker, president of the National Negro Business League, had originally urged President Roosevelt to appoint a "well qualified Negro" to the new manpower commission. Although these requests were ignored, McNutt invited black leaders to meet with him to discuss problems of black manpower. On May 11, 1942, several black leaders gathered in McNutt's office to support an active role for minorities within the WMC. McNutt greeted the group cordially and announced that he had anticipated their request and had already established a separate division to deal with minorities. A few blacks were unhappy with a division, but McNutt felt that "the consensus of [black leadership] opinion is that such a section . . . is necessary and desirable."[11]

McNutt appointed Robert C. Weaver to head the Negro Manpower Service of the WMC. Weaver, an honor student with a doctorate in economics from Harvard, had joined the New Deal early as racial advisor to Harold Ickes in the Interior Department. Although a rather shy personality, Weaver had conducted his own one-man sit-in during the 1930s. His rise to prominence as head of this job branch of the WPB reflected the success of his moderate view and his high level of professional competence. Now he began work for McNutt on the local level to remove racial barriers to hiring blacks. Field representatives from his office made contacts with forty-five plants each week and reported encouraging results. On a higher level, McNutt sought aid in promoting black employment from other members of the administration. At a meeting of the WMC on May 6, 1942, he reported that in 1941 blacks were being rejected for jobs because they were not trained. Then they were turned away from training centers because they were not employable. The cycle had been broken at the training level. Yet he still found at least six important war-production areas with a surplus of skilled blacks without jobs.[12]

To his embarrassment, McNutt soon discovered that his own organization had a hand in this problem. The United States Employment Service, reflecting its former state control, tried to work within regional mores. When employers called for white workers only, the USES complied and refused to refer blacks. Blacks were often rated at low skill levels by the USES, despite training provided by the WMC itself. In June 1942 the WMC established a policy permitting local USES offices to permit employers to decide whether or not to hire blacks. But now the USES was asked to report each case of discrimination to the Fair Employment Practice Committee (FEPC), established by Roosevelt in June 1941. The FEPC itself was transferred to McNutt's control in July 1942. Yet by August 1942 the USES policy continued to emphasize persuasion to end discriminatory specifications for worker referrals. If persuasion failed, the USES was under orders to refer workers as requested. Complaints about such practices soon poured in to the President and to Eleanor Roosevelt. Mrs. Roosevelt had long championed the cause of black Americans, much to the irritation of bigots both in the North and in the South. She now asked the President how he could square the actions of the USES with his Executive Order no.

8802. Walter White, president of the National Association for the Advancement of Colored People, raised the same objections. President Roosevelt responded to this pressure by turning to McNutt. Within days, McNutt had produced a new order for the USES which ended such discriminatory referrals. As he explained to the WMC, such an action was needed to bring the agency into line with the FEPC, now part of the team. More candidly, he admitted that the President wanted an end to such discrimination. In this case at least, the initiative for ending discrimination came from Mrs. Roosevelt rather than from McNutt.[13]

McNutt, like President Roosevelt and unlike Eleanor, was a politician forced to act with circumspection to promote black employment. Before sending blacks to a particular plant near Chicago, McNutt arranged a meeting with management, labor, and local housing authorities. All this planning preceded the arrival of five black laborers. When race riots broke out at the Mobile drydocks in May 1943, McNutt immediately called his local representative and learned that the WMC had been partially responsible for the blowup. The area director, Bowman Ashe, had initially arranged to have 7,000 blacks hired at the plant to work in segregated areas. But then Ashe had requested a general upgrading of all workers. Management proceeded to upgrade both blacks and whites, but this change led to the integration of several work teams. Rioting followed. Harvey Allen of the WMC, reporting to McNutt from Mobile, believed that the manager of the plant began the integration as a means of discrediting President Roosevelt and Executive Order no. 8802. Allen warned McNutt that the WMC should step lightly in this political jungle. McNutt took this advice and lined up support from Secretary of the Navy Frank Knox and Admiral Emory S. Land, head of the U.S. Maritime Commission. Together they sent a telegram to the regional director of Alabama's Maritime Commission endorsing a locally drafted compromise which would return blacks to segregated work areas. McNutt's crusade for black rights had definite limits. He refused, upon the objection of the MLPC, to condemn the racial violence.[14]

McNutt was a liberal, not a radical, in his approach to racial problems. But his personal attitudes mattered little given his official position. He was an agent of the President. McNutt had to do his best to please Roosevelt, the black community, and organized labor. At the suggestion of the President, McNutt repeatedly provided sinecures for individual black leaders, including Clark Foreman and Mary Bethune. Even if McNutt could not prevent Mobile-like incidents, his general outlook was liberal. Malcolm S. MacLean of the FEPC recognized McNutt's limited virtues. When MacLean heard in November 1942 that Roosevelt planned to replace McNutt with Harold Ickes, the civil rights advocate immediately intervened. MacLean warned the President that such a shift would cause an "explosion" among blacks. Despite Ickes's gaudy reputation as a defender of blacks, MacLean pointed out that when one compared the percentage of blacks working under McNutt with those under Ickes it became apparent that such a shift would be a setback for integration. McNutt survived a threatened Roosevelt purge for several reasons, but the sympathy of black Americans helped.[15]

IV

Ironically, a few months later the same black Americans called for McNutt's resignation. In July 1942 President Roosevelt transferred the FEPC from the White House to the WMC. This agency had not met with the success anticipated by American blacks. Roosevelt had approved an antidiscriminatory clause in the Selective Service Act of September 1940 and appointed William Hastie as a civilian aide to the Secretary of War. Randolph's threat of a march on Washington had generated Executive Order no. 8802. But still black laborers found it difficult to get jobs. Eleanor Roosevelt pressed Sidney Hillman on this issue. However, Hillman replied in February 1942 that the National Labor Supply Committee, the predecessor of WMC, had no plans to give representation to minority groups. With the creation of the FEPC and the appointment of McNutt to head the new WMC, blacks became more optimistic.[16]

The FEPC was mandated by executive order to investigate cases of racial discrimination in defense hiring. Blacks felt they had Roosevelt's close attention, but by April 1942 the President became convinced that logical organization required the FEPC be assigned to the newly created War Manpower Commission. In Roosevelt's view the black problem was primarily a problem of jobs, and

McNutt was now in charge of labor utilization. Malcolm MacLean appreciated Roosevelt's reasoning but still hoped that the agency might maintain its "direct connection" with the President. Despite respect for McNutt, MacLean did not think "it well to have this committee booted about in the slums. . . ." McNutt, unaware that he was running a low-rent organization, encouraged the shift of the FEPC. On May 27, 1942, the entire WMC voted unanimously to recommend that the FEPC be transferred to McNutt. As the WMC already had a Division of Negro Manpower, it should also have the FEPC. In addition, Harold Smith of the Office of the Budget warned the President that the FEPC proposed to "assume jurisdiction over discriminatory hiring practices in states, counties and municipalities and in business enterprises manufacturing for interstate commerce." Roosevelt, who established the FEPC merely as a sop to black opinion, repudiated such pretensions by the agency. The fear of excessive activism helped convince Roosevelt to transfer the FEPC to McNutt, where it could be brought under tighter political control.[17]

The transfer took place on July 30, 1942. Whatever the logic or motives for the move, it created problems for McNutt from the very first day. Although black leaders made little public protest before the transfer, MacLean had warned the President that blacks "will take it poorly" and their silence soon ended. Letter after letter poured in from NAACP branches and from locals of the Brotherhood of Sleeping Car Porters. Walter White of the NAACP wrote to McNutt complaining at "what appears to be a deliberate attempt on the part of Roosevelt's subordinates to strip the FEPC of its independence and effectiveness." White was probably correct, but when reporters asked the President about such charges on August 7, 1942, he replied that he did not know "whether they [the WMC and the FEPC] are equal or whether one has been subordinated to the other. I doubt very much if there has been any subordinating of the FEPC to the other." But McNutt would make the decisions on the role of the FEPC. On October 24, 1942, he and Fowler Harper, deputy chairman, agreed that the FEPC should be the operating agency within the WMC to investigate all discrimination. MacLean and White should have been encouraged. But while the FEPC would determine all policies relating to the enforcement and effect of

Executive Order no. 8802, the chairman of the WMC would have final approval over all actions. McNutt had to approve all FEPC instructions and to clear all hearings on discrimination. White continued to complain, but Marvin MacIntyre, presidential secretary, replied that both Roosevelt and McNutt hoped to reorganize the WMC to give strong support to questions of black rights.[18]

The confusion over the chain of command was only one ingredient in a stew rapidly boiling over and splattering McNutt's reputation. By December, Will Alexander of the WMC and Lawrence Cramer, executive secretary of the FEPC, were at each other's throats. Cramer sought to remove Alexander and Robert Weaver, who had run the old Negro Division in WMC. MacLean and Cramer put pressure on McNutt to shift Alexander and Weaver to FEPC control. McNutt refused, but Alexander, fed up with such petty squabbles, resigned. As he told Jonathan Daniels, a White House aide, the WMC was a madhouse with no one in charge. In the midst of this internal discord, McNutt began to assert his control over the FEPC. When the din of battle abated, the FEPC had left the WMC and McNutt had tarnished his liberal reputation.[19]

From its inception in June 1941 the FEPC had been investigating cases of discrimination in the nation. Not until January 1943, however, did it decide to tackle the problem of discrimination in the railroad industry. McNutt originally supported the FEPC decision to hold public hearings. In December 1942 he warned some 400 railroad executives, meeting in New York City, that racial quotas for hiring and promotion must end. The FEPC scheduled hearings to begin on January 25, 1943. The staff worked overtime preparing for the event. When FEPC members awoke on January 11, however, they read in their morning newspapers that McNutt had issued an order indefinitely canceling the hearings. Not everyone was surprised. McNutt had asked Lawrence Cramer to call off the hearings a few days before. When Cramer demurred, McNutt acted on his own. He explained to reporters that the administration planned a new approach to the entire problem of racial discrimination in war jobs.[20]

Observers wondered why McNutt changed his mind about the hearings and acted against the unanimous opinion of the FEPC. He knew that black leaders would bitterly resent such a move. Telegrams poured into the White House from Walter White, from Dr. George E. Haynes of the National Conference of Church Leaders, and from Mark Ethridge, David Sarnoff, and others protesting McNutt's action. Within days, MacLean, Harold A. Stevens, and Henry Epstein of the FEPC publicly resigned over what Epstein called an "irreparable blow to [FEPC's] prestige and . . . effectiveness." White wrote Roosevelt that the indefinite postponement "constitutes a crisis in Negro-White relations in the U. S." When would the nation begin to live up to its war aims at home, he asked? White urged Roosevelt to rescind McNutt's order and to restore the FEPC to independent status. Blacks believed McNutt had acted without the knowledge of Roosevelt, who was busy at the Casablanca Conference in Africa when the cancellation was made.[21]

McNutt tried to defend himself at a press conference by reminding reporters that the FEPC was under his control, whatever Roosevelt's private assurances to Walter White. McNutt insisted that the delay in the hearings would allow the WMC to "take care of the situation much better without using force." On January 15, some fifty-two black and white leaders requested a conference with McNutt. He agreed to meet with four of them. When the day arrived, McNutt was stunned to see forty-one persons flood into WMC headquarters. Fowler Harper went out to calm them down before McNutt came in. Harper admitted that the cancellation had come because of pressure from big business and Congress. Sheldon Tuppes, of the United Auto Workers, could not believe that the federal government, in the midst of war, had to bow to the wishes of such interest groups. A few participants called for using the military to enforce Executive Order no. 8802. McNutt, his hopes to avoid a confrontation fading, now entered the meeting and argued, with unintentional irony, that he always believed in a "place in the sun" for black Americans. To use force at this time, however, would only boomerang. He appealed for sympathy by admitting that this task was destroying his political career but that his major goal was to win the war. His listeners filed out unconverted. They protested to Roosevelt that McNutt had treated them in a "cavalier and arbitrary" manner.[22]

One leading black who worked for the WMC, Mary Bethune, sought to reassure McNutt. A close friend of Eleanor Roosevelt

and now head of the Negro Affairs Division, Bethune wrote McNutt
on January 22 that she had the "utmost confidence" in him and
knew how he had helped her people in the past. She urged him to
keep his courage. McNutt needed such encouragement because he
knew that he had not made the decision to cancel the railroad hearings. Once again, he was getting a bum rap. When the railroad
hearings were originally scheduled, protest had emerged from a
variety of sources, including the Department of the Navy and railroad management. Franklin Roosevelt, conveniently out of town,
was responsible for the cancellation. Roosevelt responded to criticism of the pending hearings by asking Attorney General Francis
Biddle to consider the problem. Biddle reported that the South was
up in arms over the threat to segregation and that the Ku Klux Klan
was growing. Furthermore, Congress was threatening an investigation of the FEPC. Biddle, acting as Roosevelt's agent, met with
McNutt and the FEPC. He recommended that the hearings be canceled and that the FEPC be reorganized. In its place Roosevelt
would appoint five national figures attached to the WMC. McNutt
canceled the hearings at the recommendation of Biddle, who was
acting for Roosevelt. Yet black protest focused on McNutt, who,
one editor wrote, proclaimed that the Four Freedoms do not extend
to American blacks.[23]

As the protest mounted and McNutt wiggled to get off the hook,
Roosevelt jerked the line again. On February 3, the President asked
McNutt to call a conference on how to reorganize the FEPC with
more power. Roosevelt's action was sheer public relations as it was
the unruly ambitions of the FEPC that had led him to cancel the
hearings. Now he called for a more powerful FEPC. McNutt, despite discomfiture, had to play his part. He convened a conference
of black spokesmen in Washington on February 19. These leaders,
predictably, called for an immediate rescheduling of the railroad
hearings, for independent status for the FEPC, more money, and
a larger staff. McNutt left the meeting midway through the presen-
tations. As he left, he promised to bring these requests to Roosevelt.
For the next two months McNutt tried to find a new head for a re-
constituted FEPC. Again, Biddle finally stepped in with the suggestion that Monsignor Francis J. Haas, a liberal Catholic priest and a
professor at Catholic University, be given the dubious honor.

McNutt jumped at the suggestion after being turned down by several other nominees. On May 27, 1943, the President announced the creation of a new FEPC headed by Haas, with the power to conduct hearings and take steps to eliminate discrimination. McNutt breathed easier when Roosevelt made the new FEPC independent of the WMC. The new agency, McNutt announced, was "in good hands and will be handled with wisdom and restraint."[24]

The FEPC continued its career throughout the war. Eventually, railroad hearings were held and twenty companies and seven unions were ordered to end discriminatory practices. Most of the companies refused and the FEPC certified the cases to Roosevelt, who failed to act. When reporters asked Roosevelt to respond to charges that he had not given the FEPC "active support," he blandly replied, "I would like to have some suggestions as to how I could give more active support to it." The reporters remained silent. Despite failure with the railroads, the FEPC did have limited successes. Some 3,835 cases were docketed during 1944. Out of these, some 3,712 were closed, with 1,324, or 35.7 percent, resulting in a satisfactory adjustment. Such results hardly constituted a revolution in race relations.[25]

V

By a strange turn of events, at precisely the same time McNutt was being pilloried in public for the apparent destruction of the FEPC, in private he worked almost alone to obtain a better deal for young black men facing military conscription. In this struggle he met prejudice and narrow-mindedness by the military establishment. The Selective Service bill, as originally passed, provided that "in the selection and training of men under this Act . . . there shall be no discrimination against any person on account of race or color." The men who controlled the mobilization program, by and large, did not share this sentiment. In the Department of War a consensus of officials agreed that attempts at integration would destroy morale. Stimson explained that the problem was made worse by radicals such as White and others who want "complete social equality." "As you know," he wrote a friend, "that is simply impossible and makes matters worse." Robert Patterson even objected to Roosevelt's decision to issue Executive Order no. 8802 and create the FEPC. As one officer expressed it, "Hold these people off until after V-E Day. . . . Wait until after V-E Day to reform the world." Secretary of the Navy Frank Knox refused to consider increased use of blacks in his branch because they would not fight and would only make trouble with whites on board ships.[26]

From the very beginning of the military draft, officials implemented racial quotas. General Lewis Hershey found the administering of such draft calls a tremendous burden. Even though rejection rates for blacks were much higher than for whites, large numbers of black 1-As remained in the civilian population while whites went to war. Individual states, especially in the South, tried to send blacks to war in numbers exceeding War Department ceilings. Congressman Lester Hill of Alabama demanded to know the proportion of both whites and blacks being drafted compared to the total of each type in the state's population. Constituents had complained that blacks were beating the draft. Hershey, however, demonstrated to Hill that while some 34.4 percent of all draft registrants in Alabama were black, Negroes were providing some 36 percent of all inductees in 1942. In other words, blacks were being inducted in a greater proportion than whites. Not all complaints could be dismissed as easily. A unique problem developed in Puerto Rico where racial draft calls helped to bring home the concept of racism to a color-blind society. Draft officials on the island did not know what to make of the racial categories on the draft forms. They soon had to learn, because they were told that 50 percent of their draftees would have to be blacks. Shortly thereafter, the National Guard became segregated for the first time. American progress had come to the island.[27]

Racial quotas in draft calls violated the letter of the Selective Service law. American blacks immediately protested such calls and Roosevelt eventually asked General George Marshall if something could be done. But Marshall and the War Department refused to give in. The military argued that it could not take in blacks without adequate preparation for segregated facilities. Hershey dutifully carried out the instructions he received from the War Department. Occasionally, a state director such as Ernest L. Averill of Connecticut tried to buck the military by ignoring race and sending men to induction stations by draft order number. The military then returned any excess blacks to the Selective Service without an examination. Averill complained to Hershey that there was no legal basis for such racial calls. In reply, Hershey warned that in the future any "Director and Local Board members who sent blacks to induction would be subject to suspension." The military would have its way.[28]

When Roosevelt gave McNutt control of the Selective Service System in December 1942 he immediately attacked the racial draft. His motives were practical. Manpower reserves were being used up rapidly; shortages were developing. If the military refused to accept blacks, it meant that whites would be taken out of important jobs to meet draft quotas. McNutt opposed racial calls not on legal or moral grounds, but from a concern with manpower distribution. If both the army and navy accepted the 10 percent figure projected on the basis of the black proportion of the total population, other white, skilled workers could remain in their jobs. McNutt immediately instructed Hershey of the need to end racial calls. Hershey assured his new boss that he knew the calls were questionable under the law. Indeed, the Justice Department had informed Hershey that a writ of habeas corpus was being filed in New York on behalf of a young black drafted under a racial quota. The attitude of the War Department, however, continued to delay reform.[29]

McNutt decided to attack the problem directly in January of 1943, the same month in which he canceled the FEPC hearings. He outlined the problems of racial calls at several meetings of the WMC. Both William Haber and Hershey agreed that an end to such calls would help eliminate a backlog of some 300,000 blacks in the draft system. The actual percentage of blacks in the military was only 5.9, far below the 10 percent norm. McNutt proposed an end to all racial calls by April 1943. Both Robert Patterson of the War Department and Ralph Bard of the navy rose to object. Patterson insisted that the army was doing its share but not the navy, and that bringing in blacks required extensive planning. Bard defended his service by insisting that the navy did not have facilities for more blacks. Donald Nelson then suggested that blacks be inducted but used in labor battalions. Patterson responded that such a scheme would not work because blacks desired assignments in all branches of the service. McNutt, after listening to the complaints, acknowledged the difficulty but insisted that he could not condone the failure to use "colored" 1-A registrants. He urged a reconsideration by the military.[30]

To insure reconsideration, McNutt began a private pressure campaign. On February 17, 1943, he wrote Stimson and explained the urgency of ending racial calls. The reduced percentage of blacks in the military meant a higher percentage of blacks in civilian life. Such racial calls forced local draft boards to disregard the order number of registrants. Some 300,000 blacks had been passed over while draft boards took in white males. Such actions "possess grave implications should the issue be taken into the courts, especially by a white registrant." The Selective Service was drafting married, white fathers and allowing single, black men to remain at home. McNutt insisted that Stimson agree to end such racial calls by April. The WMC would deliver men according to their induction number. The Secretary of War, unintimidated, ignored McNutt. The War Department had no intention of changing its policy. Since the military controlled who would be inducted, Stimson had the final say. He blandly replied to McNutt that racial calls were not "discriminatory in any way."[31]

After failing with Stimson, McNutt approached President Roosevelt during a cabinet meeting in February. McNutt reported the same argument about the growing backlog of blacks. Roosevelt was sympathetic, but refused to overrule the military. Stimson and Knox remained committed to racial calls. Knox justified the navy's failure to take a fair share of blacks by insisting that they could not fight. The army used 9 percent of all blacks in the population but considered it an "extravagant use of manpower."[32]

McNutt's campaign to end racial calls met repeated failure. By December 1943 his interest in the problem faded as the Selective Service System was removed from his jurisdiction. But General Hershey continued to be plagued with the problem throughout the war. In October 1944 he wrote Stimson saying, "I feel I must again point out the necessity of Selective Service receiving calls in which the percentage of Negroes more nearly approximates the Negro percentage of registrants available. . . ." For the record, Hershey also wrote Stimson that "we feel impelled under circumstances and under requirements of law that the selection of men . . . shall be made in an impartial manner . . . without discrimination against any person on account of race or color." Despite this formal protest, Hershey continued to fill racial calls coming in from the military. As late as February 16, 1945, he wired his State Director in San Juan, Puerto Rico, that he was authorized to deliver for induction into the army "800 white registrants net and 200 negro registrants net."[33]

VI

Having failed with the FEPC and with the racial calls, McNutt might well have considered his contribution to the progress of black Americans as marginal. Nothing, however, could silence his liberal rhetoric. His clichés about black progress became so popular that black newspapers such as the *Chicago Defender* constantly invited him to write for their pages. In one of his last efforts in December 1944, he sought to inspire the black man with hope for the future. Metz T. P. Lochard, editor of the *Chicago Defender*, warned McNutt that a few radicals were predicting race riots during the reconversion from war. Blacks held precisely those emergency war jobs where cutbacks could be expected. McNutt rose to the challenge by insisting that the government must "protect Negro manpower and all other minority manpower when the cutbacks . . . reduce jobs." Some 70 percent of all black labor was in emergency industry. But with the aid of the federal and state governments, of industrialists and economists, McNutt hoped the country could find jobs for 60,000,000 Americans, black and white.[34]

McNutt could offer only platitudes and good intentions. But the manpower mobilization experience which he guided did bring about change in the black's condition. War employment drew thousands of blacks out of the South. Some 100,000 moved to Chicago; 60,000 went to Detroit. Los Angeles alone increased its black population from 75,494 (before the war) to 134,519. Furthermore, these demographic shifts had important political implications as blacks became decisive voters in states with large electoral vote totals. The total male, black, work force in 1940 was 4,474,221. By 1945 the total had risen to 5.3 million in the civilian economy. The percentage of blacks working in war jobs stood at 4.2 percent in

1942, but rose to 8.6 percent in 1945. Blacks employed by the federal government grew from 50,000 to 200,000 during the war. These impressive statistics, however, could be misleading. Little advance had been made in placing blacks in skilled and semiskilled jobs. Black employment was concentrated in certain big war industries, such as the airframe companies of Lockheed, Bendix, and Curtiss Wright. Smaller firms seemed reluctant to hire blacks. A 1943 report concluded: "In none of the tight labor markets of the North is there a significant use of skilled blacks in war industry as a whole." Indeed, where domestic service counted for 60.2 percent of all black male employment in 1940, in 1944 the figure had *risen* to 75.2 percent. After four years of war work, more than 98 percent of the clerical and sales personnel in the nation remained white. The general proportion of black unskilled labor to the total unskilled work force remained the same.[35]

The gross increase of black employment obscured the continued problem of black workers. The figures misled men such as Carey McWilliams, who saw the war as a turning point in black-white relations. President F. D. Patterson of Tuskegee Institute was pleased with the progress of blacks and spoke of "a definite improvement in . . . conditions with a fuller utilization of the manpower in the Negro group." Ironically, a closer look at the statistics indicates that manpower mobilization pushed blacks into the unskilled laboring class. Before the war the curriculum of Tuskegee and other black colleges emphasized management and liberal arts. During the war vocational courses were emphasized. New vocational courses emerged in several cities to attract blacks. In Memphis, Tennessee, the city and the local USES established vocational courses for blacks only. Instead of learning basic educational skills, blacks moved into low-skill training. One reporter wrote glowingly of the new interest being shown by blacks in blacksmith courses.[36]

Such irony did little to disturb McNutt. His job during the war was to find workers for the war economy. As a means of promoting this objective, he advocated an end to racial discrimination. His efforts for the black man were limited because both he and President Roosevelt shared a pragmatic attitude. Another inhibiting force was the narrow view of the military establishment, which had no time for social change. Blacks did move into the American work force in large numbers during the war. Unfortunately, even after being trained for higher skills, they moved into those jobs which required the least amount of skill. They moved into industry closely tied to wartime expansion, industry which would shrivel up with the peace. The problem was only dimly perceived. McNutt continued to make public and private statements against discrimination. His rhetoric helped to gloss over the continued dilemma of the American black man. The Roosevelt administration sought to defuse the race problem while solving the more pressing problem of military victory. McNutt played a major role in this campaign of smothering the black drive for equality.[37]

Notes

1. Quote from David Hinshaw, *The Home Front* (New York: Putnam, 1943), pp. 43-44. Historians still debate the overall effect of the war on the blacks' quest for equality. See Richard Polenberg, *War and Society: The United States, 1941-1945* (Philadelphia: J. B. Lippincott, 1972), p. 113; Geoffrey Perrett, *Days of Sadness, Years of Triumph: The American People, 1939-1945* (New York: Coward, McCann and Geoghegan, 1973), p. 150; Carey McWilliams, "What We Did about Racial Minorities," in *While You Were Gone*, Jack Goodman, ed. (New York: Simon and Schuster, 1946), pp. 89, 102; James Baldwin, *The Fire Next Time* (New York: Dell, 1963), p. 68. The most recent scholarly study is Neil A. Wynn, *The Afro-American and the Second World War* (London: Paul Elek, 1976), see especially pp. 39-59.

2. Joel Seidman, *American Labor from Defense to Reconversion* (Chicago: University of Chicago Press, 1953), pp. 165-67; Polenberg, *War and Society*, p. 106; John Dos Passos, *State of the Nation* (Boston, Houghton Mifflin, 1943), p. 167; Leonard P. Adams, *Wartime Manpower Mobilization* (Ithaca, N.Y.: Cornell University Press, 1951), p. 20; *Monthly Labor Review*, January 1942, p. 49.

3. For the transit strike see Allan M. Winkler, "The Philadelphia Transit Strike of 1944," *Journal of American History* 59 (June 1972), pp. 73-89; McWilliams, "What We Did About Minorities," p. 90; McNutt speech for National Industrial Conference, May 20, 1942, Paul V. McNutt Papers, The Lilly Library, Indiana University, Bloomington, Ind.; *Monthly Labor Review*, July 1942, p. 59; Adams, *Wartime Manpower*, p. 27; Josephine von Miklos, *I Took a War Job* (New York: Simon and Schuster, 1943), p. 139; H. Sitkoff, "Racial Militancy and Interracial Violence in the Second World War," *Journal of American History* 58 (December 1971), pp. 665-72; *New York Times*, July 31, 1942, p. 1; Dos Passos, *State of the Union*, p. 97. Polenberg, *War and Society*, pp. 99-130, presents a summary of blacks during the war.

4. Minutes of Dayton Federal Coordinating Committee, May 27, 1943, box E58, Record Group 216, National Archives, Washington, D.C.; *New York Times,* July 23,

1943, p. 15; LaGuardia to Eleanor Roosevelt, August 6, 1943, box 1688, Eleanor Roosevelt Papers, Hyde Park, N.Y.; Parmett, *Days of Sadness*, p. 316.

5. *New York Times*, June 4, 1943, p. 11, and June 23, 1943, p. 12, for coverage of the riots. See also Sitkoff, "Racial Militancy," pp. 672-73.

6. Speech file of March 1, 1941, McNutt Papers; I. George Blake, *Paul McNutt: Portrait of a Hoosier Statesman* (Indianapolis: Central Publishing, 1966), pp. 107, 319.

7. Press conference, August 18, 1941, McNutt Papers; see also Winkler, "The Philadelphia Strike," pp. 73-89.

8. Speech file of May 4, 1942, and June 28, 1942, McNutt Papers; *New York Times*, September 13, 1942, sec. 4, p. 9; newsreel manuscript, October 19, 1942, and "Work for Victory," in *Boston Herald*, December 31, 1942, copies in McNutt Papers.

9. Speech file of May 5, 1943; statement to black editors, July 17, 1943; article for *Pennsylvania Federationist*, October 1, 1943, all in McNutt Papers.

10. Haber to Broughton, January 10, 1944, McNutt Papers; McNutt radio speech, February 26, 1944, *ibid.*; McNutt to Julius A. Thomas, March 4, 1944, *ibid.*; Metz T. P. Leonard, editor of *Chicago Defender*, to Ingle, December 29, 1944, *ibid.*; "Negro Manpower," by McNutt, December 21, 1944, *ibid.*; William J. Rogers to McNutt, March 26, 1945, *ibid.*, in which McNutt warned against the circulation of his article because it might hurt the WMC in seeking congressional appropriations. See also Lee Finkle, "The Conservative Aims of Militant Rhetoric: Black Protest during World War II," *Journal of American History* 60 (December 1973), pp. 692-713, who argues that black editors were playing a conservative role.

11. Dr. J.E. Walker to Roosevelt, April 14, 1942, Official File 4905A, and Fannie O. Baxter to Roosevelt, April 18, 1942, OF 4905A, Franklin D. Roosevelt Papers, Hyde Park, N.Y.; Jeanetta Welch to Eleanor Roosevelt, May 18, 1942, and McNutt to Welch, June 3, 1942, box 840, Eleanor Roosevelt Papers.

12. Weaver to General F. J. McSherry, April 25, 1942, box 20-145, E 117, RG 211, National Archives; WMC minutes, May 6, 1942, box 5-100, RG 211; for a fuller discussion of Weaver's views see his book, *Negro Labor* (New York: Harcourt, Brace, 1946).

13. Jeanetta Welch to Eleanor Roosevelt, May 18, 1942, box 840, Eleanor Roosevelt Papers; WMC minutes, June 17, 1942, and August 19, 1942, box 5-100, RG 211; MacIntyre to McNutt, September 10, 1942, box 15-H, Franklin Roosevelt Papers; WMC minutes, September 30, 1942, box 5-100, RG 211; White to Roosevelt, November 4, 1942, OF 4905, Roosevelt Papers; Byron Fairchild and Jonathan Grossman, *The Army and Industrial Manpower* (Washington, D.C.: U.S. Department of the Army, 1959), p. 159, point out that McNutt did not issue the order until a year later (September 3, 1943).

14. McNutt to Everett C. Bloom, July 29, 1943, box 1-1, RG 211; memorandum of call from Allen to Broughton, May 27, 1943, *ibid.*; McNutt to regional directors, June 2, 1943, *ibid.*; Management-Labor Policy Committee minutes, June 29, 1943, box 5-98, RG 211.

15. Grace Tully for FDR, February 12, 1944, OF 4905, Roosevelt Papers; Walter White to Roosevelt, OF 4905, *ibid.*; MacLean to MacIntyre, November 25, 1942, OF 4905, *ibid.*

16. Sitkoff, "Racial Militancy," p. 662; Joseph P. Lash, *Eleanor and Franklin* (New York: Norton, 1971), p. 693; Polenberg, *War and Society*, pp. 102-3; Hillman to Eleanor Roosevelt, February 12, 1942, box 837, Eleanor Roosevelt Papers; for a history of the FEPC see Louis Ruchames, *Race, Jobs, and Politics: The Story of FEPC* (Chapel Hill: University of North Carolina Press, 1948).

17. MacLean to MacIntyre, April 25, 1942, OF 4905A, Roosevelt Papers; McNutt to Roosevelt, May 29, 1942, OF 4905, *ibid.*; Harold Smith, Presidential Conference no. 13, in Franklin D. Roosevelt Library, Hyde Park, N.Y.

18. MacLean to MacIntyre, August 3, 1942, OF 4905, Roosevelt Papers; White to McNutt, October 13, 1942, *ibid.*; White to Roosevelt, December 8, 1942, *ibid.*; MacIntyre to White, December 14, 1942, *ibid.*; *Complete Presidential Press Conferences of Franklin D. Roosevelt*, 25 vols. in 12 books (New York: Da Capo Press, 1972), 20: 46-47 (August 7, 1942), hereafter cited as *PPC*; Fowler Harper to McNutt, October 24, 1942, box 832, Eleanor Roosevelt Papers.

19. Jonathan Daniels, *White House Witness, 1942-1945* (New York: Doubleday, 1975), pp. 94-96, 116.

20. Carol Kopsco, "President's Committee on Fair Employment Practice's Railroad Discrimination Hearings of 1943" (master's thesis, University of Miami, 1973), p. 26; Seidman, *American Labor*, p. 168; *New York Times*, January 14, 1943, p. 17.

21. *New York Times*, January 13, 1943, p. 12, and January 18, 1943, p. 8; White to Roosevelt, January 15, 1943, and White to Eleanor Roosevelt, January 19, 1943, box 858, Eleanor Roosevelt Papers.

22. Kopsco, "President's Committee," pp. 29-31; Dr. George E. Haynes to Roosevelt, January 18, 1943, Roosevelt Papers. See also Ruchames, *Race, Jobs, and Politics*, p. 51.

23. Bethune to McNutt, January 22, 1943, box 1-1, RG 211; Francis Biddle to Eleanor Roosevelt, January 27, 1943, box 858, Eleanor Roosevelt Papers; Biddle to Roosevelt, January 29, 1943, OF 4905, Roosevelt Papers; Kopsco, "President's Committee," pp. 32-33.

24. *New York Times*, February 4, 1943, p. 15; Biddle to Roosevelt, April 23, 1943, OF 4905, Roosevelt Papers; *Monthly Labor Review*, August 1943, p. 408; Kopsco, "President's Committee," pp. 35-36; WMC minutes, June 2, 1943, box 5-100, RG 211.

25. Seidman, *American Labor*, p. 168; *PPC*, 23: 215-17 (June 2, 1944); *Monthly Labor Review*, June 1945, p. 1338.

26. Stimson to Alfred E. Stearns, January 30, 1942, box 139, Henry Stimson Papers, Yale University Library, New Haven, Conn.; Fairchild and Grossman, *Army and Manpower*, pp. 158, 173; diary of Harold L. Ickes (September 5, 1943), 8155, box 11, Library of Congress, Washington, D.C. For the full story of the military and integration see Richard Dalfiume, *Desegregation of the U. S. Armed Forces, 1939-1953* (New York: Columbia University Press, 1969).

27. Hershey to state directors, November 6, 1942, staybacks, 1942, General Lewis B. Hershey Papers, Military History Research Collection, Carlisle Barracks, Pa.; Albert A. Blum, *Drafted or Deferred: Practices Past and Present* (Ann Arbor: University of Michigan Press, 1967), p. 48; Col. Wanvig to Hershey, June 13, 1941, official file, WWII, Hershey Papers; Hershey to Congressman Hill, August 21, 1942,

staybacks, 1942, *ibid.*; Major C. C. Johnson to Hershey, March 10, 1941, official file, WWII, *ibid.*

28. Blum, *Drafted or Deferred*, p. 46; Averill to CG, 1st Corps Area, November 8, 1941, official file, WWII, Hershey Papers; memorandum by LBH to Colonel Dargusch, February 20, 1942, staybacks, 1942, *ibid.*

29. Hershey to McNutt, December 30, 1942, staybacks, 1942, Hershey Papers; John J. O'Sullivan, "From Voluntarism to Conscription: Congress and Selective Service, 1940-1945" (Ph.D. dissertation, Columbia University, 1971), p. 264. For a federal case involving race and the draft see U. S. ex. rel. Lynn v. Downer, 140F 2d 397.

30. WMC minutes, January 20, 1943, box 5-100, RG 211; *ibid.*, January 27, 1943; J. Douglas Brown to Patterson, February 19, 1943, box 183, Robert Patterson Papers, Library of Congress.

31. McNutt to Stimson and Knox, February 17, 1943, official file, WWII, Hershey Papers; Stimson quoted in Blum, *Drafted or Deferred*, p. 46.

32. Diary of Harold L. Ickes (February 21, 1943), box 10-7481, and (September 5, 1943), box 11-8155, Library of Congress; minutes of White House Manpower Conference, February 26, 1943, box 324, Harry Hopkins Papers, Roosevelt Library; Wynn, *Afro-American*, pp. 35-38.

33. Hershey to Stimson, October 5, 1944, and August 5, 1944, War Department file, 1944-1945, Hershey Papers; Hershey to state director of Puerto Rico, February 16, 1945, staybacks, 1945, *ibid.* Hershey recalled that Congress appropriated money for black units and he had to fill them with racial calls. Interview with General Hershey, Bethesda, Md., May 26, 1975.

34. Metz T. P. Lochard to McNutt, December 6, 1944, McNutt Papers; McNutt, "Negro Manpower," December 21, 1944, *ibid.*; John K. Collins's speech, October 18, 1944, *ibid.*

35. For statistical information see the following: "Report on Employment of Negroes in War Industries," in WMC minutes, June 9, 1943, box 5-100, RG 211; WMC Summary of Negro Employment, October 16, 1943, McNutt Papers; Bureau of Placement Report on Negro in Postwar Economy, October 18, 1944, McNutt Papers; *Monthly Labor Review*, January 1945, pp. 1-4; *Statistical Abstract of the United States, 1944-1945* (Washington, D.C.: U.S. Government Printing Office, 1945), p. 126.

36. McWilliams, "What We Did," pp. 97-99; *Monthly Labor Review*, November 1943, pp. 952-53; Patterson quoted in *New York Times*, April 11, 1943, p. 52.

37. Sitkoff, "Racial Militancy," p. 661, argues that racial violence had the ironic effect of helping to create a civil rights movement which lost the truly radical black movement in a fog of integrationalism.

CHAPTER 8

Rosie the Riveter

As it was with blacks, so it was with women. Filling the manpower needs of the nation forced McNutt to fight prejudice against hiring women in traditionally male occupations. Superficially, women, like blacks, appeared to be making revolutionary progress from 1942 to 1945. Pearl Harbor meant many things, but one of its more prosaic consequences was full employment. Women moved into areas vacated by men, but well into 1942 their percentage of the job market remained consistent with long-term trends. Before the war was over, however, women had come into their own. The female percentage of the total United States work force rose from 24 percent in 1940 to about 33 percent in 1944. The number of women employed jumped from around 10,800,000 to a peak of some 19,000,000 in 1944-1945. By July 1944 Donald Nelson of the WPB could boast that some 36.9 percent of the total personnel employed by war industry was female.[1]

I

Whatever the figures, the manpower mobilization plan as executed by McNutt and the War Manpower Commission did little to promote a new status for women. Women's employment during the war, as conceived by recruiters and as executed by management and labor, rested upon traditional assumptions. The image of women war workers rested on an archaic rather than a modern notion of feminism. A woman was to be the helpmate of man, temporarily sharing his danger while simultaneously preserving her role as mother, wife, and homemaker. As Dorothy Thompson put it in "The New Woman in the New America": ". . . there is a typical American monument to American womanhood. In this typical monument, the woman is not sitting, nor even standing, but striding. Her brow is lifted to the sun, and her skirts are swept back from her legs by her stride. Her children cling to those skirts—and they are walking too. She is going with them, into newly discovered and opened lands. She is the Pioneer Woman."[2]

The cultural assumptions dominating American society in 1941 indicated that women should not be considered equal to men in economic matters. In the 1930s, Gallup polls reported that some 80 percent of the survey objected to women working. Although in 1942 the same pollster found that 60 percent of the public now accepted wives working in war industries, no real shift had occurred. The question was framed so as to request support for the defeat of Hitler and Tojo; it had nothing to do with assumptions about the normal role of women.[3]

The manner in which Franklin Roosevelt and Paul McNutt went about recruiting women revealed a reluctance to tamper with traditional roles. The Roosevelt administration remained largely unconcerned about recruiting women until late 1942. When eventually forced to consider this source because of the pressing need of the military, officials moved slowly. When General Hershey testified before a congressional investigation into labor migration, he predicted that the voluntary registration of female workers was a long way off. If women wanted to help they could join the Women's Army Corps. At the same time, the Catholic Daughters of America passed a resolution opposing any "regimentation of women."[4]

Three days after his appointment to head the War Manpower Commission in April 1942 Paul McNutt announced that women would not be needed. A few days later he corrected himself and admitted they might be useful in a few local areas on a voluntary basis, but for the most part *man*power would be an accurate description of his concern. The United States Employment Service in Connecticut had begun registering women because of the shortage of males in that area, an action that prompted McNutt's retraction. McNutt would allow voluntary registration, but he still insisted that the entire idea was premature and might hurt national morale. Nor did Donald Nelson of the WPB see fit to encourage women workers. The administration appeared satisfied with having women wrap bandages for the Red Cross.[5]

The potential of female labor appeared first at the local level; the message reached McNutt and Washington only later. By the fall of 1942, the military began revising upward its estimates on draft calls. From Detroit came startling news that a locally initiated, voluntary registration of women had netted some 250,000 positive responses out of 650,000 inquiries. Faced with new draft quotas and the apparent willingness of women to work, the administration finally acted. On September 4, 1942, McNutt appointed a Women's Advisory Committee, something spokeswomen had requested earlier. Margaret A. Hickey of St. Louis and eleven other prominent women representing clubs, unions, and professions, took desks in WMC's headquarters. McNutt also announced that although 1.4 million women had entered war industry since last December without being recruited by government, he would now need 5.6 million more women by the end of 1943. To insure success of this belated drive, he issued a series of guidelines: women should be granted equal pay, special counseling services, rest periods, and safety devices, and should work no more than a forty-eight-hour week. He also asserted emphatically and repeatedly that the government did not desire mothers to work and that "normal family life should be preserved and maintained to the maximum extent consistent with all-out production."[6]

McNutt's strategy of wanting women to work and at the same time hoping to maintain the traditional female role in the home revealed the administration's continued ambivalence about the issue. On the one hand, Roosevelt, returning from a transcontinental inspection trip in October 1942 spoke favorably of the female worker and hinted at voluntary registration. On the other hand, McNutt continued to insist that only local registration was needed and Mrs. Roosevelt announced her opposition to a female draft. Female activists such as Sadie Dubar, former president of the General Federation of Women's Clubs, called for bolder action. Polls of her group revealed wide sentiment for national registration, as did surveys of readers of *Woman's Home Companion.* But McNutt's hesitancy seemed more in tune with congressional sentiment. Of the seven women in Congress, six rejected any draft of women. Senator Warren Austin and Congressman James Wadsworth, sponsors of a national service bill, replied to entreaties for a female draft by explaining that public sentiment opposed such a step. Frances Perkins announced that she saw no need for a draft. The National Committee to Oppose Conscription of Women sent Mildred S. Olmsted to testify before Congress that the group favored a continuation of the war rather than a female draft. The Department of Labor released figures showing that 650,000 women were currently unsuccessful in seeking jobs. McNutt explained to Kathleen McLaughlin of the *New York Times* that compulsory registration of women, a step many feared would lead to conscription, would be too expensive for the obsolete information it would provide.[7]

In the middle of 1943, the administration suddenly changed its mind about female recruitment. General Marshall reported a need for more soldiers. General Hershey threatened to call up pre-Pearl Harbor fathers. Secretary Stimson began to advocate national service, allowing the draft of all workers, male and female. Neither McNutt nor Congress liked the national service alternative. The administration moved to recruit more women as a means of avoiding the draft of fathers and national service. Roosevelt announced that "in a profound sense, it is a woman's war." McNutt became evangelical, with personal appearances at parades and recruitment centers. He hinted that if women did not enter the work force faster it might mean taking fathers. Ironically, women were asked to work in order to save father for the American home. McNutt did insist that he wanted no mother of children under fourteen migrating to war jobs.[8]

Unfortunately, women failed to provide a substitute for the draft of fathers and in 1943 men were still leaving industry faster than women entered. McNutt now announced that he "never expected women to keep pace with the induction of men." When staff members of the WMC met in early 1944 to consider what would become the final recruitment drive for women, they were pessimistic. Women had failed to respond to earlier drives. In explanation, these experts stressed female distaste for dirty working conditions, the husband's reluctance to permit his wife to work, and the inadequacy of community services for working mothers. By 1944 women were being laid off on the West Coast.[9] As women moved in and out of the work force during World War II, the actions and attitudes of Paul McNutt and the WMC seem to have had little effect.

II

His failure can be partially explained by the traditional male bias found in the offices of the WMC. In 1940 Sidney Hillman, head of the National Defense Advisory Commission, had refused a post to a woman on his staff. This gesture set the tone maintained by McNutt throughout mobilization. Initially, the WMC had no women officers, an omission brought to light by Mary Anderson of the Women's Bureau of the Department of Labor. McNutt finally responded to criticism by Anderson, Dr. Minnie Maffett, and Olive O. Van Horn by establishing the Women's Advisory Committee (WAC), headed by Margaret Hickey. In many ways McNutt was the master of the empty gesture. When Hickey took her desk at WMC she found it empty in more ways than one. She realized quickly that she was to be a mere figurehead, gratuitously denied voting rights within the Management-Labor Policy Committee of the WMC and ignored on campaign strategy. Several communities erected little WACs, but they had no more success than the national organization. In August 1943 the New York WAC resigned en masse in protest over being repeatedly ignored by the male head of the regional WMC. Women fared just as poorly at the War Production Board, where only one of the 146 ranking officials was female. As late as June 14, 1944, a White House conference sponsored by Eleanor Roosevelt and attended by 200 women leaders complained that: "So far very few women have shared in the councils of national and international policy-making bodies."[10]

McNutt, who had no intention of granting women power in the WMC, saw nothing incongruous about asking American business and labor to reject traditional prejudices against hiring and working with women. In January 1942 a new male worker had three times the chance of being hired as a new female worker. John Studebaker, head of the Office of Education, refused to promote the training of women because he was sure management would not hire them. By mid-1943 William Haber reported optimistically that while in

January 1943, according to a survey of 12,000 plants, management was willing to hire women for only 29 percent of all jobs, by June 1943 females were acceptable for 55 percent of all jobs. Leonard Carmichael, Director of the National Roster of Scientific and Specialized Personnel, after lamenting the scarcity of technically trained women (in electrical engineering the roster had 12,000 men and twenty women), admitted that females who did take degrees in sciences could not find jobs. Neither medical nor law schools increased their enrollment of women during the war. Such was the discrimination against women that the American Association of University Women became encouraged after forcing the Civil Service Commission to stop listing women workers under the category "physically handicapped" in manuals. Female stereotypes remained intact.[11]

Management was called upon to accept so many qualifications in employing women that traditional ideas were reinforced. The federal government's pamphlet explained that women had special emotional needs on the job. Or, as one foreman complained, "women just can't take a bawling out." The WMC and the Women's Bureau issued guidelines on hiring women which stressed the importance of female counselors. These counselors provided a shoulder to cry on and were described as angels of mercy, ready with a helping hand for the distressed.[12]

Weaker than the male and four inches shorter, the average female worker needed special consideration. Studies indicated that women tired faster than men. McNutt, aware of these problems, advocated an apron-shift and hourly rest periods. By August 1944 the average work week for a female was 41.2 and for a male 47 hours per week. In many plants women worked at specially designed benches with newly designed tools. When Rhea Radin of the WMC inspected plants and shipyards in New Jersey and on the Pacific Coast, however, she was appalled at the "crowded, cluttered and indescribably dirty" washrooms. Even steel mills had to refurbish washrooms and cafeterias.[13]

Women had to do "double-duty" for the war effort. As married women and mothers moved into the factory, neither the government nor the community expected them to give up their traditional role. Rather, the community was expected to help them continue to perform as housewives and as war workers. As McNutt told the New

York State Conference of Women Workers in December 1943:
"Each community can help . . . by providing and planning correct
services to take care of transportation, housing, health, sanitation,
child care, recreation, shopping, and the medical needs of women."[14]
About 36 percent of all female workers had some responsibility for
a family and a major part of the housework. The consumer industry
based its sales pitches on how a product allowed the working-home-
maker to fulfill her dual responsibility. Heinz soup, Westinghouse
stoves, and General Electric cleaners allowed the working mother
to fly through her chores at home, rush to her drill press at the
factory, and be romantic at night.[15]

III

Despite this demand for double-duty, women proved surprisingly
capable. McNutt and the WMC presented considerable evidence
that women workers could hold their own with men in 80 percent of
all industrial tasks. Studies revealed that women did best in tertiary
work and poorest in primary work.[16] But the WMC found two
dramatic exceptions to this rule: aircraft construction and shipbuilding. The aircraft industry increased employment of women
from less than 1 percent to 28 percent of all workers. At a peak
period in 1944, women made up 44 percent of all workers in West
Coast plants such as Boeing, Consolidated Vultee, Douglas, North-
rop, North American, and others. In June 1944 the industry employed about 439,500 women. Women also contributed to shipbuilding on both coasts. Their success in these two heavy industries
sprang from good pay, innovative management, and the absence of
a large prewar male work force. In addition, WMC studies showed
that women did best in jobs more closely related to the war effort.
Women who worked for the government, especially the War Department, rated very high in performance.[17]

Unfortunately, women did have problems on the job, problems
which could be exploited to reinforce traditional stereotypes. When
the initial enthusiasm and patriotism wore off, women began to
slow down. Both management and labor presented evidence that
despite special treatment women lacked job discipline. At first
McNutt and WMC officials denied accusations that women were

quitting or taking holidays. To admit that women were leaving jobs as rapidly as they were hired would have made McNutt look ridiculous. Yet the evidence could not be denied forever. By the fall of 1943, when female recruiting had major priority, the WMC admitted that for every two women hired for war work in June, one had quit. Women who stayed on the job had an alarming tendency to take unauthorized holidays. Some 16,600 war plants reported that the quit-rate for women in June was 6.2 percent as compared to 3.9 percent for men. In July another study found that in every industry for which sex data could be compared the same trend prevailed. Even in aircraft plants, the turnover rate among women was 12.2 percent as compared to 4.2 percent for men.[18]

Several reasons explained this weakness in the female work record. Women worried more about poor housing. They caught peace fever earlier than men. They had double-duty with homes and children. They met constant resentment from male colleagues on the job. A poll taken by the American Institute of Public Opinion in June 1943 asked: "Are women able to do as well as men at the same job in the plant?" Women agreed they were just as capable as men by 83 percent. Male workers disagreed by a 63 percent margin.[19]

Management and unions must have agreed with males because they supported a discriminatory pay policy. A Gallup poll found 78 percent of the public supporting equal pay for equal work. Roosevelt, McNutt, and Perkins all advocated equal pay. But these opinions aside, women received less than men. Some industries, especially aircraft and shipbuilding, did provide equal pay for women. Such industries were exceptional. The average hourly wage for women in 1941 was about fifty-six cents; for men about seventy-two cents. By late 1944, women received seventy-six cents and men eighty-nine cents. On a weekly basis, despite a jump for women from $21.37 to $31.31, men increased their margin by jumping from $29.92 to $41.18. Various devices were employed to discriminate against women, including defining a job as a female task or as light work. One executive explained that "the differential is based on masculine prestige as much as on productivity." For example, some 800 male workers at Pullman Standard of Birmingham walked off the job when females received a raise. When the war ended, women continued to meet frustration in attempts to have Congress pass an equal-pay bill.[20]

Discrimination could have been reduced if unions had objected. But the union rank and file remained an instrument for perpetuating traditional distinctions. Such attitudes prevailed even though women joined unions in large numbers. Female membership rose from less than a million in 1941 to more than three million in 1944 when seventeen million women were employed. McNutt and the Women's Bureau both promoted female union membership. But increased membership had little effect on male leadership. A survey of New York State unions in December 1943 indicated that males controlled almost all offices; a similar pattern appeared in ninety unions in the Midwest. Some unions excluded women from leadership and worked with management to maintain differential wage scales. National union leaders called for equal pay, but they called in vain. One bright young woman volunteered to help organize the other girls in her section of the factory. The union shop leader responded by asking if she was a communist.[21]

Who could blame the female who responded to a union membership drive by saying, "for the $12 a year union fee, I can have my garbage removed," a more sensible use of her money than supporting a racket which worked to maintain male supremacy. A few women disliked unions because they appeared unpatriotic in their attention to traditional problems during the crisis of war. But without union support, the female future in the job market would be bleak. Elisabeth Christman, of the Women's Trade Union League, and R. J. Thomas, president of the United Auto Workers, warned women to look to the future.[22]

IV

McNutt had good reason to worry about the future of the female worker. Female labor leaders from twenty-three different unions met in Washington in April 1945. They called for a permanent place for women in the postwar economy and formed a committee to advise the WMC and the Department of Labor. Everyone feared that female workers would disappear when Johnny came marching home. Susan B. Anthony II wrote to convince the public that working women could be good mothers, that at least one-third of all women needed to work, and that the family would not be threatened.

But a public opinion poll of November 1943 indicated that between 80 and 90 percent of all respondents agreed that women must leave their jobs to make way for returning veterans. McNutt did what he could to prevent a repetition of post-World War I's wholesale dismissal of women workers by harping upon full employment in postwar America. In February 1944 and in March 1945, upon Margaret Hickey's recommendation, McNutt issued guidelines on the treatment of women during reconversion. Women workers should be counseled about why they were being dismissed. Notice should be given as far in advance as possible. Women should receive information on retraining, transfers, and social security rights. McNutt urged that part-time workers be laid off first and that separation should be based on skills and on seniority. Despite such good intentions, management rushed females out of the work force with unseemly haste.[23]

A month after V-J Day, McNutt admitted that millions of women had already been fired. In fact, dismissals had begun much earlier. In January 1944 Bendix Aviation Corporation in Philadelphia laid off 1,000 workers, 80 percent female. The Office of War Information found in February 1944 that women consistently received first notice. In March 1943 some 103,500 women worked on airplanes; by October 1945 only 10,600 were left. In two months, from September to November 1945, women's employment dropped by 300,000. From September 1945 to November 1946 around 2.25 million women left work and another million were laid-off. Women made up 60 percent of all workers laid off in the early postwar months; their layoff rate was 75 percent higher than for men.[24]

V

Women played a major role in mobilizing the American economy during World War II. But the war did not "complete female emancipation," or "radically alter the character of American society." McNutt and President Roosevelt might speak of World War II as a crusade for human rights and call for continued reform, but the war was also a fight to preserve and even export what many considered the best of all systems. Wars have a way of reaffirming traditional myths. The traditional role of the female as wife and mother had much support during the war despite mobilization. A survey of female opinion (1944) revealed that women agreed marriage and motherhood should not be put off until after the war. By 1945 magazines featured stories on women such as Lois White Eck. A concert soprano with a brilliant future, she gave up her career because it threatened her marriage. She planned to concentrate on her role as wife and mother because "it's the only lasting happiness a woman can have." Dorothy Thompson again called on women to save civilization by not being afraid "to think and feel as women, and look upon the world with the eyes of mothers, realizing that mothers and housewives are perhaps the most important national and international society on earth."[25] Rosie the Riveter never displaced the feminine mystique.

Notes

1. Vene Burnett, "Manpower Reserves," *New York Times Magazine*, February 27, 1944, p. 18; Donald Nelson, *Arsenal of Democracy* (New York: Harcourt, Brace, 1946), pp. 137-38; Byron Fairchild and Jonathan Grossman, *The Army and Industrial Manpower* (Washington, D.C.: U.S. Department of the Army, 1959), pp. 171-72; Richard Polenberg, *War and Society: The United States, 1941-1945* (Philadelphia: J. B. Lippincott, 1972), pp. 79, 146; *New York Times*, February 25, 1944; Kathleen McLaughlin, "Women's Activities," *New York Times Magazine*, March 14, 1943, sec. 2, p. 15; *The War and Women's Employment: The Experience of the United Kingdom and the United States* (Montreal: International Labour Office, 1946), pp. 159-66, 175-76; Mary E. Pidgeon, *Changes in Women's Employment during the War* (Washington, D.C.: Government Printing Office, 1944), pp. 1-22; Ethel Erickson, *Women's Employment in the Making of Steel* (Washington, D.C.: Government Printing Office, 1944), p. 24; William H. Chafe, *The American Woman: Her Changing Social, Economic, and Political Roles, 1920-1970* (New York: Oxford, 1972), pp. 135, 149, 172, 184, 193; Eleanor Straub, "Government Policy toward Civilian Women during World War II" (Ph. D. dissertation, Emory University, 1973), argues women made little headway toward equality; Chester Gregory, "The Problem of Labor during World War II: The Employment of Women in Defense Production" (Ph.D. dissertation, Ohio State University, 1969), disagrees.

2. Dorothy Thompson, "The New Woman in the New America," *Ladies Home Journal*, January 1945, p. 6.

3. Chafe, *American Woman*, pp. 147-48; Josephine von Miklos, *I Took a War Job* (New York: Simon and Schuster, 1943), p. 22.

4. Mattie E. Treadwell, *The Woman's Army Corps* (Washington, D.C.: U.S. Department of the Army, 1954), pp. 95, 168, 170, 172, 189, 242; ILO, *War and Women*, p. 255; *New York Times*, January 25, 1942, p. 33, February 4, 1942, p. 14,

February 16, 1942, p. 22, February 28, 1942, p. 9, and March 27, 1942, p. 10; for debate over registering women see serial no. R1502 in *Monthly Labor Review* (December 1942), in Mary Anderson Papers, Radcliffe College, Cambridge, Mass.

5. Files for July 19, 1941, and May 6, 1942, clipping of *Birmingham News*, March 9, 1942, Paul V. McNutt Papers, The Lilly Library, Indiana University, Bloomington, Ind.; *Woman's Home Companion*, July 1942, p. 50; *New York Times*, May 2, 1942, p. 8, May 5, 1942, p. 18.

6. Fairchild and Grossman, *Army and Industrial Manpower*, p. 170; file of October 21, 1942, McNutt Papers; *New York Times*, August 11, 1942, p. 22, August 21, 1942, p. 13, September 5, 1942, p. 1, October 2, 1942, p. 28, and October 19, 1942, p. 22.

7. *Woman's Home Companion*, December 1942, p. 56; files of December 7, 1942, December 14, 1942, and December 31, 1942, McNutt Papers; *New York Times*, October 2, 1942, p. 29, October 31, 1942, p. 1, December 8, 1942, p. 31, December 15, 1942, p. 31, December 27, 1942, sec. 2, p. 2, February 22, 1942, p. 14, March 26, 1943, p. 12, April 11, 1943, sec. 2, p. 11, and February 14, 1943, sec. 3, p. 14.

8. Leonard P. Adams, *Wartime Manpower Mobilization* (Ithaca, N.Y.: Cornell University Press, 1951), p. 36; Institute of Psychoanalysis, *Women in Wartime* (Chicago, 1943), p. 24; Fairchild and Grossman, *Army and Industrial Manpower*, p. 171; Elizabeth Hawes, *Why Women Cry* (New York: Reynald and Hitchcock, 1943), p. 58; McNutt Papers, January-February 1943; April, May, June, October 1943 files; *New York Times*, April 18, 1943, p. 20, July 8, 1943, p. 15, May 23, 1943, p. 3, and August 28, 1943. The navy even offered married couples an opportunity to work side by side at the shipyard. The Office of War Information and McNutt both agreed that working women could prevent the need for a national service law; see *New York Times*, May 24, 1943, p. 12, and file of October 20, 1943, McNutt Papers.

9. Files of August 28, 1943, February 15, 16, and 18, 1944, McNutt Papers.

10. Howard Zinn, *Postwar America* (Indianapolis: Bobbs-Merrill, 1973), p. 29; Chafe, *American Woman*, pp. 151-53; Carol Riegelman, *Labour-Management Co-operation in United States War Production* (Montreal: International Labour Office, 1948), pp. 32, 56; *New York Times*, July 14, 1942, p. 16, September 20, 1942, sec. 2, p. 4, December 17, 1942, p. 43, July 9, 1943, p. 14, and September 26, 1943, sec. 2, p. 14. Miss Hickey reported privately that she had been "hurt and at first mad and astonished" by the refusal of the MLPC to give her a vote but she vowed to appeal to McNutt. When he did nothing, she decided to carry on rather than hurt the war effort by resigning. See memorandum by Helen Breenblatt, May 1, 1943, WMC Information Division, box 20-139, record group 211, National Archives, Washington, D.C.; summary statement of White House Conference, June 14, 1944, in folder 70, Clara Beyer Papers, Schlesinger Library, Radcliffe College, Cambridge, Mass.

11. File of January 26, 1942, McNutt Papers; Miklos, *War Job*, p. 138; *Woman's Home Companion*, June 1943, editorial, and December 1944, p. 35; ILO, *War and Women*, pp. 177, 187, 252-53; *New York Times*, May 16, 1943, sec. 2, p. 10, June 29, 1943, p. 40, August 8, 1943, p. 24, August 12, 1943, p. 16, August 13, 1943, p.

14, August 14, 1943, p. 14, and December 5, 1943, p. 63; WMC minutes, June 2, 1943, box 5-100, RG 211; also box 20-137, June 1943, *ibid.*; Chafe, *American Woman*, pp. 136-38. Older women were always discriminated against and industry outdid the railroads in keeping out females. See files of May 4, 1942, and December 3, 1943, McNutt Papers; *New York Times*, December 4, 1942, p. 19.

12. Hawes, *Why Women Cry*, p. 106; *Women in Wartime*, p. 1; *New York Times*, January 21, 1944, p. 14, August 8, 1943, sec. 2, p. 9, September 2, 1943, p. 22, November 13, 1943, p. 10, and December 7, 1943, p. 22; *Women in Steel*, pp. 28-29; ILO, *War and Women*, p. 229.

13. Margaret K. Anderson, *Women's Wartime Hours of Work: The Effect on Their Factory Performance and Home Life* (Washington, D.C.: Government Printing Office, 1947), pp. 3-4; Fairchild and Grossman, *Army and Industrial Manpower*, p. 169; ILO, *War and Women*, pp. 178, 299-305; files of March 14, 1943, August 7, 1943, McNutt Papers; *Women in Steel*, pp. 29-32; WMC, Record Group 211, box 20-139, June 29, 1943; *New York Times*, February 12, 1943, p. 32, March 18, 1943, p. 20, July 20, 1943, p. 16, August 30, 1943, p. 12, November 7, 1943, sec. 2, p. 11, January 2, 1944, p. 37, and February 3, 1944, p. 24.

14. *New York Times*, August 22, 1943, sec. 2, p. 9; file of December 11, 1943, McNutt Papers.

15. Anderson, *Women's Wartime Hours*, pp. 3, 4; file of December 11, 1943, McNutt Papers; *New York Times*, August 22, 1943, sec. 2, p. 9, and January 28, 1944, p. 20; *Woman's Home Companion*, September 1942-September 1945, passim.

16. *New York Times*, June 17, 1943, p. 18, May 22, 1943, p. 8; file of June 12, 1945, McNutt Papers.

17. See folder 185 in Elinore Herrick Papers, Schlesinger Library, Radcliffe College, Cambridge, Mass., for testimonials on the patriotism of females in shipyards; ILO, *War and Women*, p. 173; John Dos Passos, *State of the Nation* (Boston: Houghton Mifflin, 1943), p. 15; Scott Hart, *Washington at War, 1941–1945* (Englewood Cliffs, N.J.: Prentice-Hall, 1970), p. 35; Miklos, *War Job*, pp. 177-84; *New York Times*, April 16, 1943, p. 17, May 23, 1942, p. 10, June 16, 1943, p. 18, August 7, 1943, p. 14, and January 20, 1944, p. 16; copy of radio address, file of October 24, 1942, McNutt Papers; Lucy Greenbaum, "I Worked on the Assembly Line," *New York Times Magazine*, March 28, 1943, pp. 18-38.

18. See especially Fraser Report, folder 77, Herrick Papers, which concludes on absenteeism: "No solution to the problem ever emerged." ILO, *War and Women*, pp. 225, 285; Anderson, *Women's Wartime Hours*, pp. 2, 3; *Women in Steel*, p. 32; *New York Times*, January 23, 1943, p. 10, July 26, 1943, p. 16, August 24, 1943, p. 10, August 29, 1943, sec. 2, p. 9, and October 6, 1943, p. 26.

19. *New York Times*, March 9, 1943, p. 16, March 6, 1942, p. 10, and February 23, 1944; Anderson, *Women's Wartime Hours*, pp. 1-2, 6, 8; *New York Times*, August 22, 1943, pp. 9, 11, July 11, 1943, p. 34, September 13, 1943, p. 16, August 26, 1943, p. 25, and February 6, 1942; ILO, *War and Women*, pp. 278-79; Elizabeth Hawes, "Woman War Worker: A Case History," *New York Times Magazine*, December 26, 1943, p. 9; *New York Times*, June 12, 1943, p. 10, and October 29, 1943,

p. 24; WMC, Record Group 211, box 20-137, June 1943; Chafe, *American Woman*, p. 139; *Women in Steel*, p. 3; Miklos, *War Job*, pp. 48, 88, 112, 191; Hawes, *Why Women Cry*, pp. 58-62; *New York Times*, April 23, 1943, p. 15.

20. See especially file 40 in M. Anderson Papers and *Monthly Labor Review*, December 1942; Baker, *Women in War*, p. 44; Chafe, *American Woman*, pp. 155-58; ILO, *War and Women*, pp. 206, 211, 214-17; *New York Times*, February 13, 1942, p. 11, April 4, 1943, sec. 2, p. 15, October 14, 1943, p. 18, February 22, 1944, p. 28, May 9, 1943, p. 7, and September 8, 1944, p. 32.

21. Seidman, *American Labor*, p. 154; ILO, *War and Women*, pp. 237-46; Chafe, *American Woman*, p. 144; Riegelman, *Labour-Management Co-operation*, p. 294; file of March 20, 1943, McNutt Papers; McNutt made various speeches advocating women's rights before union groups; *New York Times*, February 3, 1943, p. 9, September 25, 1943, p. 12, September 30, 1943, p. 18, and May 17, 1943, p. 7; Hawes, *Why Women Cry*, p. 150; ILO, *War and Women*, pp. 246-47; Baker, *Women in War*, pp. 20, 29, 47.

22. Hawes, *Why Women Cry*, p. 124; Miklos, *War Job*, p. 28; *New York Times*, November 16, 1943, p. 23, and February 26, 1944, p. 17; but union leaders did support equal pay for women if men had enough jobs: see file 40, Anderson Papers, Radcliffe College.

23. Nancy Craig interview of Elinore M. Herrick, October 3, 1945, folder 187, Herrick Papers; see also speech by Herrick, May 18, 1944, folder 186, *ibid.*; Riegelman, *Labour-Management Co-operation*, p. 294; *Women in Steel*, p. 33; ILO, *War and Women*, pp. 264-65; Elinore M. Herrick, "What about Women after the War?" *New York Times Magazine*, September 5, 1943, p. 7; *New York Times*, February 15, 1943, p. 12, October 24, 1943, p. 19, January 21, 1944, p. 1, January 12, 1944, p. 26, February 1, 1944, p. 24, and September 20, 1944, p. 19; Susan B. Anthony II, "Is it true what they say about women?" *Woman's Home Companion*, June 1945, p. 22; *ibid.*, April 1943; *New York Times*, June 7, 1943, p. 10, June 19, 1943, p. 10, August 16, 1943, p. 12, October 31, 1943, p. 51, November 15, 1943, p. 24, November 16, 1943, p. 20, and November 20, 1943, p. 10; Mary Anderson, "16,000,000 Women at Work," *New York Times Magazine*, July 18, 1943, p. 18; McNutt to H. A. Koehler, August 31, 1943, McNutt Papers; file of October 1, 1943, *ibid.*; *New York Times*, September 26, 1943, p. 31, November 2, 1943, p. 16, December 3, 1943, p. 28, December 13, 1943, p. 24, February 18, 1944, p. 12, and February 20, 1944, p. 29.

24. ILO, *War and Women*, pp. 258-68; Pidgeon, *Changes*, vi; McNutt estimated that by December 1943 some 2.5 million women would be looking for jobs, 1.5 million of them former war workers: see file of October 1, 1943, McNutt Papers; but also see Chafe, *American Woman*, pp. 174-84, who argues that as women were laid off they were also hired so that "two years after the war ended, women had regained many of the losses suffered in the immediate postwar period and started toward new peaks of employment." Yet in 1945, taking an average of the four quarters, women made up 35 percent of the total work force. In 1946, taking the same average, women made up only 29 percent of the work force which had increased by a total of 4.7

million workers. See *Statistical Abstract of the United States, 1946* (Washington, D.C.: Government Printing Office, 1946), p. 173; ibid., *1947* (Washington, D.C.: Government Printing Office, 1947), p. 173.

25. Margaret B. Pickel, "A Warning to Career Women," *New York Times Magazine*, July 16, 1944, pp. 19, 32; Margaret Mead, "The Women in the War," in *While You Were Gone*, Jack Goodman, ed. (New York: Simon and Schuster, 1946), pp. 279-80; *New York Times*, January 9, 1944, p. 41; Pickel candidly recommended that females avoid economic competition with males and resume their roles as "helpers and servers." See also Booth Tarkington, "I Gave Up My Career to Save My Marriage," *Ladies Home Journal*, April 1945, pp. 131-33; Dorothy Thompson, "A Call to American Women," *ibid.*, August 1945, p. 6.

CHAPTER 9

The Military Equation

Even if McNutt had mastered the problem of discrimination against women and blacks, he would not have solved the manpower problem. In a total war the military establishment could legitimately lay claim to all manpower. President Roosevelt and Paul McNutt always admitted the primacy of military manpower needs. In theory, however, they recognized the need to man the civilian economy. McNutt had to balance the needs of the military with the needs of war industry and essential civilian services. Few men faced a more formidable and less-rewarding task. To a degree no longer fashionable, the generals and admirals of World War II called the tune on the mobilization of the economy. Civilians, especially politicians, fell over themselves trying to satisfy the needs of General George Marshall. Military leaders such as Secretary of War Stimson and Secretary of the Navy Knox agreed that no limit should be imposed on them in fighting the war. As such opinions were supported by the public, McNutt would have had difficulty challenging them.[1]

I

Throughout the years 1941 to 1945, leading military figures such as Marshall, Stimson, and Robert Patterson consistently pressed for a larger and larger army. The size of the army would naturally be a vital determinant in the availability of civilian manpower for industry. Uncertainty about the total personnel needs of the military complicated McNutt's job of projecting civilian labor supplies. He understood the problem of military leaders. He sympathized, he deeply sympathized, but his problem was made worse because original military estimates were much too low. In 1940 the Selective Service bill passed by Congress had aimed at an army of 900,000 men. By the summer of 1941, Congress revised the draft law to remove the total strength ceiling. When Roosevelt asked military leaders for an estimate of how many men would be needed to defeat any potential enemy, they refused to commit themselves. When Roosevelt put together his Victory Program in 1941, he envisioned an army of close to nine million men.[2]

As sophisticated techniques revealed the actual manpower needs for meeting industrial production goals and civilian needs, an increasing number of Americans began to question the size of the military manpower pool. In the summer of 1942, the War Department proposed that the army reach a level of 8.2 million by the end of 1943. After including similar increases to staff the navy and marines, the total figure for military manpower amounted to more than 10.9 million. These enlarged estimates upset both McNutt and Donald Nelson, who felt the military had pulled the totals out of a hat without considering the problem of coordinating civilian and military manpower needs. The executive order creating the WMC had specified that such military manpower figures be coordinated with McNutt, but he had been ignored. McNutt claimed his coordinating responsibility with the military in September by writing General J. R. Deane of the Joint Chiefs of Staff that "based on current estimates the maximum number of men which can be made available for the Armed Forces without hurting the balance of support production as of December 31, 1943 is 9,000,000." McNutt urged a periodic staff conference with the military, the War Production Board, and the War Manpower Commission to settle the problem. Both Donald Nelson and Robert R. Nathan of the WPB agreed to McNutt's proposal. Two World War I mobilization experts, Herbert Hoover and Bernard Baruch, warned that too large an army would destroy the economy.[3]

These arguments had an effect on Roosevelt. The President informed General Marshall in early October 1942 that the "total of the Army and the Marine Corps would be limited to 7,300,000 up to the end of 1943, amounting to about a limit of 6,700,000 for the Army alone.'' At the President's urging the Joint Chiefs met with representatives of both the WPB and the WMC. McNutt, at first glance, seemed victorious in gaining control of manpower. But neither Marshall nor Stimson intended to lower their manpower figures or concede civilian control over such decisions. Marshall did agree to provide the WMC with the estimated rate of inductions up through December 1943 to allow McNutt time to plan for corresponding withdrawals from industry. But the general stood firm on the need for a larger army and finally obtained Roosevelt's agreement to such limited increases as the military mission dictated, up to a total of 8.2 million for the army alone by December 1943. The War Department thereby obtained its large army and maintained autonomy.[4]

McNutt quickly recovered from this defeat and counterattacked. Ironically, he was aided by War Department planners who now submitted an inflated figure of 14,086,557 men in uniform as the goal for the end of 1944. Marshall and Stimson both quickly recognized that such a total would generate considerable opposition within the Roosevelt administration. In an attempt to deflate opposition, they met on December 9, 1942, with WMC officials, politely requesting information on how much manpower would be available in 1944. Marshall consistently refused to allow McNutt control over military strength, but the general now accepted the need for some coordination with the WMC. McNutt provided the requested estimates of available manpower for 1944 to Stimson and Marshall, who both realized the impossibility of reaching their projected goals without new legislation. Specifically, they wanted a national service act and by February 1943 Congress was debating just such a bill. Marshall hurried over to Capitol Hill to tell the Senate Appropriations Committee that he needed 8.2 million in the army by the end of 1943. Stimson testified that the nation must put 8.5 percent of the entire population in uniform. Both men argued that the only means of reaching their goal was through passage of a national service act. President Roosevelt now announced the need to have a total of eleven million men in all branches of the military by the end of 1943. A special White House committee investigated the manpower problem and reported that the nation could support a military establishment of eleven million, provided that improved recruitment and utilization techniques were used.[5]

As 1943 drew to a close the War Department had approval for a total of 11,264,000 men for all branches by December 1944. The strength of the military by May 1945, when war in Europe ended, peaked at 12,124,418. The final figure was surprisingly close to estimates made as early as 1940. Stimson and Marshall appeared victorious in the debate over the size of the military. But the objections raised by McNutt, Nelson, and others and the failure of national service legislation forced the War Department to pay more attention to data provided by the WMC. McNutt alerted the military to the importance of considering how a large draft call would affect production of military equipment. While McNutt never gained any control over total manpower, he did broaden the perspective used by the military in making a decision. Moreover, the debate weakened the reputation of the military leaders as experts in manpower problems.

By the end of 1944 military estimates of manpower needs seemed less and less infallible. General Somervell kept telling everyone that manpower shortages caused problems at the front. But other military men in Europe admitted to the press that no battle had been lost because of too little equipment. Eventually, Somervell admitted that adequate supplies were reaching the unloading areas. Undersecretary Patterson began complaining about the excessive turnover rate in the munitions industry. He took his complaint to McNutt who had no difficulty in demonstrating that the quit-rate in 1944 did not "differ substantially" from that of 1943. McNutt's statistics showed that the quit-rate among factory workers making civilian goods was running about 29 percent above those workers making war goods in 1944. The quit-rate in the munitions industry remained stable. Patterson could not believe these figures because he was bombarded with complaints from friends in the field. McNutt and Haber admitted there might be a few local problems but, nationally, the situation looked good.[6]

As Stimson and Patterson publicly campaigned for a national service law they received private reports which indicated that "on the whole, labor shortages are not significantly impeding the achieve-

ment of ASF [Army Service Forces] procurement objectives."
Colonel Ralph F. Gow of the War Department reported to Patterson on the domestic manpower picture. On April 17, 1945, he wrote
that "total ASF deliveries in March exceeded those in any previous
month since Pearl Harbor." Gow predicted that imminent cutbacks
in tank, truck, and artillery production would clear away all manpower shortages. Under such circumstances McNutt's optimism
about the manpower problem, irritating to certain military leaders
and politicians, was not as Pollyanna-ish as some supposed.[7]

II

Disagreements between McNutt and the military sprang from
personal factors as much as from conflicts inherent in their separate
missions. Secretary of War Stimson came to the cabinet in 1940
with a considerable reputation achieved under three presidents. He
was an eastern Republican, an internationalist, and a private man.
McNutt, a midwestern Democrat, had the personal aggressiveness
of a career politician. As members of the Roosevelt cabinet, however, both men tried to play with the team. In November 1941
McNutt cooperated with Stimson. The Surgeon General's office,
which was under McNutt's Federal Security Administration, published information critical of the War Department. Stimson became furious but calmed down when McNutt came over personally
to apologize for what he called an unjustified attack. Over the next
few weeks both men worked together and harmony prevailed.[8]

After McNutt was appointed to head the new WMC in April
1942, he came into closer contact with Stimson. The Secretary of
War appointed an old friend and law partner from New York,
Goldthwaite Dorr, as departmental representative on the WMC.
Although Dorr was old and ill, Stimson insisted to Roosevelt that
he "had to have people that I knew around me to do my work."
Initially, McNutt accepted the appointment. Dorr took his seat on
the WMC and even helped McNutt maintain the services of several
military officers scheduled for active duty.[9]

This era of good feeling could not endure because McNutt understood his role as manpower director to include control of the draft.
By October 1942 he was hard at work to capture the Selective Ser-

vice System. McNutt emphatically rejected the theory, popular in the War Department, that the WMC was merely to control whatever men were left after the military took what it wanted. He insisted on being involved in decisions affecting military manpower levels. Stimson and Patterson, in contrast, viewed with alarm McNutt's attempt "to get his clutches on the Selective Service Commission." By mid-October Stimson had concluded that McNutt was seeking more and more power. The Secretary worried because "while he [McNutt] is an able man himself, according to credible reports he has a very feeble staff—a lot of callow New Dealers with more ambition than brains." Stimson and Patterson even began promoting Bernard Baruch to replace McNutt. On November 11, 1942, Stimson had a long talk with Baruch on the problem. Baruch agreed with Stimson that the military and civilian manpower programs should be kept distinct and that McNutt was inadequate in his job. But while Stimson was away from Washington on December 5, 1942, Roosevelt issued an executive order putting McNutt in charge of Selective Service.[10]

Roosevelt's tactics made things even worse. Stimson became furious when Roosevelt hinted that McNutt had been given his new authority despite the personal impugnation of the Secretary of War. Stimson feared that the President had deliberately sought to provoke a feud between McNutt and the military. To his diary, Stimson confided that up to now "I have been on very friendly terms with him and I have found him a pretty decent fellow." To show that no hard feelings existed, Stimson invited McNutt up for an hour and a half of talk in which both men reassured each other about their sincerity. In truth, suspicions remained on both sides. McNutt knew that the War Department had intrigued against him in Congress and in the press. He was convinced that Dorr was a mere stooge for Stimson and an obstructionist on the WMC. Stimson sensed McNutt's antagonism toward Dorr. The Secretary swore to McNutt that Dorr had defended the WMC position in War Department staff meetings. As the conference closed Stimson believed he had McNutt's promise to allow Dorr to remain with the WMC. He warned Dorr that a housecleaning at the WMC seemed imminent and that he should keep his mouth shut, but report back all he heard.[11]

Whatever Stimson's assumptions, McNutt had no intention of allowing Dorr to remain on the WMC. Despite Stimson's reassurances, McNutt believed Dorr was a garrulous obstructionist. McNutt and Harold Smith, Director of the Budget, insisted to Roosevelt that Dorr be removed. On December 17, 1942, Roosevelt responded with a note to Stimson asking that Dorr be replaced by John McCloy. Stimson exploded: "McNutt has been more slimy than I had hoped." The Secretary was indignant not only at having wasted ninety minutes courting McNutt, but because the President had presumed to pick a replacement for Dorr. Stimson called Roosevelt and threatened to resign unless he received an immediate hearing. Roosevelt retreated. He conceded that the Secretary should have the last word on who would replace Dorr. This concession only mildly placated Stimson who now viewed McNutt with undisguised hostility. Roosevelt sent Justice Felix Frankfurter to make peace. After talking with McNutt, Frankfurter became convinced that there had been no deliberate double cross of Stimson. The real villain, to Frankfurter, was Roosevelt's sloppy administrative technique. Stimson, however, remained unmollified and told Roosevelt on December 24 that "it does not fit in with my plans to accede to your suggestion that I designate Mr. McCloy." Stimson appointed Patterson to sit with the WMC, but kept Dorr around as a special advisor on manpower and as a constant reminder of McNutt's perfidy.[12]

III

Such personal disagreements notwithstanding, McNutt and the military did cooperate during the war on several important problems. Most people recognized early in the war that the assignment of war contracts should be made with some knowledge of the availability of labor in particular regions. Early in the war, when a labor surplus still existed, the assignment of contracts could be based primarily upon facilities needed, proximity to transportation, and safety from enemy attack. As one scholar writes: "In the four months immediately following the attack on Pearl Harbor, the labor supply factor was almost forgotten in the rush to get . . . construction." Gradually, however, the military began to take man-

power into consideration. During the war Patterson ordered a reduction in procurement for several areas because of manpower
shortages.[13]

Soon after assuming office McNutt realized that his hopes to
bring control to civilian manpower depended upon his ability to
control the character of military manpower withdrawals from the
economy. Volunteering had a long and honorable history in America. During the first year of the war the various military services
conducted high-pressure campaigns to recruit volunteers. Such
campaigns led to serious manpower problems by late 1942. McNutt
strove to end the volunteer program on the grounds that it upset
manpower planning. After much argument, Stimson was converted.
He wrote to Roosevelt in November that sooner or later "we must
have a single selection process without any volunteering." The
Secretary had been influenced by fears that the navy received a
disproportionate share of high-intelligence recruits due to the volunteering system. He wanted his share. A month later McNutt
obtained Roosevelt's approval to end volunteering as part of a general expansion of the WMC's powers. The President told the press
that although he liked volunteering during World War I the time
had arrived where "I had to discard sentiment and end enlistments."
His order ended all military recruitment campaigns. McNutt breathed
a sigh of relief.[14]

McNutt and the military might cooperate during the war, the use
of prisoners of war for labor being another case in point, but little
harmony existed. Given the rather narrow perspective adopted by
Stimson, Knox, and Patterson, disagreements were inevitable. The
military thought it had the main job in the war; McNutt's work
appeared trivial. Stimson and Patterson resented any attempts by
McNutt to extend his manpower management principles to civilian
personnel in the War Department. By 1944 neither Stimson nor
Patterson bothered to attend the meetings of the WMC. They sent
James Mitchell of the Industrial Personnel Division of the War
Department. Mitchell returned from one meeting and reported to
Patterson: "Meeting convened at 2:30 p. m. and adjourned at 4:15
p.m. Mr. Appley presided. Mr. Haber talked. Nothing happened."[15]

McNutt and the military disagreed over the question of union
rights during mobilization. McNutt bent over backwards to preserve

union rights. Stimson and Patterson considered such problems mere bagatelles. When the army took over a plant it had the power to recommend cancellation of all employment privileges. In one case at a Western Electric plant in Maryland, Patterson insisted that McNutt change his traditional policy of not referring new workers to plants on strike. As this plant was now being operated by presidential decree, Patterson wrote: "Please see that employment requisitions covering these plants submitted to local USES are promptly filled." The military would fight the war and let the National Labor Relations Board worry about enforcing labor rights.[16]

McNutt took a holistic view of American manpower and its responsibilities. Political and pragmatic, his view represented a more sophisticated understanding of the problems of mobilization in a free society. For Stimson and Patterson, total war meant that every man should be ready to bear arms at any time. McNutt disagreed with this view but never challenged the supposition that winning the war was the primary mission of all members of the administration. He simply argued that men might help win the war by not serving in the military. John J. McCloy later complimented McNutt on the outstanding job the WMC did in obtaining workers for the Manhattan project. Both McNutt and the military eventually came to a limited understanding of each other's point of view. When regional manpower directors met in Washington in September 1944, McNutt invited Patterson and other military leaders to appear and make their plea for continued high production.[17] Such cooperation, however, could only go so far given the obvious competition between the military and McNutt for manpower. In the middle of this competition sat the formidable figure of General Lewis Hershey, head of the Selective Service System.

IV

McNutt's ability to control manpower depended to an extraordinary degree upon the success of his collaboration with General Hershey. At first, prospects for close cooperation seemed high. Both McNutt and Hershey had a deep commitment to a decentralized approach. Hershey's draft system revolved around the volunteer, local boards which were largely autonomous of Washington's con-

trol. Both men came from Indiana, although Hershey was no New
Dealer. A strapping six-footer, with flaming red hair, he had been
directed toward noncombat duty because of a polo accident which
had cost him the sight of one eye. Raised in Angola, Indiana, he
had rejected farming as a vocation and turned instead to teaching
as a career. After the war Hershey joined the regular army. By 1936
he was still only a major but was serving as Secretary of the Joint
Army and Navy Selective Service Committee in Washington. By
1940 he knew more about the draft system than any other man. In
August 1940 he was promoted to lieutenant colonel and three
months later he had his first star. Although Roosevelt selected
Clarence A. Dykstra, president of the University of Wisconsin, to
head the newly enacted Selective Service System in September 1940,
by April 1941 he had resigned. Hershey became head of the agency
in July 1941. For the rest of the war and for many years thereafter,
Hershey played a key role in the mobilization of American manpower.[18]

The Selective Service Act provided Hershey's power and insured
competition with McNutt. Although designed primarily to recruit
manpower for the military, the act held important implications for
general mobilization of American society. The most obvious implication revolved around section 5, which dealt with the question of
deferments.[19] McNutt correctly anticipated problems with the military over the issue of occupational deferment. The screening of
men with an eye to their essentiality in the domestic war economy
was a major part of McNutt's task. The War Department, however, took a dim view of such deferments. In 1941 it supported
unrestricted volunteer enlistments by any worker who wanted to
join the service, no matter how critical his job skill.[20] Secretary
Stimson eventually accepted industrial deferment in principle, but
he felt that particular workers should not have a continuous deferment. As for Patterson, General Hershey recalled that his "soul
was always hurt when he had to ask for the deferment of anybody."[21]

McNutt always believed that the manpower of the United States
represented a unity that could not be divided in an arbitrary fashion.
Although originally President Roosevelt refused to face the issue
squarely, he soon realized that the military could not be permitted
to pull men out of the economy in a random fashion without serious
consequences for the efficiency of mobilization. General Hershey

also understood the problem but felt that his new agency could handle both military and civilian manpower. Before the creation of the WMC in April 1942, Hershey had already warned workers in one plant to either work or be drafted, an action which led to public criticism. This reaction, plus the suspicions of Harold Smith and Donald Nelson about the dangers of military men controlling the economy, hurt Hershey's chances of being appointed manpower czar. Organized labor refused to consider him. When Roosevelt established the WMC on April 18, 1942, he turned instead to McNutt, who began his task of mobilizing manpower at a distinct disadvantage. For several months Hershey had been busy with the same job.[22]

The executive order (no. 9139) which created the WMC made clear McNutt's power to control Hershey. The order authorized McNutt to issue policy and operating directives to direct governmental agencies as to the proper allocation of available manpower. The Selective Service System was mentioned specifically as an agency which had to conform to such directives, regulations, and standards "with respect to the use and classification of manpower needed for critical industrial, agricultural and governmental employment."[23] Nothing could have been clearer. McNutt indicated he understood this language when a reporter asked him to clarify his relationship to Selective Service. He announced that "we will tell them who to defer by groups, regions, or localities." The reporter replied that Hershey was on record as opposed to group deferments. McNutt answered confidently, "Well, after all it is a question of where the determination of policy will be made." Apparently, he believed he had the authority to control Hershey. Events would prove otherwise.[24]

In early 1942 the two Hoosiers enjoyed a brief dalliance. On May 13, 1942, at an early meeting of the WMC, Hershey gave a speech on his duties. In discussing the all-important issue of job deferments, he said: "The industry must be necessary and . . . the man must be needed by industry and irreplaceable." He granted, however, that the WMC "must decide what is an essential industry. Local boards cannot do that." In fact, local boards were doing just that all across the country even as Hershey spoke. As McNutt complained a few days later, some local draft boards viewed all deferments as close to treason, while others were too liberal in granting them. McNutt had hopes that the newly published facts by the WMC on the essentiality of certain skills would be used by local boards to develop a more consistent policy. To insure compliance, the WMC issued a directive to Hershey instructing him to take action so that workers in essential war work would be temporarily deferred from induction and workers not in essential work, but qualified for it, would have time to shift jobs.[25]

The directive had little effect. Local boards acted on the basis of local prejudices in granting job deferments. No one knew why one man remained on the job and another went to fight. To make matters worse, General Hershey failed to appreciate McNutt's position. On October 5, 1942, Hershey wrote to Admiral Emory S. Land that "in no instance can the listing of an occupation as critical by an occupational bulletin [of the WMC] be considered as automatic exemption from the military. Such determination can be made only by the registrant's local board." After this statement McNutt realized that his program had little hope of success without a reorganization of his relationship with Selective Service.[26]

McNutt could bring order to manpower mobilization only if the Selective Service System marched in better step with the WMC in general and the USES in particular. Hershey had issued independently a work-or-fight order for 200,000 men in lumbering and mining, threatening to have local boards draft the men if they did not return to their jobs. McNutt now began urging upon Roosevelt a reorganization order for the WMC which would place Hershey under control. McNutt wanted all hiring done by the USES and sought to have a WMC official work directly with each local draft board to insure proper deferment policy. McNutt's thinking was logical but he ignored political reality if he expected a mere executive order to master Hershey. McNutt's organization lacked political backing. Hershey had the support of the military and Congress. The War Department fought desperately to keep Hershey independent. When Hershey heard of McNutt's campaign he emphasized his loyalty to the WMC. To John J. Corson, head of the USES, Hershey wrote that he had fought for a larger budget for that organization. "Had I been activated by narrower considerations," he explained, "I would have avoided giving assistance to what in detail might have seemed a competitor."[27]

Despite such assurances and the resistance of Stimson, Roosevelt finally gave McNutt his way by signing Executive Order no. 9279 on December 5, 1942. Roosevelt acted in the face of opposition of several governors and of the War Department which feared that local boards would lose their nonpolitical aura if given over to McNutt. The executive order authorized the chairman of the WMC to issue mandatory directives to local draft boards. At a press conference McNutt assured reporters that Hershey would be retained but that only the chairman of the WMC would make policy. While he promised to establish uniform deferment standards he also promised that local boards would remain autonomous, as they had to under the law. The contradictions escaped reporters.[28]

General Hershey had little to fear from McNutt's new unified plan. Confident of support in Congress and in the military establishment, Hershey expected and received McNutt's endorsement for independent operation. The general telegraphed all state directors on December 7, 1942, that McNutt had directed the system to operate as heretofore. In a memorandum of understanding as to Hershey's powers within the WMC, McNutt confirmed the general's independence and gave him power "to do all the other acts and exercise all the other powers, duties, and functions exercised by him prior to the issuance of Executive Order No. 9279." McNutt was only being realistic in granting Hershey such independence. Both Hershey and the local draft board system were too popular to tamper with. More importantly, Hershey's entire organization had the sanction provided by legal statute, while McNutt operated under the dispensation of a mere executive order. Yet McNutt's failure to use this opportunity to assert control over a consistent mobilization plan for all manpower guaranteed the continuation of confusion, including an inconsistent deferment policy. Given the reluctance and suspicions of Congress and the military and the temporizing of Roosevelt, perhaps a unified manpower mobilization plan was impossible, but McNutt did not really assert himself.[29]

V

Outwardly, the new arrangement seemed to work harmoniously. War as well as politics could make strange bedfellows. The two

Hoosiers, one a liberal Democrat, the other a conservative army officer, did their best to make the new system work. McNutt began 1943 by trying to force workers to stay in critical jobs under the threat of immediate induction if they left. He also released a list of nondeferrable jobs, occupations which could easily sacrifice men to the military. Hershey cooperated fully. On January 3 he ordered local boards in twelve states to draft any of the 200,000 employees in nonferrous metal mining and lumber industries who left their jobs without clearance. When the WMC issued a list of essential occupations, Hershey passed the data on to the local boards. Although Hershey continued to insist that the law prohibited any blanket deferment by occupation, he did urge local boards to give key individuals special consideration for deferments. This cooperation by Hershey had a healthy effect in recruiting war labor. After the nondeferrable list appeared, more than 30,000 men in New York City rushed into seven local USES offices looking for war work where they would be safe from the draft. Hershey sent detailed instructions to state directors of the SSS on how to cooperate with the WMC to insure the success of employment stabilization programs, such as those covering lumber, logging, and mining in the West.[30]

Even in the midst of this cooperation, however, several signs appeared pointing to the basic incompatibility of Hershey's and McNutt's ideas on manpower mobilization. Despite pages of information put out by the WMC and Hershey's directives, some local boards continued to give priority to family status over occupation in providing deferments. In Washington, McNutt wanted to draft fathers rather than cripple war industry. But local draft boards refused to believe that young, single men were irreplaceable in war industry, no matter what their skill. All the orders and directives by McNutt and Hershey could not change this attitude.[31]

McNutt's stubborn attempt to substitute job deferment for dependency deferment led to a serious reversal. Few institutions were more sacred than the American family. As late as March 1944 the American public overwhelmingly preferred to draft single women for nonfighting military jobs rather than draft fathers. Both McNutt and Hershey realized that it would be unpopular to remove the unofficial deferment granted to pre-Pearl Harbor fathers early in the war. Yet they had to do something during 1943. Given the existing manpower supply, McNutt predicted that if fathers remained exempt he would be 446,000 short for the military. His task was further complicated by the Tydings Act of November 1942 which provided exemptions for 1,567,000 farmers. The only large pool of young men remaining consisted of 5,988,000 fathers.[32]

Drastic action was needed soon. McNutt confronted the military's need for 1.5 million soldiers and sailors and also the industry's need for an additional 3.2 million workers in 1943. In January 1943 he published a list of some twenty-nine different nondeferrable jobs. Men eighteen to thirty-eight in such jobs could expect a call from the draft board unless they transferred to a war job by April. Even fathers would be drafted from such nondeferrable jobs: dependency exemptions were now ended. McNutt hoped this new order would also help him find the 3.2 million war workers who would be needed. At first glance the new order seemed reasonable. The nondeferrable jobs included such tasks as tending bar, shining shoes, teaching dance, and similar activities. Even if a man's job was listed, he could retain his deferred status by visiting a local USES office and offering to take an essential job in either civilian or war production.[33]

McNutt had bit the bullet. The war could not be won without the full participation of young married men. Although such sentiments were perfectly reasonable, McNutt had blundered badly by not preparing both the public and the Congress for this innovation. The *New York Times* editorialized that both Hershey and McNutt had exceeded their legal power by revoking dependency as a criterion for exemption. To many critics, McNutt's actions amounted to an indirect national service act, something Congress had already rejected. Was this why Roosevelt had put Hershey under McNutt?[34]

Several congressmen asked the same question. A few days after McNutt's announcement, Congressman Paul J. Kilday of Texas proposed a bill which granted married men a deferment until all eligible men without dependents were drafted. By February 18, 1943, the House Military Affairs Committee approved the bill by a vote of twenty-three to two and similar action was pending in the Senate.[35]

A running battle between Congress and the WMC began, a battle which would eventually lead to a loss of power for McNutt. Although Hershey, Stimson, and even Roosevelt agreed with McNutt that dependency deferments be removed, upon McNutt fell the onus for attacking the American home. He waited until April 12 to issue his order which put all men eighteen to thirty-eight in the 1-A category with the exception of those with deferments for essential jobs in industry and agriculture. A few hours later the House voted 143 to seven to approve the Kilday bill which required that the Selective Service induct men in a rigid order of dependency. The Kilday bill moved to the Senate and McNutt was on a collision course with Congress.[36]

At this point Senator Burton Wheeler introduced an amendment to the original Selective Service bill, granting a blanket deferment for all fathers until January 1, 1944. Wheeler, a stern isolationist, suspected that the military sought too large an army. The Roosevelt administration opposed both Wheeler's amendment and the Kilday bill. But McNutt knew the strength of public opposition and explained to Roosevelt that the main reason fathers had to be drafted was because the high physical standards of the navy and the army caused 60 percent of all registrants to be rejected. Roosevelt agreed with McNutt that the military should take more men on a limited service basis. By late May 1943 a compromise seemed possible. On May 28 the Senate Military Affairs Committee tabled the Kilday bill by unanimous vote. A few days later, McNutt announced that the navy had lowered its physical standards for draftees and that this might slow up the rate of induction of fathers. He now expected the father-draft to be delayed until early August.[37]

In approaching the father-draft, McNutt tried to act as schoolmaster to the nation. He preached the importance of sacrifice and repeated the "Don't you know there is a war on" theme. Hershey, in contrast, was more a political realist and less a moral crusader. He knew congressional opposition to such a draft could not be displaced by rhetoric. He also knew that the average citizen would never be convinced of the virtues of a system which drafted fathers while permitting young, single men to remain at home. Theoretically, McNutt was correct in calling for a substitution of dependency deferment with job deferment. Practically, however, the idea was difficult to sell. McNutt willingly carried the brief but occasionally expressed disappointment at the lack of support he received from the rest of the administration. Finally, in a cabinet meeting of July 23, 1943, he won unanimous support for his campaign against dependency deferment. Patterson even assured him that the War

Department would support his campaign with statements that large numbers of men were still needed.[38]

The public, however, remained confused over when fathers might be drafted. Hershey and McNutt had both announced that the induction would begin October 1 and that as many as 300,000 such men might be in uniform by the end of the year. Local draft boards were told to reclassify all fathers from ages eighteen to thirty-seven. Simultaneously, the WMC listed some 149 critical jobs which would provide temporary deferment to fathers who accepted them. But it was one thing to direct local boards to draft fathers and give deferments to essential workers. It was quite another thing to enforce such a policy. Local draft boards continued to go their own way. Both the USES and employers waited in vain for the rush to essential jobs. General Hershey confused the issue by announcing on August 23 that although 446,000 men with dependency deferment would be inducted in 1943 he felt that such fathers should be called only after the supply of all other men had been exhausted. Hershey seemed to be contradicting McNutt's plan for replacing dependency with job deferment. No wonder Senator Robert R. Reynolds, chairman of the Military Affairs Committee, called for an end to the contradictions between Hershey and McNutt. Congress again began to demand a definite policy on the drafting of fathers.[39]

McNutt tried to retrieve the situation through a national radio address on August 25. He stressed his need for 3,600,000 more men and women for the military and for war industry by July 1944. Some 446,000 fathers were needed by the end of the year to fill Hershey's quotas. To those who called such actions an illegal attempt to use the draft to force men into industry, McNutt shouted, "I say that is nonsense." Economic status rather than family status had to govern. In conclusion, McNutt insisted that he expected "close collaboration" between local draft boards and the USES to institute the new policies.[40]

Hershey had no such expectations. In a WMC meeting he predicted that all nondeferred single males would be drafted by November. Unless the WMC tightened up occupational deferments, the public would protest young bachelors staying home while fathers marched to war. By early September local draft board officials began resigning en masse rather than implementing the father-draft.

Hershey dismissed the entire local board no. 76 from Haverhill, Massachusetts, because it refused to draft fathers until all bachelors had been taken. The President tried to help during a press conference on September 14, 1943. When asked about the father-draft, his tongue slipped into the following malapropism: "If a married man with a child is in an essential industry in this war, he would not be drafted, but there are a good many fathers laying around who are—a good way of putting it—who are neither in the Army—nor performing any essential service."[41]

In addition to mass resignations by draft officials, McNutt and Hershey were also faced with congressional protest. Senator Sheridan Downey of California, chairman of the Senate Subcommittee on Military Affairs, supported Congressman Andrew J. May's call for a temporary halt of all inductions pending a total review of the manpower problem. Once again, to Roosevelt's dismay, manpower had become a source of congressional bickering. The President had repeatedly reviewed the manpower problem. In April 1942 the review had led to the WMC under McNutt. In December 1942 another review had led to McNutt's control of the Selective Service System. Now another review threatened beyond White House control.[42]

The Senate Military Affairs Committee called both McNutt and Hershey to appear on September 16 to clarify the manpower picture. McNutt testified but refused to budge from his support of a father-draft. He told the committee that military requirements for 1,221,000 men by the end of the year could not be met without taking pre-Pearl Harbor fathers. Few congressmen objected to meeting military needs but they did object to forcing fathers into war jobs. The senators urged instead a careful canvass of all job deferments and physical deferments. They cited cases of labor waste brought to their attention by constituents. McNutt admitted that there was no overall manpower shortage and that improper utilization had much to do with the problem, but he still insisted that fathers be drafted. When the senators invited him to suggest new legislation which would improve his control, he answered that he knew of nothing that could be done that had not been done. McNutt failed to see his opportunity. His answer was not only inaccurate, but also inappropriate. National service had not been tried. It should have been

clear to him that Congress intended to do something about manpower. By refusing to suggest reform, McNutt insured that any new
proposal would be hostile to his own position. A Gallup opinion
poll revealed that 68 percent of all Americans favored drafting
bachelors from essential jobs in war industry rather than taking
fathers. He seemed to be inviting Congress to tie his hands. To a
national radio audience he declared that the induction of men with
dependent children was not debatable. Of course, he added senten-
tiously, "it is entirely within the rights of the people of the United
States, through their Congress, to repeal these instructions." Congress agreed.[43]

VI

As early as August 13 Congress began hinting how it intended to
punish McNutt for drafting fathers. Wheeler gave up on his bill to
defer fathers, but Senator James J. Davis of Pennsylvania proposed
that Congress remove the Selective Service from McNutt's control.
Behind this suggestion was the belief that McNutt preferred to
draft fathers rather than tighten up occupational deferments. Hershey, in contrast, had the reputation of being more opposed to occupational deferments for single men. On September 20 he warned
that public morale would break down unless employers stopped
asking for job deferments for young, single males. This get-tough
outlook endeared Hershey to Congress but made enemies elsewhere.
McNutt and Patterson were both upset at the inappropriateness of
Hershey's remarks. Patterson suggested that Hershey be removed,
but Secretary Stimson demurred. Stimson regretted Hershey's
frequent forays in public print but feared that his removal would
only delay draft calls. Instead of removal, Stimson called Hershey
in and reprimanded him.[44]

If Hershey's reputation slipped with the War Department, it rose
steadily in Congress. Senator Davis's bill took shape in November.
The measure amended the original Selective Service law and called
for a review of occupational deferments. Most importantly, the bill
directly attacked the WMC's entire program by providing that pre-
Pearl Harbor fathers could only be drafted "after the induction of

other registrants not deferred, exempted, or relieved from liability. . . .'' The next section of the bill struck directly at McNutt's
work-or-fight directives by providing that "no individual shall be
called for induction because of their occupation, or by occupational
group. . . .'' This provision prevented McNutt from forcing fathers
from nondeferrable jobs into war jobs by threat of the draft. Finally,
to complete the dismantling of McNutt's efforts, the bill specified
that the President was permitted to delegate the power of the draft
only to the Director of the Selective Service. Roosevelt's executive
order of December 1942, granting McNutt control of Hershey, was
now to be revoked by Congress.[45]

McNutt recognized the threat before the bill was passed on
December 5. He immediately wrote to Senator Edwin C. Johnson
that splitting the Selective Service from the WMC would be disastrous.
Sponsors of the bill thought such an action would remove the emphasis on occupational deferment and slow the draft of fathers.
But McNutt stressed the irony of such thinking because Hershey
had been one of the first officials to stress jobs over dependency.
Now McNutt found he was to be punished by Congress for Hershey's
idea. McNutt further argued that the Davis bill was unpalatable because it divided responsibility for manpower mobilization and
made the proper allocation of workers impossible. The Truman
Committee, the Tolan Committee, and the Kilgore Committee, all
congressional investigations into manpower, had stressed the importance of a single, responsible head for the entire problem. The
Davis bill would prevent the President from integrating the draft
with the overall manpower program. In a word, the bill would
sabotage the existing manpower program.[46]

McNutt argued logically, but he missed the point. Congress had
to take some action because of the increasing public resentment
over drafting fathers. For the American public, the preservation of
a stable social order had priority over the efficiency of manpower
mobilization. Furthermore, many Americans held a quaint Jack-
sonian view of the economy. Such people refused to believe that
one man was more essential than another because of his job skill.
McNutt's attempt to push fathers into essential jobs had led to
further problems. His work-or-fight orders seemed an attempt to
implement national service without bothering with enabling legisla-

tion. Congress resented this presumption of power by a man whose political partisanship was well known. Hershey, however, would represent no such threat. He appeared to be a nonpolitical military man, honestly seeking to do his difficult task as effectively as he could. By passing the Davis bill Congress could satisfy the voters by appearing to protect fathers and at the same time punish McNutt for his overweening behavior.

Congressional action can be understood, but not Roosevelt's decision to sign the bill early in December despite McNutt's protest. The bill repudiated much of what Roosevelt had said about the importance of integrating manpower. When queried by reporters about this decision, Roosevelt justified his action by explaining that only part of the bill was bad and that a general revision of Selective Service procedure was needed. Roosevelt admitted that the bill "made for a very poor administration." Under the old system McNutt and Hershey sat side by side and that "system was going awfully well." But now, "Congress in its wisdom—always put that in—decided that they shouldn't meet any more. . . ." He explained to reporters that he was working on a new executive order by which he could follow the new law "but try to work out some liaison between them [McNutt and Hershey]."[47]

Roosevelt, in the words of Henry Wallace, was a great waterman. He could row in one direction and look in another with little effort. He seemed to be equivocating with reporters. McNutt and Hershey seldom sat side by side. The system was not "going awfully well," as witness the confusion among the public and Congress over manpower politics. More importantly, there was very little in the new bill which was needed for control of the draft. Outside of the War Department, no one in the Roosevelt administration supported the bill. When Roosevelt signed the bill it meant an end to his manpower program and should have led logically to the resignation of McNutt. Why then did Roosevelt sign it? One reason was Stimson's and Patterson's desperate desire to liberate Hershey from McNutt's control. With McNutt out of the way, Stimson expected fewer obstacles to War Department ideas.

Without the political turmoil associated with the father-draft, the President might have refused to cooperate with Stimson. Despite presidential and WMC statements, the public refused to accept the need to draft fathers. McNutt, however, had made his stand on this issue. If Roosevelt decided to buck Congress on this bill and stand behind McNutt, the legislature would become more obstreperous and uncooperative on other issues. McNutt had now become a political liability because of his stubborn support for the controversial work-or-fight program with its plan to remove dependency deferment.

In keeping with his long-standing preference, the President sought to avoid such a frontal conflict with Congress. Instead, he tried to finesse a solution by signing the law, but using a new executive order to reestablish harmony within his manpower program. On December 20, 1943, Roosevelt had Hershey in for a talk about cooperating with McNutt. The general, succumbing to the Roosevelt charm, agreed to a newly drafted executive order which was signed on December 23. The order implemented the Davis law by establishing the Selective Service as a separate agency. But a companion executive order directed Hershey to consult with McNutt before making major policy decisions. At a meeting of the WMC on December 30, Hershey, now the gracious victor, affirmed his desire to maintain continued close relations with McNutt, who would be allowed to keep his mules for the spring plowing.[48]

Regardless of Roosevelt's executive orders and Hershey's goodwill, McNutt had suffered a severe drubbing. No longer could he insist that Hershey implement WMC policy. The War Department, having already gained independence from Nelson and the War Production Board, had now succeeded in gaining independence from McNutt and the War Manpower Commission. Local draft boards continued to draft bachelors from critical jobs while avoiding fathers. The American home was safe but President Roosevelt's desire for cohesion and logic in manpower mobilization went out the window.[49]

VII

Problems arose almost immediately. McNutt and Hershey were soon at odds over the problem which had originally led to congressional intervention—the legitimacy of occupational deferments. In early 1944 several different factors provoked a crisis. The Selective

Service had recently fallen behind in filling military quotas. At the end of 1943 the army was 200,000 men short of what it was supposed to have. Stimson and Patterson believed that the only solution to the problem was a severe cutback of occupational deferments. To make the situation even more complex, General Marshall now announced that the army should have only young men from eighteen to twenty-six years old because they made the best soldiers and were easier to train. Since Stimson and Patterson thought the military the best judge of which civilian war jobs should receive deferment consideration, they hoped to work their will through Hershey without interference by McNutt.[50]

Originally, Hershey had agreed with McNutt on occupational deferments, but now he moved closer to Stimson's position. Hershey had a practical problem. His agency had failed to meet quota calls by approximately 100,000 men a month since October 1, 1943. He believed that his failure in mission was caused by occupational deferments as well as by the untouchable fathers and farmers, who were protected by congressional edict. As of February 1, 1944, the Selective Service operated with a pool of 22,200,000 men, ages eighteen to thirty-eight. Of this number some 3,204,000 had industrial deferments; 1,689,000 had agricultural deferments. Hershey had checked over the 4-F list and other groups and was convinced that these two deferred groups offered the only legitimate, additional supply of draftable men. Hershey concluded that there had to be a drastic cut of industrial deferments. He was fed up with the entire notion of a "critical" job. In his experience "once an activity becomes critical it never thereafter loses that critical character."[51]

Despite occasional exceptions, the War Department agreed with Hershey. In early February 1944 Stimson, Patterson, and Marshall launched a campaign to enlist Roosevelt's help in cutting such deferments. At a cabinet meeting of February 18, 1944, the President seemed to agree on the need and wondered whether it would be possible to have Hershey and McNutt "squeeze" young men out of deferred jobs in both industry and agriculture, replacing them with women. McNutt argued against any immediate drastic action and nothing was decided. The next week, McNutt left town for a speaking tour with the issue still up in the air. While he was away, on February 26, 1944, Roosevelt issued a directive to both Hershey

and McNutt ordering immediate review of some five million occupational deferments in order to find younger men for the draft. The
President also announced that the administration had been too
lenient with deferments for young men; he expected veterans and
women to take up the slack. This entire statement had been drafted
by General Marshall and had not been staffed with Hershey, McNutt,
or Nelson.[52]

Hershey, as a good soldier, simply followed orders. He immediately instructed all local draft boards to review all occupational
deferments of men ages eighteen through thirty-seven. The entire
concept of occupational deferments seemed in jeopardy. McNutt,
no soldier, exploded when he heard of the President taking such a
step without consultation. After being demoted in December 1943,
McNutt was in no mood for additional embarrassments. He had
always believed that industrial deferments were an essential tool in
promoting an efficient war economy. He also felt strongly that the
question of such deferments should be kept out of military hands,
where it would be if Hershey were left unchecked.[53]

The failure of Roosevelt to clear the new directive with him
added to McNutt's irritation. Ironically, McNutt was giving a speech
in Des Moines, Iowa, praising the occupational deferment system,
on the day Roosevelt pulled the rug. Returning to Washington,
McNutt stormed into the next cabinet meeting on March 3, 1944,
raging against the President. The directive, according to McNutt,
"was the most terrible body blow. It is just upsetting everything.
We can't give you the production with this order; we just can't give
it to you." Roosevelt, always uncomfortable in the midst of such
acrimony, pleaded ignorance about the order. After general pan-
demonium among cabinet members over who had been responsible,
with Roosevelt insisting "I never heard of the order" and asking
"who did it," Stimson finally admitted that he had asked Marshall
to draft the statement after clearing it by phone with the President.
Sensing that the War Department had pulled a fast one, James
Byrnes, Donald Nelson, and Harold Ickes supported McNutt's
contention that such an order would destroy the war industry. The
entire scene appeared to be out of Lewis Carroll. The President of
the United States claimed total ignorance of an order which bore
his name and which meant the drafting of thousands of young men,
single and married, industrial workers, and farmers.[54]

McNutt now began a campaign to recover his lost authority. By March 13 he had composed a memorandum for Roosevelt's signature which sought to undo the harm of the earlier presidential directive. McNutt's draft called for a review of all occupational deferments, but also insisted that needed men in plants whether under or over age twenty-six "must not be withdrawn until replacements can be obtained." The WMC would provide the SSS with direction on occupational deferments. Clearly, if Roosevelt signed this memo he would be returning to McNutt all the power he had lost and would be repudiating the War Department. Despite the odds, McNutt seemed optimistic as he left the White House on March 13 after delivering his draft. The War Department had other ideas.[55]

As a matter of course the President asked the War Department for its opinion on the proposed statement. The response was predictable. Patterson recommended to Stimson that Hershey immediately cancel all occupational and dependency deferments of men ages eighteen to twenty-one. No exceptions should be made. Next, for men ages twenty-two to twenty-five, Patterson wanted to cancel all occupational deferments except in a case when a state SSS director found a man irreplaceable in vital war industry. Finally, for men ages twenty-six to thirty-seven, Patterson felt occupational deferments should be liberalized. As McNutt sought Roosevelt's aid in affirming occupational deferments, Stimson and Patterson sought to pressure Hershey into eliminating them. Hershey, with good political sense, procrastinated because of the current uproar. Stimson refused to wait and called Hershey to a conference. He got tough and Hershey promised to cooperate. After straightening out Hershey, Stimson turned to Roosevelt. On March 13 Stimson and General Marshall arrived at the White House to plead with the President not to accept McNutt's draft statement. Marshall, always effective in such encounters, had precise figures on what the military needed. Roosevelt seemed sympathetic, as usual, but refused to commit himself.[56]

Roosevelt finally revealed his decision at a press conference the next day. The military had carried the day. McNutt had suffered another setback. In his remarks, the President emphasized the need for more young men to fight for General Marshall. Roosevelt thought that such men (under age twenty-six) would not be indispensable in industry. He ordered Hershey to have his state directors review all industrial deferments of men ages eighteen to twenty-five. No man could be considered a key worker without the recommendation of the Selective Service Director. On the surface, McNutt seemed vanquished on all fronts. Not only would the decision to remove all deferments from young men stand, but Hershey would be in charge of approving such deferments. The military apparently controlled all manpower.[57]

<h2 style="text-align:center">VIII</h2>

McNutt, stubborn as ever, refused to concede that his position had been overrun by the War Department. If he could not reverse Roosevelt's decision about drafting young men, perhaps he could insure that Hershey did not create havoc in the economy by disregarding nonmilitary factors when drafting such men. McNutt now hoped, with Nelson's support, to have the WMC act as an advisory agency to the draft boards on what was an essential deferment and what was unessential. Patterson of the War Department rejected this plan. Stimson and Patterson feared that an advisory system would be the means by which McNutt could reassert his control over Hershey, despite the statute of December 1943. In the War Department's opinion, McNutt's list of essential activities and critical occupations "have never been of any real benefit in determining deferments."[58]

After the congressional setback of December 1943 and the presidential reversal of March 1944, McNutt's ability to continue the struggle against military domination of manpower seems a remarkable testimony to his doggedness as an administrative fighter. A less-experienced or less-confident man would have resigned. Some of McNutt's stubbornness sprang from his sincere conviction that civilian control was best for the nation in the long run. But he probably also realized that his entire political future would be jeopardized by a resignation during wartime. He had little choice but to fight on if he hoped to maintain his position in national politics. He still remembered how close he had come to the vice-presidential nomination in 1940.

In reviving his career, McNutt was aided by increasing evidence that local draft boards did need help in dealing with occupational deferments. On the West Coast local draft boards pulled in highly skilled, irreplaceable, aeronautical engineers because they were under twenty-six. Donald Nelson predicted war production would be slowed. On March 18, McNutt put his cards on the table for the President. He asked Roosevelt if he wanted the WMC to perform the duties assigned to it by executive order or to hand these responsibilities to the generals and admirals? Knowing that Congress was increasingly suspicious of attempts to militarize the entire economy, McNutt was on safe ground. Roosevelt could not dismantle the WMC at this late date. Nor could he afford to alienate totally McNutt, who had support from Nelson on occupational deferments. Both McNutt and Nelson agreed that the military should have first call on men. But the needs of the military for more men made it urgent that a more definite deferment program be established.[59]

McNutt's counterattack had some prospect of success because of the support he received from other officials, especially Nelson and Harold Ickes, and also because of the uncertainty with which Hershey assumed his new responsibilities. As late as March 18, 1944, Hershey wrote Roosevelt asking him to revoke the section of Executive Order no. 9410 which required the Director of Selective Service to consult with the WMC. When Roosevelt asked James Byrnes about this request, the latter replied that the law of December 1943 had effectively canceled the executive order. Hershey, however, seemed unsure of his new authority. McNutt made use of such indecision to recover ground. At the next full cabinet meeting McNutt insisted that without deferments there would be coal shortages. Radar and rubber production would also be hurt. Yet Stimson continued to stand firm against deferments. The President seemed "more or less indifferent," according to Harold Ickes. Roosevelt had heard enough about the problem. A temporary compromise was announced on March 18 by which some 40,000 men under twenty-six in key jobs could retain deferments. McNutt had momentarily prevented a military take-over of manpower mobilization.[60]

Repeatedly at cabinet meetings McNutt assumed the authority to decide who should be drafted and who deferred. This power had passed to Hershey by law in December of 1943. Yet Roosevelt refused to challenge McNutt's continued assumption of the prerogative. McNutt was an imposing advocate at cabinet meetings, frequently offending others by shouting and lecturing. In late March he presented a new program to control occupational deferments for men ages twenty-two to twenty-five. The plan called for the WMC to request from the procurement agencies of the government a list of occupations which required deferment. The WMC would then weigh these recommendations against the needs of the military and the civilian economy. The WMC would determine the priorities for deferment and, in collaboration with Hershey, establish quotas of the maximum number of persons in the age group to be deferred for approved programs by each procurement agency.[61]

To the War Department's dismay, Roosevelt seemed receptive to McNutt's idea. The President agreed to the creation of an Inter-Agency Committee on Occupational Deferments, incorporating many of McNutt's recommendations. Under this system a man seeking an occupational deferment had to be certified by the employer, by the government procurement agency involved, and by the State Director of the Selective Service. Stimson lamented, "If only he [Roosevelt] would see what a failure McNutt has been. . . ."[62] James Byrnes pointed out to Roosevelt that the law gave Hershey full power to act without the aid of McNutt, but the President had tired of the dispute and sought a compromise.[63]

As could have been predicted, the compromise soon collapsed because it failed to resolve the fundamental question, Who was in charge of manpower—McNutt or Hershey? The showdown took place over the decision by the Inter-Agency Committee to refuse deferments to coal miners and medical and science students. McNutt opposed the decision. When an issue could not be resolved by the committee, it was supposed to be submitted to McNutt. But in this case a clear majority of the committee had supported the decision. McNutt now approached Roosevelt for a reversal. At a cabinet meeting on Friday, April 7, 1944, Roosevelt, just recovered from a lingering viral infection, brought the problem up by announcing that he favored deferments for coal miners. Now, as he was on the brink of success, McNutt revealed the strain he had been under by losing control. Instead of merely accepting Roosevelt's statement and using it to obtain a reversal by the committee, McNutt lashed out at the many problems which had been besetting him over the past weeks. He denounced the Inter-Agency Committee, the WMC, and Hershey. He announced that he would make recommendations to Hershey, regardless of what the committee recommended. The executive order creating the WMC had provided such authority and McNutt now wanted Roosevelt to either affirm his commitment or dismantle the agency. The President, stunned by McNutt's aggressiveness, refused to take a stand until a particular issue came up. As McNutt became more contentious, Roosevelt responded in kind. Stimson, fearing for the President's health, jumped in to attack McNutt and defend Hershey, who was absent. Byrnes reminded McNutt that Congress wanted Hershey to have the final decision. When tempers cooled McNutt realized he had failed to bully the President into reasserting WMC control over Hershey. The President resented McNutt's tone and could no longer be counted on for support. Stimson left the meeting convinced that "the whole manpower problem and evil centers around the personality of McNutt."[64]

Hershey, while missing the battle, emerged the clear victor in the fight with McNutt. From this time until the end of the war, anyone who wanted action on occupational deferments knew that Hershey, not McNutt, was in charge. McNutt continued to make recommendations through the Inter-Agency Committee but he had no control over decisions. The essential job list of the WMC was temporarily resurrected by Byrnes in January 1945, but Hershey used it only as a guide. From March 1944 onward Hershey took orders from Byrnes and Roosevelt, not from McNutt.

Ironically, the battle may have been fought over an imaginary problem. The crisis resulted in part from the dire need of the military for more young men in early 1944 (1,160,000 from January to June 30). The army insisted it needed quality and quantity. But as Hershey fought McNutt and began a review of some two million deferments, the army changed its mind. Millard White, the GI at the War Department, told Hershey in early April that the "Army would soon be overstrength if the draft continued." The War Department now asked Hershey to stop inductions for April. On May 11, 1944, as a result of decreased military manpower demands, Hershey issued orders staying the induction of most men ages twenty-six through twenty-nine for at least six months and deferring older men indefinitely. He announced that if men over thirty stayed in vital war work they would not be called. The Senate Committee Investigation of Defense Industry, to further embarrass the military, disclosed through its new chairman, Senator James M.

Mead of New York, that a study of the draft of formerly deferred young, highly trained experts revealed that most of them ended up doing clerical work. Hershey's new draft policy, said Mead, had been a mistake.[65]

Throughout the rest of the war General Hershey managed to resist McNutt's embrace. Although Hershey was always reluctant to yield any authority to McNutt's "conglomerate of an organization," the two agencies did work together in the field. When the administration made its last attempt to pass a national service act in January 1945, Hershey asked for reports from state directors on how well the voluntary manpower program was working. Uniformly, the various regions reported a high degree of cooperation among the WMC, the USES, and the SSS. This cooperation soon became an essential part in the major task of 1945, reconversion to a peace-time economy.[66]

Notes

1. See Bruce Catton, *The War Lords of Washington* (New York: Harcourt, Brace, 1948), pp. 114ff, for the sad lament of a civilian administrator over the military control of the economy. Donald Nelson, *Arsenal of Democracy* (New York: Harcourt, Brace, 1946), pp. 385-90, makes the same point. But for the other side see Byron Fairchild and Jonathan Grossman, *The Army and Industrial Manpower* (Washington, D.C.: U.S. Department of the Army, 1959), p. 20, who argue that the military was forced to assume a vigorous role in industrial manpower because of the weakness of the civilian agencies.

2. Digest of War Production Board minutes, October 6, 1942, box 12, Donald Nelson Papers, Huntington Library, San Marino, Calif.; Albert A. Blum, *Drafted or Deferred: Practices Past and Present* (Ann Arbor: University of Michigan Press, 1967), p. 33; John J. O'Sullivan, "From Voluntarism to Conscription: Congress and Selective Service, 1940-1945" (Ph.D. dissertation, Columbia University, 1971), p. 223; Fairchild and Grossman, *Army and Manpower*, p. 45.

3. Digest of WPB minutes, October 6, 1942, box 12, Nelson Papers; McNutt to Deane, September 16, 1942, official file (OF) 4905, Franklin Roosevelt Papers, Roosevelt Library, Hyde Park, N.Y.; Blum, *Drafted or Deferred*, pp. 36-38; O'Sullivan, "Voluntarism to Conscription," p. 247; *New York Times*, September 23, 1943, pp. 1, 16.

4. Quote from Stimson Diary (October 2, 1942), 40: 120, Henry Stimson Papers, Yale University Library, New Haven, Conn.; Stimson memorandum to Marshall, October 2, 1942, box 140, folder 30, Stimson Papers; Fairchild and Grossman, *Army and Manpower*, pp. 47-49; *New York Times*, December 20, 1942; Blum, *Drafted or Deferred*, p. 36.

5. Fairchild and Grossman, *Army and Manpower*, pp. 50-52; *New York Times*, February 11, 1943, p. 1, February 14, 1943, p. 6, March 14, 1943, sec. 4, pp. 2, 7, and March 17, 1943, p. 15.

6. Allen Drury, *A Senate Journal, 1943-1945* (New York: McGraw-Hill, 1963), pp. 302-3; Haber to Patterson, December 1, 1944, box 155, Robert Patterson Papers, Library of Congress, Washington, D.C.; Patterson to Haber, December 8, 1944, *ibid*.

7. Colonel Gow to Patterson, April 17, 1945, May 15, 1945, and July 10, 1945, box 184-5, Patterson Papers; Herman M. Somers, *Presidential Agency: OWMR, The Office of War Mobilization and Reconversion* (Cambridge: Harvard University Press, 1950), pp. 120ff.

8. Stimson Diary (November 17, 1941), 36: 31 (January 1, 1942), 37: 3 (January 30, 1942), 37: 78.

9. *Ibid*. (April 21, 1942), 38: 133 (April 27, 1942), 38: 147-48 (May 12, 1942), 39: 7, (June 29, 1942), 39: 130; cabinet meeting notes, April 24, 1942, box 171, series 11, folder 14, Stimson Papers.

10. Blum, *Drafted or Deferred*, pp. 24-26; minutes of War Manpower Commission (WMC), October 24, 1942, box 5-100, Record Group (RG) 211, National Archives, Washington, D.C.; Stimson Diary (October 14, 1942), 40: 152 (October 20, 1942), 40: 165 (October 30, 1942), 40: 185 (November 5, 1942), 41: 12, and (November 11, 1942), 41: 37.

11. Stimson Diary, (December 10, 1942), 41: 79, and (December 11, 1942), 41: 83.

12. Presidential Conference no. 13, December 18, 1942, Harold Smith Papers, Franklin Roosevelt Library; Stimson Diary (December 18, 1942), 41: 100-1 (December 19, 1942), 41: 103 (December 20, 1942), 41: 104-5, and (December 21, 1942), 41: 107; Stimson to Roosevelt, draft letter, December 24, 1942, box 141, Stimson Papers; Roosevelt to Stimson, December 17, 1942, *ibid*.; Stimson to Roosevelt, December 18, 1942, *ibid*.

13. Quote from Fairchild and Grossman, *Army and Manpower*, p. 104; see also *ibid*., pp. 107-17, 119-20; Nelson, *Arsenal*, p. 150; McNutt to Patterson, March 22, 1943, Patterson Papers.

14. Albert A. Blum, "Sailor or Worker: A Manpower Dilemma during the Second World War," *Labor History* 6 (Fall 1965), p. 232; Stimson to Roosevelt, November 18, 1942, OF 4905, Roosevelt Papers; Stimson and Knox to workers, November 20, 1942, box 183, Patterson Papers; *Complete Presidential Press Conferences of Franklin D. Roosevelt*, 25 vols. in 12 books (New York: Da Capo Press, 1972), 20: 290-91 (December 11, 1942), hereafter cited as *PPC*; McNutt, "Allocation of Manpower," June 26, 1943, Paul V. McNutt Papers, The Lilly Library, Indiana University, Bloomington, Ind.

15. Notes of cabinet meeting, February 6, 1942, box 171, series ii, folder 11, Stimson Papers; James Mitchell to Patterson, January 13, 1944, box 182, Patterson Papers.

16. Fairchild and Grossman, *Army and Manpower*, pp. 35-37; Patterson to McNutt, December 23, 1943, box 184, Patterson Papers.

17. Cabinet meeting notes [n.d.], Stimson Diary, 43: 123; McCloy to McNutt, June 28, 1944, box 185, Patterson Papers; McNutt to Patterson, March 16, 1944, box 184, *ibid.*; Appley to Patterson, August 9, 1943, box 184-5, *ibid.*; McNutt notes, September 23, 1944, McNutt Papers; McNutt to Major General Henry Aurand, October 20, 1944, *ibid.*; McNutt to Lieutenant General Brehon Somervell, March 28, 1945, *ibid.*; McNutt speech at Army Day luncheon, April 6, 1945, *ibid.* The army also helped McNutt import alien labor from the West Indies.

18. Blum, *Drafted or Deferred*, p. 28; O'Sullivan, "Voluntarism to Conscription," pp. 122, 144, 315; Hershey to Alma Richardson, November 8, 1942, staybacks, 1942, General Lewis B. Hershey Papers, Military History Research Collection, Carlisle Barracks, Pa.

19. Blum, *Drafted or Deferred*, p. 13; O'Sullivan, "Voluntarism to Conscription," pp. 55, 72.

20. Blum, "Sailor to Worker," p. 233; Hershey to Stimson, March 16, 1942, and March 26, 1942, staybacks, 1942, Hershey Papers; *New York Times*, January 10, 1943, p. 27.

21. Blum, *Drafted or Deferred*, p. 26; O'Sullivan, "Voluntarism to Conscription," p. 318; Patterson to McNutt, March 12, 1943, box 184, Patterson Papers.

22. Hershey to Roosevelt, March 28, 1942, staybacks, 1942, Hershey Papers; Stimson Diary (September 29, 1941), 23: 96; interview with General Lewis B. Hershey, Bethesda, Md., May 26, 1975; Hershey to Colonel Frank McSherry, January 30, 1942, staybacks, 1942, Hershey Papers.

23. Samuel I. Rosenman, ed., *The Public Papers and Addresses of Franklin D. Roosevelt*, 13 vols. (New York: Harper and Row, 1938-1950), 11: 201.

24. McNutt news conference, April 20, 1942, McNutt Papers.

25. W.MC minutes, May 13, 1942, box 5-100, RG 211; McNutt speech file, May 20, 1942, McNutt Papers; *Monthly Labor Review*, August 1942, p. 225.

26. Hershey to Admiral Land, October 5, 1942, staybacks, 1942, Hershey Papers; *New York Times*, September 20, 1942, sec. 4, p. 7; Hershey to J. P. Schaefer, November 4, 1942, staybacks, 1942, Hershey Papers; Henry Morgenthau Presidential Diary (October 2, 1942), 5: 1188, Franklin Roosevelt Library; Stimson Diary (September 24, 1942) 40: 98, and (September 29, 1942), 40: 108.

27. *New York Times*, September 20, 1942, sec. 4, p. 7, October 27, 1942, p. 19, November 1, 1942, sec. 4, p. 7, November 3, 1942, p. 1, and November 24, 1942, p. 16; Hershey to Corson, December 2, 1942, staybacks, 1942-1943, Hershey Papers.

28. Lubin to Hopkins, October 21, 1942, file 324, Harry Hopkins Papers, Roosevelt Library; Stimson to Roosevelt, November 5, 1942, OF 4905, Roosevelt Papers; Smith to Roosevelt, October 14, 1942, *ibid.*; see also OF 1413, *ibid.* for governors' reaction; *Monthly Labor Review*, January 1943, pp. 26-27; minutes of McNutt press conference, December 4, 1942, McNutt Papers.

29. Hershey to State Directors, December 7, 1942, staybacks, 1942-1943, Hershey Papers; Administrative Order no. 26 by McNutt, December 5, 1942, copy in index file, Hershey Papers; quote from Lt. Col. Shattuck to B. C. Gavit, December 9, 1942, index file, Hershey Papers.

30. *New York Times*, January 4, 1943, sec. 9, p. 6, and February 14, 1943, p. 1; *Monthly Labor Review*, May 1943, p. 1025; Hershey to Patterson, March 19, 1943, staybacks, 1942-1943, Hershey Papers.

31. McNutt speech, October 20, 1943, McNutt Papers; *New York Times*, May 25, 1943, p. 17, quote from September 5, 1943, p. 1. Hershey and McNutt also disagreed over the procedure to insure that job deferments would be only temporary. Both men agreed that such deferments would be limited to a few months but disagreed over how to implement the limit. Hershey favored a replacement schedule by which each employer would submit a schedule to the state director of Selective Service of when local boards could draft men currently deferred. McNutt felt such a system relied too much on the good faith of the employer. The WMC pressed for a manning-table system to determine whether or not these deferred workers were really essential. In the end, both systems were used. See *New York Times*, November 24, 1942, p. 16, and May 18, 1943, p. 15.

32. George Gallup, ed., *The Gallup Poll: Public Opinion, 1935-1971*, 3 vols. (New York: Random House, 1972), 1: 435; McNutt speech [n.d.], 1943, McNutt Papers; Hershey to Colonel Kramer, March 2, 1942, staybacks, 1942, Hershey Papers; Blum, *Drafted or Deferred*, pp. 57-61, says eight million men were deferred because of dependency in 1943.

33. *Monthly Labor Review*, May 1943, p. 1025; *New York Times*, February 3, 1943, p. 1, and February 14, 1943, p. 1; McNutt radio address, February 13, 1943, McNutt Papers.

34. *New York Times*, February 4, 1943, p. 22, and February 7, 1943, sec. 4, p. 6.

35. *Ibid.*, February 6, 1943, p. 1, February 19, 1943, p. 1, and February 21, 1943, sec. 4, p. 1.

36. Hershey to Roosevelt, March 28, 1942, staybacks, 1942, Hershey Papers; *New York Times*, March 9, 1943, p. 15, March 31, 1943, p. 12, and April 13, 1943, pp. 1, 13; *Monthly Labor Review*, August 1943, p. 399.

37. *New York Times*, April 11, 1943, sec. 4, p. 7, May 1, 1943, p. 20, May 6, 1943, p. 9, and May 23, 1943, sec. 4, p. 12; Stimson cabinet meeting notes, May 7, 1943, box 171, Stimson Papers; WMC minutes, May 13, 1942, box 5-100, RG 211; *New York Times*, May 29, 1943, p. 1, and June 1, 1943, p. 25.

38. *New York Times*, June 4, 1943, sec. 4, p. 9, June 15, 1943, p. 1, and June 20, 1943, sec. 4, p. 2. Major Emmett Solomon of the Selective Service announced in mid-July that pre-Pearl Harbor fathers would not be drafted until well after October at the earliest. *New York Times*, July 16, 1943, p. 1; Patterson to Stimson, July 23, 1943, box 171, Stimson Papers; Harold L. Ickes Diary (July 25, 1943), 10: 8021, Library of Congress, Washington, D.C.

39. *New York Times*, August 3, 1943, p. 1, August 15, 1943, p. 1, August 17, 1943, p. 1, August 24, 1943, p. 1, and August 22, 1943, p. 15; *Monthly Labor Review*, November 1943, p. 1038.

40. McNutt speech, August 25, 1943, McNutt Papers.

41. WMC minutes, August 26, 1942, box 5-100, RG 211; *New York Times*, September 9, 1943, p. 52; *PPC* (September 14, 1943), 22: 96-98.

42. *New York Times*, September 12, 1943, sec. 4, p. 2, and September 14, 1943, p. 15.

43. *New York Times*, September 17, 1943, p. 1, September 19, 1943, sec. 4, p. 10, September 21, 1943, p. 1, and September 24, 1943, p. 15; McNutt speech, September 19, 1943, and September 21, 1943, McNutt Papers.

44. *New York Times*, August 13, 1943, p. 10, and October 1, 1943, p. 13; Stimson Diary (October 11, 1943), 44: 186.

45. U. S., *Statutes at Large*, vol. 57, pt. 1, pp. 596-99, 78th Cong., 1st sess., 1943.

46. McNutt to Johnson, November 22, 1943, McNutt Papers.

47. *PPC* (December 17, 1943), 22: 224-26. Roosevelt signed the bill while attending the Teheran Conference.

48. *PPC* (December 21, 1943), 22: 235-36; *New York Times*, December 24, 1943, p. 19, December 25, 1943, p. 6, and December 19, 1943, p. 41; WMC minutes, December 30, 1943, box 5-100, RG 211.

49. When Hershey gained his independence a pool of some 5,917,000 pre-Pearl Harbor fathers was stagnating around the country. By February 1, 1944, some 3,367,000 were reclassified to 1-A. Of these, 2,505,000 were either drafted or deferred. Of those drafted, only 161,000 were actually inducted into the military. Congress had done its work well. See Hershey to Stimson, February 26, 1944, War Department correspondence, 1944-1945, Hershey Papers.

50. Blum, *Drafted or Deferred*, pp. 125-32; Stimson Notes, February 18, 1944, box 172, Stimson Papers; Stimson Diary (March 13, 1944), 46: 94 (March 22, 1944), 46: 118 (March 27, 1944), 46: 131, and (December 13, 1944), 49: 90.

51. Patterson to Hershey, February 12, 1944, box 183, Patterson Papers; Hershey to Stimson, February 26, 1944, staybacks, 1943-1944, Hershey Papers; Hershey to Bard, January 19, 1944, index file, *ibid.*

52. Stimson Notes, February 18, 1944, box 172, folder 1, Stimson Papers; William D. Hassett, *Off the Record with F.D.R., 1942-1945* (New Brunswick, N.J.: Rutgers University Press, 1958), p. 237; Blum, "Sailor or Workers," p. 237; Blum, *Drafted or Deferred*, pp. 125-32; *New York Times*, February 27, 1944, p. 1; Stimson Diary (March 13, 1944), 46: 94 (March 22, 1944) 46: 118 (March 27, 1944) 46: 13, and (December 13, 1941), 49: 90.

53. Catton, *War Lords*, p. 236; Hershey to Stimson, February 28, 1944, War Department correspondence, 1944-1945, Hershey Papers; *New York Times*, March 10, 1944, p. 1.

54. *New York Times*, January 11, 1944, p. 21; Morgenthau Presidential Diary (March 3, 1944), 5: 1334; Ickes Diary (March 11, 1944), 11: 8702.

55. Digest of WPB minutes, March 7, 1944, box 12, Donald Nelson Papers, Huntington Library, San Marino, Calif.; *New York Times*, March 14, 1944, p. 1; draft of memorandum, Roosevelt to McNutt, March ?, 1944, box 184, Patterson Papers.

56. *New York Times*, March 14, 1944, p. 1; Patterson to Stimson, March 12, 1944, box 184, Patterson Papers; Stimson Diary (March 13, 1944), 46: 95; Patterson to Stimson, March 15, 1944, box 184, Patterson Papers.

57. *New York Times*, March 15, 1944, p. 1, March 16, 1944, p. 1, and March 18, 1944, p. 1.

58. Patterson to Stimson, March 15, 1944, box 184-5, Patterson Papers; Clay to Patterson, March 15, 1944, *ibid.*; Patterson and Knox to Roosevelt, March 18, 1944, OF 4905, Roosevelt Papers.

59. *New York Times*, March 12, 1944, p. 29, and March 17, 1944, p. 1; McNutt to Roosevelt, March 18, 1944, OF 4905, Roosevelt Papers.

60. Hershey to Roosevelt, March 1, 1944, OF 4905, Roosevelt Papers; Ickes Diary (March 20, 1944), 11: 8724; digest of War Production Board minutes, March 21, 1944, box 12, Nelson Papers; Ickes Diary (March 21, 1944), 11: 8745; John Blum, ed., *The Price of Vision: The Diary of Henry A. Wallace, 1942-1946* (Boston: Houghton Mifflin, 1973), p. 312.

61. Memorandum, March 23, 1944, box 184-5, Patterson Papers; Morgenthau Presidential Diary (March 17, 1944), 5: 1349.

62. Somers, *Presidential Agency*, p. 164; Blum, *Drafted or Deferred*, pp. 133-37; Stimson Diary (March 22, 1944), 46: 118 (March 27, 1944), 46: 131, and (December 13, 1944), 49: 90.

63. Stimson Diary (March 23, 1944), 46: 122, and (March 24, 1944), 46: 124-25; Clay to Patterson, March 24, 1944, box 184-5, Patterson Papers; Stimson to Byrnes, telephone notes, March 24, 1944, box 172, Stimson Papers.

64. Clay to Patterson, April 6, 1944, 181, box 184-5, Patterson Papers; Stimson Diary (April 7, 1944), 46: 164-65; Ickes Diary (April 9, 1944), n.p.

65. *New York Times*, March 26, 1944, sec. 4, p. 4, and May 12, 1944, p. 1; interview with General Lewis B. Hershey, Bethesda, Md., May 26, 1975; Blum, *Drafted or Deferred*, p. 43; Catton, *War Lords*, pp. 237-38.

66. Quotes from O'Sullivan, "Voluntarism to Conscription," p. 249; for Hershey's sense of superiority to McNutt see Hershey to Larry MacPhail of the Brooklyn Dodgers, January 22, 1942, staybacks, 1942, Hershey Papers, in which the general announced that "only the SSS can determine where a man should go in industry or war production." See also U.S., Congress, House, Committee on Military Affairs, hearings on *Mobilization of Civilian Manpower*, H.R. 1119, 79th Cong., 1st sess., 1945, pp. 110-15; speech by Colonel Keesling, January 12, 1945, index file, Hershey Papers; Carol Riegelman, *Labour-Management Co-operation in United States War Production* (Montreal: International Labour Office, 1948), pp. 281-82; reports from the field, January 16, 1945, 79th Cong. file, Hershey Papers; McNutt file of January 9, 1945, McNutt Papers.

CHAPTER 10

The Mandate Lost and Reconversion

McNutt's struggle with Hershey and the War Department represented only one more aspect of the gradual deterioration of his manpower mandate. As he sought to bring order to the manpower problem, McNutt faced constant political challenges from Congress and from other members of the administration. In early 1943 he looked toward a promising future. On January 9, at his first press conference of the year, Roosevelt told reporters that "marked progress has been made in mobilizing manpower." Industrial production was up by 46 percent, agricultural production by 15 percent. The new year, however, would present even greater challenges. Although some ten million people had been added to both industry and the military since the summer of 1940, some six million more would be needed in both areas in 1943. The supply would soon be stretched taut.[1]

I

Several days after this press conference President Roosevelt issued an executive order requiring a forty-eight hour week in all war industry. The idea of such a work extension had been debated for several months. The Fair Labor Standards Act of 1938 established the forty-hour week as the norm in industry engaged in interstate business and required that the employer pay time and a half for anything beyond this limit. Neither McNutt nor Roosevelt, as friends of organized labor, desired to sacrifice this social advance on the altar of economic mobilization. Throughout 1942 there seemed little need for any new ruling on the average work week. Workers flocked into industry. Management remained unworried about paying over-time beyond the forty-hour limit because of lucrative government contracts. In April 1942 McNutt asserted that production had not been delayed by the forty-hour week. Production did not rise in direct proportion to the number of hours worked. Instead, absen-teeism and turnovers rose. McNutt sought optimum hours, not maximum hours.[2]

As was the case with so many issues during Roosevelt's presidency, the question of establishing a forty-eight-hour work week soon be-came part of a political debate. Whenever a manpower shortage was reported in the country, Congress responded by considering measures to reduce the power of organized labor, which had waxed strong under the New Deal. By early 1943 antilabor leaders in Con-gress began pushing the forty-eight-hour week idea. According to their arguments, war production was being hindered by the Fair Labor Standards Act with its overtime pay requirements. Several bills emerged in Congress designed to gut the Fair Labor Standards Act. Roosevelt and McNutt saw these bills as a product of congenital antilabor attitudes combined with an ignorance of the nature of the manpower problem. Oscar Cox, a New Dealer serving in the Justice Department, immediately advised Roosevelt to anticipate and frus-trate such antiunion legislation by issuing an executive order ex-plaining that the FLSA did not prevent men from working more than forty hours and that many industries were exceeding this norm. Secretary of Labor Perkins, in contrast, urged the President to stay out of the dispute. Perkins believed the entire labor-management structure in the United States was now in a precarious balance. A heavy-handed intervention by the President might have disastrous results.[3]

As Perkins expressed her opinion, McNutt appeared before the Senate Subcommittee on Appropriations on January 28, 1943. He informed the senators that a pending bill raising minimum hours before overtime pay to forty-eight per week would not help the manpower problem. "It is the considered judgment of all of the procurement agencies," he insisted, "that any attempt to change the 40 hour week, that is, the wage aspect of it, would cause more loss of production than any one thing that could be done today, because of the necessity of renegotiating all these contracts."[4]

McNutt had as much sympathy for labor as had Cox, but the latter was dissatisfied with such statements. Cox pursued his plan by drafting an executive order for Roosevelt but first staffing it with McNutt. A secret poll conducted by the Office of War Information showed that some 83 percent of the public thought the number of hours worked should be increased and 33 percent thought forty-eight hours should be the new minimum. The Cox order would give McNutt power to increase the minimum hour limit wherever it was needed. McNutt knew of Cox's plan even as he assured senators that raising the minimum hour norm would be of little use.[5]

Despite the potential for confusion, Roosevelt signed the Cox draft as Executive Order no. 9301 on February 9, 1943. The order provided that "for the duration of the war, no plant, factory, or other place of employment shall be deemed to be making the most effective utilization of its manpower if the minimum work week therein is less than 48 hours per week." Roosevelt gave McNutt the responsibility for determining all questions about the implementation of the order. Finally, the President ordered that nothing in the statement should supersede or conflict with any federal, state, or local law limiting hours of work; "nor shall this Order be construed as suspending or modifying any provisions of the Fair Labor Standards Act."[6]

The real purpose of the order, the political purpose, was stated last—the defense of the FLSA from unfriendly congressional attacks. The preceding provisions made little sense. Surely the President did not intend that every factory in the nation must change to a forty-eight-hour week or be charged with inefficiency. McNutt had worked to insure that nondefense-related industry remained understaffed and underworked. McNutt himself blinked in puzzlement over the order and called on Attorney General Francis Biddle for an explanation of the legal problems. He asked how he could enforce an order involving hours of work when this subject was usually established by a contract between unions and employers.[7]

Whatever McNutt's confusion over the order, he wasted little time carrying out his new responsibility. Within twenty-four hours he had extended the forty-eight-hour rule to thirty-two labor-short areas by prohibiting companies working less than the minimum from recruiting additional workers. William Green of the AFL approved of Roosevelt's order and McNutt's action but warned against trying to impose a work week beyond forty-eight hours.[8]

Although the forty-eight-hour order owed its origins to an attempt by the administration to defend the Fair Labor Standards Act, neither Roosevelt nor McNutt could admit mere political motivation. Instead, McNutt drew up an elaborate program of implementation and the entire idea developed its own momentum. After ordering the plan into effect for labor-short areas, he delegated authority to regional directors to extend the coverage wherever the longer shift would help cure a shortage. McNutt cautioned against applying the order in "areas and industries where its net effect would be merely to release workers who could not be readily absorbed in employment. . . ." Ironically, a literal implementation of Roosevelt's order might create unemployment.[9]

McNutt added provisions for exceptions justifying a work week of less than forty-eight hours. In several industries such a work week was impracticable because of triple-shift arrangements. In other cases, working forty-eight hours was unsuited to the task at hand. In several areas the forty-eight-hour week conflicted with state and local law. Despite these obstacles, McNutt continued to insist that there would be no blanket release from the order and warned that plants refusing to cooperate would be denied additional labor. McNutt also designated eleven cities for immediate application of the forty-eight-hour rule. Plants in these cities had to follow McNutt's guidelines: no new labor could be hired unless plants went on a forty-eight-hour schedule and they had to release any surplus labor generated by the longer work week.[10]

Most Americans applauded the forty-eight-hour order. Walter Reuther of the United Auto Workers joined William Green in praising the idea but wanted McNutt to extend the order to all war industry. Labor leaders had an eye on the increased paychecks which would come to their constituents. Management was not as enthusiastic as labor. Eric Johnson, president of the Chamber of Commerce of America, warned that the longer work week would merely fan the flames of inflation. Management officials of the WMC repeated this complaint and grumbled that McNutt had once again demonstrated his prounion bias.[11]

In executing the order McNutt revealed again his commitment to Jeffersonianism, to winning the war and to holding the line on the labor advances of the New Deal. While he could have extended the order to the entire nation, he did not feel it was needed. The manpower problem remained a network of local problems. McNutt rejected the notion that one answer dreamed up in Washington would be superior to plans conceived in a local area by a regional director in immediate contact with local management-labor committees. He assured his critics that the WMC represented a "sincere and earnest effort to show that a Federal agency can operate in such a way as to leave home town decisions to home town people. . . ."[12]

By October 1943 McNutt had expanded the forty-eight-hour rule to cover some seventy-one areas with labor shortages. By May 1944 the order covered nonferrous mining and smelting, metals, logging, iron and steel, lumbering, and cotton textile industries. A total of 136 urban areas operated under the rule. *Business Week* announced that here was one WMC rule that "really is working."[13]

II

In addition to coping with the forty-eight-hour rule, McNutt also had to deal with the politically sensitive task of draft deferments for members of the federal government. Nothing could embarrass the President more, nor delight his enemies more, than the administration being a haven for draft dodgers. Under the executive order of December 1942, McNutt had overall responsibility for such deferments. An old friend, Frank M. McHale of Indianapolis, wrote McNutt, warning, "if you don't do something soon you will be destroyed, so protect yourself now." McNutt agreed and proceeded on the assumption that government workers should receive the same treatment as anyone else. He called for an immediate reduction in personnel for all work not directly related to the war effort. If necessary, McNutt threatened to seek legislation from Congress. Duplication of service "shall be dealt with summarily," he promised. He also asked all government officials to perform an act of self-examination about the essentiality of their task. The WMC stood ready to provide assistance on improving labor utilization.[14]

McNutt preached a strong line on limiting deferments but he lacked the political muscle to push around Harold Ickes, the Secretary of the Interior, and Francis Biddle, the Attorney General. Both men sought deferments for key personnel in their departments. When McNutt refused to satisfy them, they went to Roosevelt who responded with a note supporting their cause. Privately, the President wrote McNutt that "a liberal attitude should be taken . . . where the Department requests classification of key positions." Roosevelt urged McNutt to meet with Ickes and Biddle to iron out the problem. Such a compromise was difficult to execute. McNutt, Smith, and several members of Congress felt the executive branch should set an example of sacrifice for the nation. Biddle, in contrast, could not accept McNutt's attitude that one lawyer was as good as another. As a former dean of a law school, however, McNutt had more insight in this area than did Biddle. The disagreement became heated during the cabinet meeting of July 23. As the President entered he heard McNutt, Ickes, and Biddle shouting at each other. Biddle and Ickes accused McNutt of having an absurd criterion for deferment. McNutt defended his position and denounced his critics for appealing over his head to Roosevelt. The shouting died down as the President took his seat, but Biddle refused to end the argument. At the first opportunity he spoke of the mess in manpower and of the illegality of military men such as General Hershey passing on deferment appeals. McNutt explained that the military men in question were only reservists. In the middle of the dispute Byrnes suggested to Roosevelt that an impartial arbiter such as Judge Sam Rosenman be brought in to solve the problem. Roosevelt jumped at this chance to freeze the conundrum while a new review could be made. But McNutt had suffered a setback. The executive order creating the WMC had specifically authorized McNutt to prescribe basic policy on the manpower needs of the federal bureaucracy.[15]

Rosenman could handle the special pleas of Ickes and Biddle, which was all Roosevelt desired, but the judge could not assume the task of passing on all federal deferments. A WMC appeal board handled hundreds of cases from federal workers. McNutt had grounds for defending his work because federal deferments were well within reason. In September 1943 General Hershey reported that only 42,296 single civilians of draft age had government deferments.[16]

Despite this record, part of McNutt's authority was removed. Roosevelt's decision to appoint Rosenman, however, had other implications than the deferment program. The President was upset at the political squabbles between Ickes, Biddle, and McNutt. Roosevelt was disappointed in McNutt's inability to compromise and solve disputes before they reached the cabinet level or Congress. In Congress Senator James E. Murray and Congressman Paul J. Kilday suggested that McNutt be fired. Even Harold Smith, who had been instrumental in expanding McNutt's power in December 1942, now became disillusioned. McNutt did not seem to know how to use his new powers effectively. Roosevelt could not afford to allow manpower mobilization to become enmeshed in personal political feuds. The War Department was already calling for national service. The President decided to appoint Rosenman to head a special ad hoc committee to investigate manpower.[17]

In early March 1943 Roosevelt asked Bernard Baruch, James Byrnes, Admiral William D. Leahy, and Harry Hopkins to join Rosenman on this committee. These men had Roosevelt's confidence and much political experience. Their general knowledge of manpower, however, was rather primitive. Hopkins, for example, mistakenly believed that the administration had to find twelve million additional workers during 1943 to staff war industry. None of the members of the committee had kept up with recent manpower developments, but in the next few weeks they held six meetings and heard testimony from a variety of experts including McNutt, Nelson, Wickard, Hershey, and others. Reporters, hearing of the committee's activities, spread the word that McNutt's head was on the block.[18]

During the investigation various individuals presented testimony which only confirmed their public positions. Military representatives called for more men and younger men for the draft. Organized labor representatives opposed any talk of national service. Donald Nelson opposed a labor draft but reported that war industry would need an additional 1,800,000 war workers by November 1943. Both Nelson and Charles Wilson of the War Production Board urged the removal of union restrictions on factory procedures and the adoption of an incentive payment plan to solve the manpower crisis. McNutt appeared and defended the success of his agency.[19]

The committee heard additional testimony before finally rendering a report to Roosevelt on March 14. McNutt's future hung in the balance. The committee concluded that it would be impossible to satisfy all labor needs for 1943 under current arrangements. Although McNutt's administration could be vastly improved, "even with a 100 percent administration, the job can just about be done on a voluntary basis." As a solution the committee recommended that "under no circumstances should the 11,100,000 figure for the military be changed." Second, the administration of the WMC had to be improved. The WMC's major problem seemed to be poor relations with other federal agencies and with Congress. McNutt had made a mistake in delegating authority to Wickard for farm labor. The committee felt Wickard incompetent and urged his removal. As for McNutt himself, the committee admitted that part of the problem was the fault of Congress which refused to support the WMC. While "the economy of the country has not yet been mobilized to meet the demands being made upon it for total war," the WMC did have a good plan based on voluntarism. The committee concluded: "We recommend that the set-up in the WMC be continued and given a chance to carry out their [sic] program, but that help be given . . . especially to obtain necessary Congressional action." Because there was considerable congressional resentment to McNutt, "further consideration should be given to the question of changing the Chairman of the Manpower Commission."[20]

President Roosevelt could not bring himself to swing the ax. The President disliked firing anyone. Reporters were anxious to learn if the confidential committee report had ended McNutt's career, but Roosevelt dissembled in reply. He insisted to reporters that there "aren't any, no findings of fact." Reporters had to accept such obfuscation, but Roosevelt still had to do something about manpower mobilization. Instead of firing McNutt, Roosevelt adopted an old procedure of adding someone new on top of the disgraced official.[21]

More and more James Byrnes became the man Roosevelt looked to for a solution. The bouncy, optimistic Byrnes was a veteran political warrior. Born in South Carolina in 1879, he had made a legal career in an area where Irish Catholics were a rare breed. Byrnes became an Episcopalian when he married and, after a stint in journalism, he was elected to the state legislature. In 1930 he won election to the United States Senate. Although by 1936 Byrnes had become disenchanted with the New Deal, he always remained a loyal Democrat and a personal retainer of the President. Appointed to the Supreme Court in 1941, he took leave of this post, which ill-suited his activist temperament, to become Director of Economic Stabilization for Roosevelt in 1942. Now in April 1943 Byrnes urged Roosevelt to issue a "Hold the Line" order to control the domestic economy. The order froze prices and wages but also authorized McNutt, with the concurrence of Byrnes, to freeze labor. Few people were surprised when, on May 27, 1943, the President issued another order creating the Office of War Mobilization with Byrnes as director. He would now supervise the entire mobilization machinery, including McNutt and manpower.[22]

Roosevelt's juggling of personnel was as skillful as ever. He tossed one man up while allowing another to drop, but no one hit the floor. Congress, however, remained dissatisfied with the performance. Legislators remained upset at McNutt because in the course of carrying out the new Roosevelt-Byrnes freeze he began attacking the draft deferment of fathers. Breaking up the family raised the hackles of congressional constituents. Byrnes now began resurrecting the earlier plan of replacing McNutt with Ickes, but Roosevelt disliked the idea. Congress soon took the initiative out of the President's hands. In late 1943 Congress passed a bill amending the Selective Service and Training Act of 1940. The amendment repudiated McNutt's handling of manpower by throwing out his nondeferrable list and providing that fathers as a class could not be inducted before available volunteers and nonfathers, regardless of job. Adding insult to injury, the amendment also reestablished the independence of the Selective Service and put Hershey directly under the President. The manpower scene was a political jungle scattered with casualties.[23]

McNutt no longer had priority in the manpower field. Byrnes made decisions for Roosevelt and coordinated the overlapping functions of Hershey, Nelson, and McNutt. Within the Roosevelt cabinet Harold Ickes, Francis Biddle, and Henry Morgenthau continued to criticize McNutt and urge his removal. When the President hinted to Morgenthau that McNutt might make a good running mate in 1944, the Secretary of the Treasury pleaded: "I will crawl from here to the Capitol on my stomach and back again if it will keep you from taking McNutt. . . . The man's record is very bad."[24]

III

McNutt was not obtuse. He realized his loss of prestige and power. Occasionally, he reminisced about the Democratic convention in 1940, when he had stood so close to the vice-presidency, and the convention had cheered his name. Now, a few years later, his career appeared over. In an earlier age he might have volunteered for a dangerous military mission with the hope of ending his career in a blaze of glory. But no such heroic opportunities were available now. He had plenty of fight left in him and he refused to live in the past. He had enlisted for the duration and would serve at the President's pleasure. He still had plenty to do. From its creation in 1942 to February 1, 1944, the WMC had expanded to 227 regional, state, and area offices covering the entire nation. Within the last twelve months the USES had placed over 9,500,000 workers.[25]

McNutt could feel confident because, despite his demotion, he continued to enjoy good personal relations with the President, who sent over little notes of encouragement from the White House. Roosevelt appreciated the imbroglio which was manpower mobilization and sympathized with McNutt's difficulties. As the President told reporters in March 1944, the manpower "thing, it's awfully difficult." The military demanded not just men but young men. But if you drafted such men in vital factories it might slow production. "It's a little like a cross-word puzzle—Yes, a jigsaw puzzle,'' Roosevelt admitted.[26]

Majority opinion in 1944 supported less controls rather than more restrictions. To an increasing number of citizens the war appeared already won. The question now concerning many people was how the end of the war would affect their job status. The problem of reconversion to peacetime became an important issue months before the last shot was fired. The war worker grew apprehensive over future employment opportunities. The entire reconversion issue was even more complex than the average worker suspected. The complexity sprang partially from political rivalry between the presidency and Congress. For several years Congress had labored under a reduced status while giving full support to the war. As the prospects for peace increased, it became anxious to reassert its authority and prerogative. The President, in contrast, impressed with the efficiency of the military organization and knowing of the vast problems which would confront the nation in the postwar world, believed demobilization could best be handled from the White House.

Adding to the contentiousness of reconversion was disagreement, not merely over jurisdiction, but over purpose. To many men, including President Roosevelt, the reform impulse of the New Deal had been only temporarily sidetracked by the war. The New Dealers, with McNutt as a leading flag bearer, sought to use reconversion as a means of launching a new ship of reform. These aspirations met staunch opposition in Congress where a conservative coalition had come to power in 1938 and still held sway. Legislative suspicion about Roosevelt's wartime powers were compounded by a difference in outlook about the postwar world. Many congressmen suspected that the President might attempt to make permanent the vast concentration of federal power which had evolved during the war. Such a concentration, layered on top of existing New Deal measures, frightened congressmen yearning for a period of stability and retrenchment.[27]

McNutt supported the connection between reconversion and reform. He agreed with Bruce Catton, a liberal historian working for the WPB, that reconversion would be the last chance to show that the war had been fought for more than a return to the status quo, that the sacrifice had been for a brave new world. Reconversion would also be the last chance for McNutt to salvage his reputation.[28] The President set the reform tone in August 1944 by identifying reconversion with full employment. The phrase "60 million jobs for Americans" became a favorite slogan for liberals. Paul McNutt became a booster of reconversion to full civilian employment for all Americans, regardless of age, race, sex, or creed.[29]

McNutt kept telling his audience that the postwar economy had to supply "10 million to 15 million more jobs than existed before" the conflict. His motto became "jobs for all Americans who want to work." His audience, recalling at firsthand the suffering of the depression, applauded enthusiastically. In one speech to the American Federation of Labor in November 1944, McNutt insisted that "the pay envelope of the workers is the business barometer of America." In 1945 he wrote that "American business can never again afford involuntary unemployment in America." Total victory over the enemy should insure total victory over unemployment. The choice for the future was clear to McNutt: either a future of rocket wars or one free of war and want. President Roosevelt could hardly have expressed the reform dream more succinctly.[30]

But how could such a noble dream be realized? Already in 1944 signs appeared that women and minority workers would be pushed out of the economy with the return of peace. Many Americans seemed to desire a return to the status quo, but not McNutt. In his mind national survival required full employment and a waste of manpower was a threat to democracy. Full employment could be achieved, he argued, by the continued cooperation of the "great American team of labor, management and government," which was winning the war. Recognizing the legitimate desire of businessmen to be rid of government red tape, McNutt insisted that the close coordination of the economy which existed under wartime mobilization could be maintained while still giving "full scope to honest, private initiative—full opportunity for fair and reasonable profit." In other words, McNutt called for a planned economy with enough flexibility for private enterprise to function.[31]

Specifically, McNutt and his aides believed that the key to full

employment in the postwar world could be found in the full use of
the scientific techniques of manpower management which the
WMC had developed during the war. Cooperation by labor, management, and government meant in particular the implementation
of utilization studies, of personnel management schemes that had
been part of the WMC work. The agency, for example, had demonstrated the value of female labor and had explained how to convert
skilled positions into several lower-skilled jobs. As McNutt told his
regional directors, "America is both industrially and psychologically
equipped to solve the problem of full employment." The solution
required the continued application of the WMC's wartime policies,
especially in employment stabilization plans and the continued use
of the USES for placing veterans and nonveterans.[32]

McNutt's ideology of full employment intersected neatly with the
thinking of other members of the administration who looked greed-
ily at opportunities for new world markets for the United States.
Full employment could be achieved only if the United States
dominated a healthy share of the markets of the world. The attitude
of domestic liberals on full employment dovetailed with traditional
business attitudes on international trade. Roosevelt had no intention
of losing opportunities for new trade outlets to the British, even in
Yugoslavia. The President reassured American businessmen keen
to capture trade opportunities opened up by American forces of
liberation. He promised American industry a fair share in world
markets. McNutt agreed with the connection between full employment at home and a "fair share of world markets." He felt the days
of economic nationalism were over for the United States. The
American economy would be the key economy of the entire postwar
world and, McNutt wrote, "We Americans can be the key people in
a new world."[33]

IV

Less agreement existed when the discussion of reconversion
moved from an ideological level to such mundane questions as
when to convert a particular factory from war production to civilian
production. McNutt played an important role in the debate over

the timing of reconversion. Stripped of rhetoric, the decision to renew civilian production would have a tremendous impact on manpower mobilization. President Roosevelt could give only infrequent attention to the reconversion problem, but occasionally he was forced to act. James Byrnes began to urge the President to draw up a reconversion plan before Congress usurped this responsibility. In August 1944 Roosevelt insisted that, as soon as the Japanese surrendered, war agencies should be liquidated with dispatch. The President also sympathized with Henry Morgenthau's fears that if the war ended suddenly hundreds of thousands of workers would be laid off with calamitous effects for the Democratic party in the November elections. But Morgenthau felt Roosevelt was tired of such questions. Indeed, Roosevelt seemed more interested in material surplus than manpower. He seemed willing to leave reconversion to be debated by such subordinates as Nelson, McNutt, Byrnes, and Stimson.[34]

These underlings disagreed over the meaning and timing of reconversion. The debate intensified in early 1944 when Byrnes asked Bernard Baruch and John Hancock to make recommendations. The issue seemed pressing as public smugness increased about inevitable victory and as war workers departed for more secure jobs. After several weeks of study, Baruch and Hancock submitted their findings to Byrnes on February 15. The report included the following recommendations: (1) establish a special office of reconversion under Byrnes; (2) take the government out of all manufacturing, with immediate payment of all debts and disposal of surplus property; (3) place all war agencies under a running review so they can be dismantled as the war winds down; (4) extend laws on price control and priorities; (5) prepare a public works program to anticipate any unemployment of war workers; (6) extend credit to veterans and small business groups.[35]

For the next few months a debate took place within the administration over the advisability of adopting the Baruch proposals. Donald Nelson of the War Production Board led a group advocating early reconversion. He argued that a reconversion program would announce to war workers that the government was planning jobs for them when the conflict ended. If the government waited until the last enemy surrendered, argued Nelson, economic chaos would face the nation. The War Department, in contrast, disliked any plan which even hinted that the war was already won, or that the American worker could afford to give less than one hundred percent. The army drew support from representatives of big corporations which were deeply committed to war contracts. Such corporations feared that a staged reconversion would provide a head start to small companies in the race for the postwar dollar. Senator Kenneth Wherry even accused the automobile industry of trying to block reconversion "until the big corporations have completed their contracts and everyone can start together."[36]

Nelson began urging reconversion as early as April 1943. In November 1943 war production reached an all-time high and began a general decline. Nelson began to plan for conversion to civilian production in certain local areas. At this time (November 1943) McNutt agreed with Nelson on the advisability of reconversion, provided sufficient manpower was available in local areas. Neither Patterson of the War Department nor Ralph Bard of the navy, sitting on the War Production Board, raised objections to Nelson's plans at this time. But on January 11, 1944, the military made clear its opposition to any reconversion of the economy. Surprisingly, McNutt now sided with Patterson and opposed any relaxation of controls because he feared that such an action would have an unfortunate impact on public opinion. McNutt had changed his mind because he expected reconversion would make more difficult the task of recruiting idle manpower for war jobs.[37]

At this point in the debate, Byrnes, with Roosevelt's encouragement, asked Baruch to make his study of the problem. The subsequent report gave encouragement to Nelson to continue to press for a return to civilian production in certain local areas. But McNutt and the military reacted by pointing to the critical shortages of manpower in such areas as foundry work. Nelson replied to these objections by announcing that "we must not be misled by occasional lapses here and there, on the part of shortsighted elements in our economy, into thinking that either management or labor, as a whole, has failed in patriotic and whole-hearted devotion to the interests of our fighting nation." War production was higher than ever. The army seemed to think that if machinists were thrown out of work by a cutback in production they could be forced into empty jobs at foundries. Nelson insisted that such workers simply disappeared from the war economy. It made good sense to allow them to work in new civilian industry instead of hiding in unessential tasks. Despite opposition, in June 1944, one week after D day, Nelson presented his reconversion plan to the War Production Board. The plan permitted manufacturers to use scarce aluminum and magnesium for civilian production, granted rights to construct experimental models for civilian products, and allowed the ordering of machine tools needed for the return to peacetime production.[38]

At this critical chiasma, with the issue still in doubt, Nelson fell ill. He planned to issue his reconversion order on July 4, 1944, but found himself too sick to attend the WPB meeting. Charles Wilson sought to defend Nelson's plan. But McNutt offered a compromise resolution which would postpone the plan. Wilson tried to resist but Patterson warned that the army would appeal Nelson's plan to Byrnes. McNutt and Patterson tried to convince Wilson that Nelson's order would hurt war production, nullify the effect of the WMC's new manpower controls, discourage the transfer of workers to critical areas, encourage migration out of labor-short areas, and even hurt the morale of soldiers. Wilson was a divided man. Personally sympathetic to the military, he felt obligated by his office to push Nelson's plan. The opposition, however, soon became too strong. A few days after the meeting, on July 7, Admiral William Leahy, Roosevelt's chief of staff, wrote a public letter to Nelson arguing that the military leaders believed early reconversion would "prolong the war." Byrnes now told Nelson to delay reconversion. Nelson conceded defeat for his plan with great reluctance. He wrote his assistants that he had decided to reschedule reconversion, because of "the urgent representations of the WMC" for time to make its new manpower controls effective.[39]

At this point Byrnes stepped in with a directive of August 4, 1944, expanding the WMC's employment ceiling program to the entire nation. Nelson went down fighting, but he went down. He was forced to accept a compromise worked out by McNutt and Byrnes. This plan permitted Nelson's reconversion order to stand but insisted that before it could take effect, the WMC had to certify that the order would not interfere with manpower recruiting. McNutt obtained a veto over reconversion. Only with his approval could reconversion begin under what was called "spot authorization." McNutt obtained this expansion of authority because he had the backing of Byrnes, Roosevelt, and the War Department.[40]

Within the next few days the President informed Nelson that he was needed in China, a polite way of giving him the gate. Julius Krug, an industrialist much closer to the McNutt-War Department view on reconversion, took over the WPB. According to Byrnes's new order, the WMC would supervise reconversion. McNutt had mixed feelings in accepting this new role. His Jeffersonian philosophy made him sympathetic with a program which would prevent the uncontrolled growth of economic monopoly. Although he had earlier agreed with Nelson on the need for reconversion, by 1944 he had changed his mind. He now began to talk as though manpower controls would be needed well after the defeat of the enemy. With Byrnes's order in his pocket, McNutt began to explain manpower shortages as due to a "victory psychosis," an overconfidence by the public.[41]

In his new role McNutt faced the unenviable task of satisfying the War Department, which saw no reason for any reconversion until the last enemy had surrendered, and the Congress, which hoped to protect the small businessman. McNutt never wavered in his commitment to provide manpower for war industry, but at times he must have wondered how he inherited such a mess. On November 17, the WPB reported that some 2,235 plants had converted to civilian production under McNutt's approval. When the WPB asked McNutt to decentralize the authority to allow reconversion, he refused. But now in late November 1944 he discovered that even his limited program had offended the War Department. Once again military leaders began a publicity campaign implying that early victory in Europe had been foiled by labor shortages in America. Supplies were short; missions cut back. Byrnes reacted to such complaints on December 1 by ordering an abrupt halt to reconversion programs in some 126 cities. For a ninety-day period no further spot reconversions would be authorized. He also ordered that in an area where war production lagged because of labor shortages and where needed labor was available in other industry such labor should be shifted to war plants even at the cost of reducing production of less urgently needed civilian goods. The administration panicked over reconversion and manpower even before the Germans began a counterattack at the Ardennes Forest.[42]

In this case, the War Department's overreaction to reconversion created a credibility problem. Donald Nelson, recently returned from China, happily testified in December 1944 before a special Senate committee that the needs of the military had been met, that all critical munitions programs were up to par, and that unemployment was growing. Senator James M. Mead, the chairman of the committee, called General Somervell to testify and clear up the conflicting impressions. Somervell explained that the supply shortages were purely local and the result of military transportation problems. He now admitted that "no one so far has suffered from a lack of supplies." The fighting men in Europe "have everything that they could possibly move to the front . . . . No military campaigns have been delayed because of material shortages." Secretary of War Stimson agreed. Krug of the WPB then presented evidence that the primary cause in any existing shortages was the fluctuating demands by the military. Senator Meade concluded his report to the Senate by stating that the military had misrepresented the problem of supply by trying to blame it on manpower shortages in the United States. Both Nelson and McNutt appeared vindicated. Even as Meade spoke, however, on December 16, German tanks began assembling under cover in the forest of Belgium. Oddly enough, they would assist the War Department in recovering the initiative in the debate over reconversion.[43]

Poor flying weather had allowed the Germans to mass troops for a counterattack which smashed through shallow Allied defenses in the Ardennes Forest. In the United States civilians rushed to support the War Department. All criticism of military opinion on manpower ceased. Byrnes cursed the easy optimism of Americans and dashed off an order closing all racetracks and nightclubs, a somewhat incongruous reaction to the Battle of the Bulge. He also began a critical review of the draft deferments of professional athletes. Krug announced that he was now operating under the assumption that the war would go on indefinitely. McNutt gave assurances of his commitment to full manpower mobilization. He also announced plans for a visit to the fighting front.[44] This reaction was perhaps the most curious of all.

V

The debate over reconversion had ended with a clear victory for the military point of view. Victory was snatched from the jaws of defeat by civilian reaction to the German counterattack, an attack which would soon peter out. McNutt's attention now moved toward the returning veteran, who would play a major role in any conversion to peacetime production. As with the issue of reconversion, the subject of planning for returning veterans did not attract White House attention. Roosevelt seemed reluctant to cater to the veteran for fear of downplaying the important role of the civilian war worker. The impetus for veteran benefits, including the "GI Bill of Rights" of June 1944, came from Congress, under massive pressure from veteran lobbies.[45]

The President had appointed a Postwar Manpower Conference in 1942 to consider the problem of rapid versus slow discharge of veterans. The conferees' efforts to find a solution, however, were hampered by Roosevelt's refusal to commit himself on what he considered a premature problem. The conferees handed in a report in June 1943 calling for the speedy demobilization of troops but also recommending the granting of three months leave or furlough pay to ease the transition by veterans to civilian status.[46]

McNutt stepped into this policy vacuum. He had several reasons for concerning himself with this phase of reconversion, including his general reformist outlook. Primarily, he became interested in veterans because he hoped to use the returning men to fill critical war jobs. As early as September 1941 McNutt lamented the failure of veterans to keep active registrations with the USES so that they could be quickly placed into war industry. Already men were being discharged from the military and their high motivation and security from the draft made them particularly attractive for war jobs. By February 1943 more than 80,000 veterans over the age of thirty-eight had been released.[47]

During 1943 McNutt campaigned to guarantee the WMC a leading role in the reconversion of veterans. A Veterans Bureau was established within the USES machinery for obtaining jobs for returnees. But not everyone appreciated McNutt's efforts. Critics charged that he was more interested in ending manpower shortages than in finding suitable jobs for veterans. McNutt denied this but did admit that he sought to use veterans to fulfill the primary mission of the WMC. These same critics argued that the Veterans Administration, headed by Frank Hines, should have total control over returnees.[48]

By December 1943 McNutt had established six experimental centers in different regions of the country to provide reemployment advice and guidance to the veteran, and help him reenter American life. The Veteran Employment Service Center (VESC) worked closely with the USES as a clearinghouse for jobs. McNutt hoped to expand the VESC program to cover all 1,500 USES centers by 1944. The basic principle guiding the WMC was that "every returning soldier is entitled to a job and he is entitled to aid in getting the job he is best suited for." Rather than have the veteran running from one government agency to another, McNutt sought one single locale where the ex-GI could find all the answers to his questions plus find a job. The VESC would be such a clearinghouse. Logically, McNutt should then be czar of veterans' affairs.[49]

Logic has always had limited application in American politics. McNutt knew that his critics feared the rights of veterans were being subordinated to the needs of the war economy by the WMC. On January 20, 1944, speaking to the American Legion, an organization he had once commanded, McNutt reassured skeptics by explaining how the VESC worked. The veteran was told of his rights and opportunities, was directed to a job or job training which suited him, and was helped to adjust in other ways. In McNutt's opinion, the prosperity of the veteran was synonymous with the prosperity of the nation. By April 1944 he expected to have the VESC functioning in all major cities with job analysts working to obtain the best-paying jobs for veterans. Naturally, he would urge them to enter war work, but the men would have full freedom to ignore him.[50]

Before McNutt could move on, however, President Roosevelt

entered the scene. In late February 1944 he instructed the Civil Service Commission to place special emphasis on recruiting and placing veterans in federal jobs. As Roosevelt wrote the heads of executive departments, "there is no reason whatsoever why, taking into consideration the present manpower situation, the Departments and agencies should not delegate this authority [to hire new personnel] to the Commission." Roosevelt also issued an executive order (no. 9427) creating a new agency, the Retraining and Re-employment Administration. This agency was given primary responsibility "to have general supervision and direction of the activities of all Government agencies relating to the retraining and re-employment of persons discharged or released from the armed services. . . ." As almost an afterthought, the order insisted that "in developing such programs, special regard shall be given to the necessity of integrating them with wartime manpower controls." This new agency was created on the same administrative level as the WMC. Frank Hines, not Paul McNutt, was named as its head.[51]

On paper McNutt had suffered another serious setback, but it failed to slow up his work. The WMC continued to operate through the VESC and USES, while Hines's new agency had only supervisory status. By February 1944 McNutt had seven experimental placement centers functioning in Denver, Philadelphia, New Haven, Houston, Los Angeles, Minneapolis, and St. Louis. He had also worked out a joint agreement with Hershey and the Selective Service which assured the WMC a major role in returning veterans to civilian jobs. Some 1,058,000 men had been discharged from the military since Pearl Harbor and by April 1944 the WMC was processing veterans back into the civilian economy at the rate of 75,000 each month. Of every 100 veterans who went through the service centers, eighty were placed immediately. Job placement interviews were given in hospitals, convalescent centers, and demobilization points. During the first eight months of 1944 USES placements totaled some 282,391, of which 65 percent were veterans. By winter 1944 discharges were running to 2,000 per day.[52]

In the midst of this avalanche McNutt sought to establish clear policy guidelines. He made clear that the veteran had first shot at his old job through the Reemployment Committee of local Selective Service Boards. If the veteran sought a new job, compatible with newly acquired skills, the Veterans Division of the USES was there to administer a battery of tests at seven demonstration centers. By April 1944 the tests were being administered at all 1,500 USES offices. McNutt told the press that his objective was "satisfactory placement" of all veterans in accord with the recommendations of the Baruch-Hancock report. At the same time, he wrote the National Vice Commander of the Army and Navy Legion of Valor that the USES sought to place veterans "in jobs where they can continue their war-usefulness." Despite criticism, McNutt still sought to exploit the veteran to solve manpower problems. By the summer and fall of 1944 the WMC placed about 50,000 to 70,000 veterans per month, the majority in war jobs.[53]

Returning veterans helped McNutt solve his shortage problems, but it was always clear that such men were to receive special treatment. On September 27, 1944, the WMC announced that all manpower controls for veterans would be lifted. A veteran was defined as "any individual who has served in the armed forces subsequent to December 7, 1941, and has an other than dishonorable discharge." By September 1944 the work of the VESC demonstration centers was absorbed into an expanded guidance and placement service for veterans in 1,500 USES offices. More than a half million jobs had already been found for the 1,279,000 veterans who had returned home. In November 1944 the WMC announced that wages earned by veterans who qualified for apprenticeship training would be supplemented by monthly allowances provided by the GI Bill. Approximately 9,300 veterans were taking advantage of war production training courses.[54]

By 1945 McNutt's campaign to place veterans in war jobs was moving smoothly. Representatives from the USES stationed themselves in each of the seventeen army separation centers in the nation. Here and elsewhere manpower experts tried to help the veteran discover, analyze, and evaluate his potential abilities. The USES staff members provided current information on job requirements and opportunities, and put the veterans in touch with training schools. In overseeing the training program, McNutt insisted that veterans not be "high-pressured" into any program, regardless of shortages. Following V-E Day, McNutt spoke proudly on national radio of how the WMC helped veterans by maintaining labor market information, by providing information on the kind of job and the type of community in which the plant was located. By June 1945 such placement services were being given to 100,000 veterans per month.[55]

VI

As the end of the war approached McNutt found himself caught in a cross fire. He had to walk a narrow line between discouraging postwar planning for manpower until the fighting ended and, simultaneously, taking steps to insure that mass unemployment did not confront the nation after victory. Although he had taken a stand with the military against Nelson's ideas about early reconversion, McNutt never entirely rejected the need for planning. The WMC cooperated with reconversion through spot authorization until Byrnes overreacted to War Department complaints. As of January 5, 1945, some 5,658 applications were received for reconversion. The WMC approved some 4,357. In public, McNutt took a determined line against reconversion. As late as April 1945 he promised to disappoint anyone who expected a speedy return to civilian production. Privately, he went about planning for peace.[56]

Like most high government officials, McNutt had hopes and plans on how he and his agency could contribute significantly to a prosperous postwar world. Some of these ideas he made public; others he kept within his agency. He fully expected his work to endure and continue in some form after the war. As the major problem of demobilization would be unemployment, he expected the role of the WMC to be recognized. As it had found men for jobs, it could also find jobs for men. In June 1944 McNutt had written down some of his assumptions about what would happen in the manpower field when the war ended. First, he expected the labor force to recede to a level consistent with normal growth, despite the inclination of more women to stay on the job. Second, the national economy could "be expected to operate at about the relatively high 1941 level of production and employment." But with the end of war production and the discharge of seven million veterans, McNutt envisioned unemployment reaching five million. One year later, following V-E Day, McNutt upped his anticipated unemployment figure to 7.5 million men and women who would be out of work one year after the defeat of Japan. With such a dismal picture confronting the nation, McNutt believed it more essential than ever that the public work projects of the New Deal be renewed.[57]

He hoped there would be a role for the WMC in such a drama. But he also recognized congressional sentiment. As early as September 8, 1944, he had promised that when the war ended in Europe, all employment ceilings, priority referrals, and stabilization programs would probably cease. The Mead Committee of the Senate agreed. Congress remained suspicious of any renewal of reform under the guise of demobilization. McNutt still insisted that the work of the 1,500 USES offices, the labor market reports on supply and demand, and other personnel functions of the WMC should continue. He felt these services would be useful in finding peacetime jobs for veterans and war workers. If Congress allowed him to continue, McNutt felt confident that the WMC could service both management and labor in a noncompulsory way. He saw his major postwar objectives as the reemployment of veterans and displaced war workers, providing counseling and job information for all, expediting the transfer of workers from surplus to shortage areas, and establishing the best possible balance between employment opportunities and labor supply.[58]

He was particularly optimistic about maintaining a vigorous federal USES. Both the worker and the employer could benefit from the services of the USES. The agency would give workers the knowledge of where jobs were located and minimize job-hunting time. This information would also facilitate the interarea transfer of workers and thereby help national businesses in planning for the future. Even the AFL agreed with McNutt on the continued importance of the USES.[59]

The USES and the WMC had developed a national, coordinated system of facts and figures on employment. During the war McNutt's agency had created methods for assembling data to show where jobs were and where workers were. By the end of the war he could boast of the WMC's ability to predict up to four months in advance where labor demands would appear and what kinds of demands they would be. In addition, new personnel management services were available to employers. The research done during the war to speed placement had led to new tools and methods which would now be available to the private sector. These tools included skills in analyzing job content, methods for comparing skills and aptitudes of applicants, and methods for relating an applicant's qualifications to the requirements of a job. The aptitude tests and physical appraisal techniques used to place women and the handicapped would now be at the disposal of business.[60]

Big business already used these services, but McNutt foresaw that they could be made available to small businesses without the cost of research. The information could be used to indicate trends and levels of employment and opportunities in various industries. The data provided information on how local wage rates compared with national averages, how minorities were treated, the opportunities for advancement, the training needed, and the condition of community services for women workers. McNutt hoped to pass on the knowledge accumulated in mobilizing manpower to the private sector.[61]

Anticipating cutbacks in war orders in 1944, McNutt urged the procurement agencies to eliminate contracts in the following order: (1) those areas where released workers could be used to relieve shortages impending urgent war work; (2) those areas where workers could be transferred to other war production; (3) in areas where workers could be transferred to civilian production; and (4), as a last resort, in areas where cutbacks would create unemployment. When instructed by Byrnes to oversee reconversion through spot authorization, McNutt ordered his staff to allow industries to assign planning engineers and technicians for developing programs for resumption of civilian production. However, the actual resumptions authorized were small. The military refused to accept the need for detailed reconversion and refused to cooperate with McNutt's priority program.[62]

With the continued collapse of German arms during early 1945, McNutt's task became somewhat easier. Beginning in mid-April 1945 the War Department no longer had apprehensions over manpower shortages. In the beginning of the year Patterson and General Somervell held weekly meetings to consider the manpower program and to urge passage of a national service law. But these meetings grew less frequent and finally ceased by April as chances for national service legislation faded. From May through August, Colonel Ralph F. Gow, the Director of Industrial Personnel under Somervell, provided weekly reports on the WMC program. The reports were uniformly optimistic. On May 29, the WMC program "looks satisfactory," and its estimates of cutbacks fair. Week after week Gow reported to Patterson that "no significant manpower shorts were impeding military procurement." With the exception of a crisis in manpower for western railroads which led to the assignment of 2,500 soldiers to civilian jobs, the entire manpower situation was rosy.[63]

VII

As President Harry Truman assumed office upon the death of Franklin Roosevelt on April 12, 1945, McNutt began dismantling his program of manpower controls. From March to June munitions plant employment dropped from nine million to 8.4 million. The WMC reclassified some twenty-nine labor areas, ending their priority rating. In May McNutt announced a new policy for the defeat of Japan: (1) manpower controls in low-priority areas (3 and 4) could be lifted at the discretion of area directors; (2) employment stabilization programs, ceiling programs, priority referrals, and the forty-eight-hour week would be kept on in high-priority areas (1 and 2); (3) in case of large unemployment during the transition, blanket or open referral cards would be issued permitting workers to accept any job. When McNutt explained these plans to a special Senate Subcommittee on Demobilization, he emphasized the flexibility of his approach, but also stressed that he was checking on small plants with 100 workers or less who wished to begin civilian production. He estimated that within the next three months the manpower requirements for war work would drop by 2.8 million. Some 700,000 workers could be shifted to civilian duty. Unfortunately, he also expected that unemployment would increase from 800,000 to two million in the next three months. He concluded optimistically that the increase in unemployment would be only "moderate" in relation to the total labor force of sixty million.[64]

From V-E Day to V-J Day (May 8 to August 14), McNutt gave area and regional officials the power to change or modify all controls. Labor controls remained only in limited areas. On August 23 he announced by radio that all manpower controls were ended. Labor was free again. Now McNutt hoped the various services of the WMC would prove useful in continuing to channel labor into more permanent employment.

He would be disappointed. Congress had already drafted legislation which would return the USES to state control within ninety days after the end of hostilities. As for manpower controls, Congress followed the same approach with most war agencies: the bloated wartime bureaucracy was a threat to normality, a temptation for more federal control and of no use in the postwar world. Congress slayed the dragon.

McNutt had too much political experience to miss the writing on the wall for his agency, despite his rhetoric. He knew the WMC had enemies in the administration as well as in Congress. In the White House, on April 26, 1945, President Truman explained that he hoped to consolidate all labor functions under the Department of Labor, a course which Frances Perkins had been pressing since early in the war. Truman also approved drastic cuts in the budget for the WMC in July 1945. McNutt now sought relief from a position which had brought him little merit over the last few years. His presidential ambitions shattered and without a firm political base, he eagerly sought and received a presidential appointment to return to the Philippines as American High Commissioner. Truman announced the appointment on September 6, 1945. Two weeks later the President announced the transfer of the duties of the War Manpower Commission to the Department of Labor.[65]

Demobilization continued rapidly without McNutt. Twelve months after V-J Day the military had been reduced from twelve million to a little over three million. Veterans found jobs because, after a short period, the economy began to race forward. The period of postwar prosperity was beginning. Money was abundant and few people tried to remember the "lessons" of World War II, lessons of labor, management, and government cooperation, lessons of a national labor placement agency. The American public had entered the war without a bold vision of transforming domestic society. Wars were aberrations to be fought and won quickly so that citizens could return to normality. McNutt's program for labor-management cooperation sounded too much like reformism. By 1945 Americans had had enough change; McNutt could experiment with Filipinos.

Notes

1. *Complete Presidential Press Conferences of Franklin D. Roosevelt*, 25 vols. in 12 books (New York: Da Capo Press, 1972), (January 9, 1943), 21: 85E-85F, hereafter cited as *PPC*.

2. Roland Young, *Congressional Politics in the Second World War* (New York: Columbia University Press, 1956), pp. 59-60; McNutt speech files of April 29, 1942, and December 14, 1942, Paul V. McNutt Papers, The Lilly Library, Indiana University, Bloomington, Ind.; *Monthly Labor Review*, May 1942, iii, 1061. See also Nelson N. Lichenstein, "Industrial Unionism under the No-strike Pledge" (Ph. D. dissertation, University of California, Berkeley, 1974), pp. 240-50, on overtime pay.

3. Transcript of telephone conversation, Cox to Perkins, December 16, 1942, daily calendar of Oscar Cox, Franklin D. Roosevelt Library, Hyde Park, N.Y.

4. U.S., Congress, Senate, Subcommittee on Appropriations, hearings on *Investigation of Manpower*, 78th Cong., 1st sess., 1943, pt. 1, p. 7.

5. Transcript, Cox to Perkins, December 16, 1942, Cox Calendar, Roosevelt Papers; Cox to Wayne Coy, December 19, 1942, *ibid.*; Cox to Ben Cohen, February 8, 1943, *ibid.*

6. Samuel I. Rosenman, ed., *Public Papers and Addresses of Franklin D. Roosevelt*, 13 vols. (New York: Harper and Row, 1938-1950), 12: 69-70.

7. Isador Lubin to Cox, February 9, 1943, and Ben Cohen to Cox, February 16, 1943, Cox Calendar, Roosevelt Library.

8. *New York Times*, February 10, 1943, p. 1, and February 11, 1943, p. 13; Patterson to McNutt, February 10, 1943, box 183, Robert Patterson Papers, Library of Congress, Washington, D.C.; *Monthly Labor Review*, May 1943, p. 1030.

9. McNutt to Byrnes, February 18, 1943, pack 5, pt. 2, James Byrnes Papers, Clemson University Library, Clemson, S.C.

10. Copy of WMC order part 903, February 1943, pack 5, pt. 2, Byrnes Papers; McNutt to Byrnes, February 18, 1943, *ibid.* The cities affected included the following: Bridgeport and Hartford, Conn.; Springfield, Mass.; Buffalo, N.Y.; Baltimore, Md.; Akron and Dayton, Ohio; Detroit, Mich.; Mobile, Ala.; Beaumont, Tex.; San Diego, Calif., and Seattle, Wash.

11. *New York Times*, February 11, 1943, pp. 1, 18, February 12, 1943, p. 14, and July 22, 1943, p. 27; file for April 14, 1943, McNutt Papers.

12. Quoted in CBS speech manuscript, March 7, 1943, McNutt Papers.

13. *New York Times*, October 21, 1943, p. 11; *Monthly Labor Review*, February 1944, p. 457, and September 1944, p. 660; *Business Week*, May 13, 1944, p. 102.

14. McHale to McNutt, December 23, 1942, McNutt Papers; Carol Riegelman, *Labour-Management Co-operation in United States War Production* (Montreal: International Labour Office, 1948), p. 290; McNutt file, May 1943, McNutt Papers; *Monthly Labor Review*, August 1943, p. 399. To supplement these efforts the Presi-

dent signed an act creating two committees, one in the judicial and one in the legislative branch of government to pass on the occupational deferments of federal employees. General Hershey was asked to make monthly reports to Congress on federal deferments.

15. Roosevelt to McNutt, July 21, 1943, official file 4905, Franklin D. Roosevelt Papers, Hyde Park, N.Y.; diary of Harold L. Ickes (July 25, 1943), 10: 8004, 8018, Library of Congress, Washington, D.C.; Patterson to Stimson, July 23, 1943, box 171, Henry L. Stimson Papers, Yale University Library, New Haven, Conn. The draft law provided that civilians would control appeals, but this idea failed in practice.

16. Ickes Diary (August 1, 1943), 10: 8044; Byrnes to Roosevelt, August 11, 1943, Byrnes Papers; Hershey to Byrnes, September 24, 1943, White House file, 1941-1943, General Lewis B. Hershey Papers, Military History Research Collection, Carlisle Barracks, Pa.; Hershey to Rosenman, December 7, 1943, staybacks, 1943-1944, *ibid.*

17. Jonathan Daniels, *White House Witness, 1942–1945* (New York: Doubleday, 1975), pp. 137-38; *New York Times*, February 24, 1943, p. 1; Ickes Diary (January 17, 1943); Senator Murray to Roosevelt, March 1, 1943, OF 4905, box 285-C, Roosevelt Papers; William D. Hassett, *Off the Record with F.D.R., 1942–1945* (New Brunswick, N.J.: Rutgers University Press, 1958), p. 160.

18. Rosenman to Roosevelt, March 14, 1943, file 59 (1), Byrnes Papers; Cox Daily Calendar, March 6, 1943, Roosevelt Library; Hassett, *Off the Record*, p. 160; *New York Times*, March 7, 1943, p. 1.

19. Minutes of manpower hearing, March 4, 1943, box 324, Harry Hopkins Papers, Roosevelt Library; Appley statement, file 59 (1), Byrnes Papers; Haber to Rosenman, March 12, 1943, box 324, Hopkins Papers; minutes of manpower hearing, March 10, 1943, box 324, Hopkins Papers.

20. Memorandum to Roosevelt, March 14, 1943, box 324, Hopkins Papers; see also same memorandum in file 59 (1), Byrnes Papers.

21. *PPC* (April 9, 1943), 21: 273-74.

22. Joel Seidman, *American Labor from Defense to Reconversion* (Chicago: University of Chicago Press, 1953), p. 160; Herman M. Somers, *Presidential Agency: OWMR, The Office of War Mobilization and Reconversion* (Cambridge: Harvard University Press, 1950), p. 38; James Byrnes, *All in One Lifetime* (New York: Harper and Row, 1958), pp. 176-77, 184-86, 188. Baruch called on Roosevelt to dump McNutt in late March. See Daniels, *White House Witness*, p. 157.

23. Senator Guffey to Roosevelt, October 16, 1943, OF 4905A, Roosevelt Papers; *New York Times*, December 11, 1943, p. 1; Byrnes, *All in One Lifetime*, pp. 190-91; Ickes Diary (December 5, 1943), 11: 8414; *Monthly Labor Review*, February 1944, p. 463; Hershey to Roosevelt, December 15, 1943, White House file, 1941-1943, Hershey Papers.

24. Ickes Diary (January 30, 1944), 11: 8600, and (April 29, 1944), 11: 8844; war diaries of Henry Morgenthau (March 17, 1944), 5: 1351, Roosevelt Library; quote from John M. Blum, ed., *From the Morgenthau Diaries: Years of War, 1941–1945* (Boston: Houghton Mifflin, 1967), p. 281.

25. *New York Times*, January 7, 1944, p. 19; file of December 23, 1944, McNutt Papers; file of February 1, 1944, *ibid.*

26. Roosevelt to McNutt, February 21, 1944, McNutt Papers; *PPC* (March 14, 1944), 23: 104-5.

27. For a general overview of reconversion see especially the following: J. Carlyle Sitterson, *Development of Reconversion Policies of the War Production Board* (Washington, D.C.: U.S. War Production Board, 1945); Jack Peltason, "The Reconversion Controversy," in *Public Administration and Policy Development*, Harold Stein, ed. (New York: Harcourt, Brace, 1952), pp. 242-43.

28. Bruce Catton, *The War Lords of Washington* (New York: Harcourt, Brace, 1948), p. 226.

29. *PPC* (August 29, 1944), 24: 77-79; McNutt speech to American Legion, September 21, 1943, McNutt Papers; *New York Times*, November 11, 1943, p. 19; Alonzo L. Hamby, "Sixty Million Jobs and the People's Revolution," *Historian* 30 (August 1968), 578-98.

30. McNutt speech, April 13, 1944; manuscript, August 25, 1944; McNutt to Colonel W. W. Rose, October 6, 1944; McNutt speech to AFL, November 21, 1944; article manuscript, October 1945; radio interview, August 23, 1945; newsreel statement, May 12, 1945; press release, April 16, 1945, all in McNutt Papers.

31. Conference on Postwar Adjustment of Women, December 4, 1944, record group 86, National Archives, Washington, D.C.; McNutt radio interview, August 23, 1945, McNutt Papers; press release, August 14, 1945, *ibid.*; McNutt address to AFL, April 13, 1944, *ibid.*

32. Speech by John Collins, October 18, 1944, McNutt Papers; McNutt to George J. Seedman, March 4, 1944, *ibid.*; McNutt manuscript on Negro Manpower, December 21, 1944, *ibid.*; McNutt speech, June 1, 1945, *ibid.*; McNutt speech to Veterans Employment Representatives, May 29, 1945, *ibid.*; McNutt manuscript for National Paint, Varnish and Lacquer Association, September 25, 1944, *ibid.*; McNutt speech, May 15, 1945, *ibid.*

33. Anna M. Rosenberg to Roosevelt, October 11, 1944, PPF 8101, Roosevelt Papers; Maurice Survis to Rosenberg, October 16, 1944, OF 4025, *ibid.*; McNutt review, February 5, 1945, McNutt Papers. The literature on how the philosophy of the "Open Door" in international trade influenced American foreign policy has grown rapidly over the last few years. See especially Walter LaFeber, *America, Russia, and the Cold War, 1945-1975*, 3d ed. (New York: Wiley, 1976), and Lloyd C. Gardner, *Economic Aspects of New Deal Diplomacy* (Madison: University of Wisconsin Press, 1964).

34. *New York Times*, September 5, 1943, p. 21; David R. B. Ross, *Preparing for Ulysses: Politics and Veterans during World War II* (New York: Columbia University Press, 1969), p. 127; Rosenman to Roosevelt, August 30, 1944, 285-C, OF 5584, Roosevelt Papers; memorandum of conversation between Morgenthau and Roosevelt, August 25, 1944, vol. 6, 1389, Morgenthau Presidential Diary, Roosevelt Library; Roosevelt to Byrnes, October 3, 1944, 932, OF 5584, Roosevelt Papers.

35. Bernard Baruch and John M. Hancock, *War and Postwar Adjustment Policies* (Washington, D.C.: American Council on Public Affairs, 1944); see also Bernard Baruch, *The Public Years* (London: Odhams Press, 1960), pp. 304-7.

36. Donald Nelson, *Arsenal of Democracy: The Story of American War Production* (New York: Harcourt, Brace, 1946), pp. 406-8; Wherry quoted in Allen Drury, *A Senate Journal, 1943-1945* (New York: McGraw-Hill, 1963), p. 147; Catton,

War Lords, pp. 245, 259; Richard Polenberg, *War and Society: The United States, 1941-1945* (Philadelphia: J. B. Lippincott, 1972), pp. 216, 230.

37. Nelson, *Arsenal*, pp. 391-402; reconversion folder, box 12, Donald Nelson Papers, Huntington Library, San Marino, Calif.; digest of WPB minutes, November 30, 1943, box 12, *ibid.*

38. Nelson, *Arsenal*, pp. 391-402; notes for speech, May 29, 1944, box 15, Nelson Papers; Polenberg, *War and Society*, p. 231.

39. Digest of WPB minutes, July 4, 1944, box 12, Nelson Papers; Drury, *Journal*, July 8, 1944, p. 215; Catton, *War Lords*, pp. 243, 264-66; Nelson to vice chairman, July 7, 1944, box 12, Nelson Papers.

40. Somers, *Presidential Agency*, pp. 185-190; press release, August 15, 1944, McNutt Papers; *New York Times*, August 16, 1944, p. 1.

41. McNutt statement before Senate Committee, September 8, 1944, McNutt Papers; McNutt statement before House Committee, April 26, 1945, *ibid.*; McNutt address at Detroit, January 21, 1944, *ibid.*; press release, July 29, 1944, *ibid.*; *New York Times*, August 3, 1944; reconversion file, box 12, Nelson Papers; *New York Times*, August 18, 1944, p. 15, and August 22, 1944, p. 27.

42. *New York Times*, August 25, 1944, p. 1, and December 2, 1944, p. 9; reconversion folder, box 12, Nelson Papers; *New York Times*, December 2, 1944, p. 1.

43. Somervell's testimony can be found in U.S., Congress, Senate, hearings on *Investigation of the National Defense Program*, 78th Cong., 2d sess., pt. 26 (1944), pp. 11989-90; *New York Times*, August 25, 1944, p. 1, and December 2, 1944, pp. 1, 9; reconversion folder, box 12, pp. 117, 133, 135, Nelson Papers; McNutt statement to House Committee, April 26, 1945, McNutt Papers.

44. Reconversion folder, box 12, p. 135, Nelson Papers.

45. Ross, *Preparing for Ulysses*, pp. 33, 43, 275-90.

46. *Ibid.*, pp. 55, 102; Therese Benedek, *Insight and Personality Adjustment: A Study of the Psychological Effects of War* (New York: Ronald Press, 1946), pp. 77, 97; Anna W. M. Wolf and I. S. Black, "What Happened to the Younger People," in *While You Were Gone*, Jack Goodman, ed. (New York: Simon and Schuster, 1946), p. 71; *New York Times*, January 26, 1943, p. 10; Drury, *Senate Journal*, p. 136.

47. McNutt speech to Virginia State Federation of Labor, September 1, 1941, McNutt Papers; speech to Veterans Employment Representatives, May 11, 1942, *ibid.*; Patterson to McNutt, February 19, 1943, box 183, Patterson Papers.

48. Radio interview, October 20, 1943, McNutt Papers.

49. *New York Times*, July 29, 1943, p. 11; Ross, *Preparing for Ulysses*, p. 142; *Monthly Labor Review*, February 1944, p. 465; McNutt to Warren H. Atherton, December 21, 1943, box 1-1, record group 211, National Archives; radio interview, October 20, 1943, McNutt Papers; McNutt to E. Tracy Sweet, December 27, 1943, *ibid.*; Philip S. Broughton to Lawrence A. Appley, December 29, 1943, *ibid.*

50. Address to American Legion, Janury 20, 1944, McNutt Papers; newsreel statement, February 2, 1944, *ibid.*; McNutt to W. E. Jones, February 7, 1944, *ibid.*

51. Ross, *Preparing for Ulysses*, p. 131; Roosevelt to heads of executive departments, February 26, 1944, Byrnes Papers; Executive Order no. 9427, February 24, 1944, in Samuel I. Rosenman, *Public Papers and Addresses* 23: 86-87.

52. *Monthly Labor Review*, June 1944, p. 1340, September 1944, p. 659; McNutt radio speech, April 26, 1944, McNutt Papers; manuscript on "Manpower Reconversion," June 6, 1944, *ibid.*; manuscript for *Encyclopedia Britannica*, December 23, 1944, *ibid.*; *New York Times*, November 28, 1944, p. 40.

53. McNutt manuscript for *Manpower Review*, March 7, 1944, McNutt Papers; press release, March 31, 1944, *ibid.*; McNutt to Earle Norton, April 26, 1944, *ibid.*; manuscript for *The Jewish Veteran*, September 19, 1944, *ibid.*; minutes of National Advisory Committee of Non-Government Agencies on Veterans Program of WMC, March 27, 1944, box 20-142, E117, RG 211; *New York Times*, June 4, 1944.

54. *Monthly Labor Review*, December 1944, p. 1322; *ibid.*, April 1945, p. 912; *New York Times*, December 10, 1944, p. 41; McNutt to W. C. Williams, October 7, 1944, McNutt Papers.

55. *Monthly Labor Review*, June 1945, pp. 1336, 1337; McNutt manuscript, January 9, 1945, McNutt Papers; McNutt to Charles King, February 28, 1945, *ibid.*; McNutt to subcomittee of House of Representatives, April 26, 1945, *ibid.*; McNutt radio address, June 18, 1945, *ibid.*

56. Somers, *Presidential Agency*, p. 190n; McNutt to Congressman Harry R. Sheppard, July 2, 1945, McNutt Papers; Patterson to McNutt, April 6, 1944, box 184, Patterson Papers; *New York Times*, February 25, 1944, p. 11; McNutt speech to AFL, April 13, 1944, McNutt Papers; McNutt radio address, September 10, 1944, *ibid.*; McNutt speech to AFL, November 21, 1944, *ibid.*; McNutt radio interview, April 22, 1945, *ibid.*

57. McNutt manuscript on reconversion, June 6, 1944, McNutt Papers; McNutt testimony before Meade Committee, July 10, 1945, McNutt Papers; McNutt to Paul B. Reinhold, February 4, 1944, *ibid.*

58. McNutt statement before Senate Committee, September 8, 1944, McNutt Papers; McNutt speech to Druggist Association, September 14, 1944, *ibid.;* McNutt speech to American Management Association, September 27, 1944, *ibid.* On April 26, 1945, McNutt testified before the House Committee on Appropriations that the WMC anticipated "sizable staffing needs and continued manpower controls" even after the European war ended. See file of April 26, 1945, McNutt Papers.

59. McNutt testimony before Senate Subcommittee on Small Business, July 10, 1945, McNutt Papers; press release, August 11, 1945, *ibid.*; minutes of Management-Labor Policy Committee, September 19, 1944, box 5-98, RG 211, National Archives; McNutt article on postwar planning, August 25, 1944, McNutt Papers.

60. Ford T. Shepherd to Judge Charles M. Hay, July 29, 1944, box 20-142, E117, RG 211; McNutt to Harold S. Buttenheim, August 25, 1945, McNutt Papers; McNutt manuscript, "Post-War Program of the USES," August 11, 1945, *ibid.*

61. McNutt to Senate Subcommittee on Small Business, July 10, 1945, McNutt Papers; McNutt manuscript, "Post-War Program of the USES," August 11, 1945, *ibid.*; McNutt manuscript, "Labor and the Post-War," August 28, 1945, *ibid.*; McNutt to Baruch, December 7, 1943, *ibid.*

62. McNutt speech at Detroit, January 21, 1944, McNutt Papers; *Monthly Labor Review*, December 1944, p. 1321; *New York Times*, September 22, 1944, p. 29.

63. Byron Fairchild and Jonathan Grossman, *The Army and Industrial Manpower*

(Washington, D.C.: U.S. Department of the Army, 1959), p. 187; see weekly reports of Colonel Gow to Patterson, May-August 1945, box 184-5, Robert Patterson Papers, Library of Congress.

64. McNutt to Truman, May 25, 1945, McNutt Papers; Riegelman, *Labour-Management Co-operation*, pp. 52-53; *Monthly Labor Review*, June 1945, p. 1205; McNutt testimony before Senate Subcommittee on National Defense, May 14, 1945, McNutt Papers; minutes of WMC, May 31, 1945, box 1-1, RG 211.

65. McNutt radio speech, August 25, 1945, McNutt Papers; minutes of MLPC, September 25, 1945, box 5-98, RG 211; Byrnes to Roosevelt, February 15, 1944, folder 73 (2), Byrnes Papers; Smith memorandum of conference with Truman, April 26, 1945, Presidential Conference 45, file 15, Harold Smith Papers, Roosevelt Library; Perkins to Smith, May 9, 1945, A 159, folder 111, Clara Beyer Papers, Schlesinger Library, Radcliffe College, Cambridge, Mass.; Harold Smith Presidential Diary (July 6, 1945), Smith Papers; Frazier J. Payton to McNutt, September 7, 1945, McNutt Papers. McNutt had told Payton twelve months earlier that he wished to return to the Philippines after the war.

CONCLUSIONS

When peace was signed with Japan on September 2, 1945, the United States seemed a different nation from the one attacked in December 1941. But was it so different? John Dos Passos wisely wrote during the war that "it is not the professed aims people are striving to achieve that set the pattern of the future but the habits of behavior they take on in the process."[1] Not the rhetoric of Roosevelt and McNutt but the methods adopted for mobilizing manpower would make the difference in society.

This distinction helps in evaluating the manpower mobilization experiment. For idealists such as Bruce Catton of the War Production Board the failure to use mobilization to promote social reform objectives of the New Deal meant a betrayal of war aims. McNutt and Roosevelt talked of a new world of full employment, of sixty million jobs, but the methods of manpower mobilization insured a return of monopolistic capitalism.[2]

McNutt failed to achieve reform because of his reliance upon voluntaristic and localistic methods for manpower mobilization. Yet in the real world of wartime America, a world of continued political, economic, and social competition, such a failure was almost inevitable. Confronted with the problem of adjusting to the demands of the various economic interest groups in America, especially the farmer and organized labor, and to continued social prejudice toward hiring blacks and women, McNutt also had to work within limits imposed by Congress, the Selective Service, and the War Department. What seems remarkable, given such parameters and the inhibitions imposed by his own philosophy of voluntarism, together with the modest support offered by Roosevelt, is that McNutt achieved anything worth remembering. Yet after the war he could write that "there was at no time a critical shortage of manpower in the urgent industries of more than 200,000." From 1942 to the end of the war the WMC made more than thirty-five million job placements through the USES, recruited more than two million workers for interstate transfers, found jobs for more than two million veterans, placed 800,000 handicapped workers, and found specialized personnel for secret military projects. Even General Hershey, no friend of McNutt's, admitted that the WMC had done a reasonable job, although too much had been expected from it.[3] Few material shortages could be traced to a failure by American labor.

In any evaluation of McNutt and manpower mobilization it is essential to remember that, despite the rhetoric of politicians who kept insisting that World War II was a total war, the American people and Roosevelt himself never accepted the idea. The study of manpower mobilization reveals how far from total war the nation remained. McNutt's experience demonstrates the power of social continuity even during war. Reform goals always took a back seat to military needs.

In many ways McNutt's career demonstrates how the weight of wartime regulations and restrictions, however limited and voluntary, soured Americans with the concept of a positive state bureaucracy. Increasingly, Americans desired a return to normality, by which they meant a more laissez-faire environment. Not only did Americans gripe about McNutt's restrictions, they frequently ignored them. They flaunted rules while simultaneously telling pollsters that they were willing to accept more regimentation to help win the war.

Sigmund Freud once wrote that the only two forces of cohesion in any community were "violent compulsion and ties of sentiment." McNutt always operated through the ties of sentiment, which Freud thought would be effective only when "they are the expression of a deeply rooted sense of unity, shared by all." Such a unity did exist within the United States during the war but there were distinct limits to the changes it would support.[4]

McNutt always hoped for more. Throughout the war he spoke of learning lessons such as the importance of cooperation between management and labor. Donald Nelson felt the war proved that "whatever this country wants to do it can do. Nothing is impossible for America." Yet only a few months after the war ended the nation was wracked by labor turmoil. The unity resting upon ties of sentiment dissolved with the end of the war. As the climate changed, McNutt went to the Philippines and manpower cooperation went to the dogs.[5]

Notes

1. John Dos Passos, *State of the Nation* (Boston: Houghton Mifflin, 1943), p. 1.

2. Bruce Catton, *The War Lords of Washington* (New York: Harcourt, Brace, 1948), p. 198.

3. McNutt quote to *Editor and Publisher*, September 27, 1945, Paul V. McNutt Papers, The Lilly Library, Indiana University, Bloomington, Ind.; McNutt radio address, November 11, 1945, *ibid.*; Frank H. Sparks to Appley, December 28, 1943, box 20-139, record group 211, National Archives, Washington, D.C.; interview with General Hershey, Bethesda, Md., May 26, 1975.

4. Freud quote in Leon Branson and George W. Goethals, eds., *War: Studies from Psychology, Sociology, Anthropology* (New York: Basic Books, 1964), p. 75.

5. Donald Nelson, *Arsenal of Democracy: The Story of American War Production* (New York: Harcourt, Brace, 1946), p. 259.

BIBLIOGRAPHICAL ESSAY

In 1971 Jim F. Heath wrote an article entitled "Domestic America during World War II: Research Opportunities for Historians," *Journal of American History* (September 1971), which provided what is still the best bibliography on the general subject. Heath's article should be supplemented with the bibliography found in Richard Polenberg, *War and Society: The United States, 1941–1945* (Philadelphia, 1972), which provides a broad survey of the home front. John M. Blum, *V Was for Victory: Politics and American Culture during World War II* (New York, 1976), is the most recent study of domestic affairs by an eminent historian. Much information on the politics of the home front can also be obtained from James M. Burns, *Roosevelt: The Soldier of Freedom* (New York, 1970). Less scholarly, but useful for popular culture are several journalistic accounts: Scott Hart, *Washington at War: 1941–1945* (Englewood Cliffs, N.J., 1970), A. A. Hoehling, *Home Front, U.S.A.* (New York, 1966), Geoffrey Perrett, *Days of Sadness, Years of Triumph: The American People, 1939–1945* (New York, 1973), and Richard R. Lingeman, *Don't You Know There's a War On? The American Home Front, 1941–1945* (New York, 1970). Eliot Janeway, *Struggle for Survival* (New Haven, Conn., 1951), is an older work in the Chronicles of America series which must be used with caution. More recently, Gordon Wright, *The Ordeal of Total War, 1939–1945* (New York, 1968), gives a worldwide perspective to the conflict in this volume which is part of the Rise of Modern Europe series.

The serious scholar interested in manpower mobilization in the United States during World War II must attend to several major manuscript collections. The papers of General Lewis B. Hershey, head of the Selective Service System, can be found at the Military History Research Collection, Carlisle Barracks, Pa. Hershey was a major political figure during this period and his papers are voluminous and revealing. At the Library of Congress two manuscript collections proved useful. The secret diary of Harold Ickes for the war years is now open to scholars. As might be expected from the chatty Ickes, the diary contains much personal information on major politicians. No military figure was more concerned with domestic manpower problems than Undersecretary of War Robert Patterson. His papers can also be found in the Library of Congress. Paul McNutt played the major domestic role with manpower mobilization and his papers, located at the Lilly Library on the campus of Indiana University in Bloomington, proved invaluable for this study. The McNutt Papers must be supplemented with the official records of the War Manpower Commission, record group 211, at the National Archives. The minutes of the WMC, the MLPC, and the WAC, were useful.

The Franklin D. Roosevelt Library at Hyde Park, N.Y., remains one of the most important depositories for the study of recent American politics. Here the researcher finds not only the papers of the President himself, but several other collections of value. These additional sources include the diaries of Secretary of the Treasury Henry Morgenthau, the diaries of Director of the Budget Harold Smith, and the papers of Samuel Rosenman and Oscar Cox, all of which aided the study. The Eleanor Roosevelt Papers, also housed at Hyde Park, provided information on the effect of mobilization on women and blacks. The Schlesinger Library at Radcliffe College in Cambridge, Mass., houses the most impressive documentary collection on women's history. The papers of Margaret Anderson and Clara Beyer contributed to an understanding of the mobilization of women. At Yale University the papers and diary of Secretary of War Henry L. Stimson revealed the attitude of the military toward civilian manpower problems. The papers of James Byrnes at Clemson University were also helpful, but Donald Nelson's papers at the Huntington Library, San Marino, Calif., were of only marginal value.

The major political figures of the Franklin Roosevelt era have assisted the work of historians by producing memoirs. Several scholarly biographies also help fill in gaps. Dean Albertson, *Roosevelt's Farmer: Claude R. Wickard in the New Deal* (New York, 1961), presents the philosophy and activities of this wartime Secretary of Agriculture. Bernard Baruch has explained his work in the higher echelons of government in several works, including *The Public Years* (London, 1960). George I. Blake presents an overly sympathetic picture of his subject in *Paul McNutt: Portrait of a Hoosier Statesman* (Indianapolis, 1966). John Blum has served the profession well by editing several major source collections on New Deal politicians, including: *From the Morgenthau Diaries: Years of War* (Boston, 1967), and *The Price of Vision: The Diary of Henry A. Wallace, 1942–1946* (Boston, 1973). James F. Byrnes wrote of his wartime service as Director of Economic Mobilization in *All in One Lifetime* (New York, 1958). Bruce Catton took time off from his interest in the Civil War to recall his services with the War Production Board in *The War Lords of Washington* (New York, 1948), which is also an indictment of the influence of big business and the military in mobilization. Grenville Clark joined Arthur L. Williston to record their unsuccessful struggle to win a national service law in *The Effort for a National Service Law in World War II, 1942-1945* (Dedham, Mass., 1947), an account which must be used carefully because of the ideological commitment of the authors. Within the White House itself Jonathan Daniels presented the view from the perspective of a presidential assistant in *White House Witness, 1942-1945* (New York, 1975). Moving away from his earlier radicalism, author John Dos Passos traveled across the country during the war and recorded his impressions in *State of the Nation* (Boston, 1943). Another novelist, Allen Drury, took advantage of his post as newspaper correspondent assigned to Congress to jot down his observations in *A Senate Journal, 1943-1945* (New York, 1963). He noted with favor the growing antagonism between Congress and the President. The presidential point of view received more sympathetic treatment by former Roosevelt secretary William D. Hassett, *Off the Record with F.D.R., 1942-1945* (New Brunswick, N.J., 1958). Donald Nelson tells his own story of struggling with the War Department to control mobilization in *Arsenal of Democracy: The Story of American War Production* (New York, 1946), but he pulls more punches than does Catton. The humanitarian side of the war can be gleaned from the last chapters in Joseph Lash's prize-winning study, *Eleanor and Franklin* (New York, 1971). For a potpourri of information on life styles in the United States during the war see Jack Goodman, ed., *While You Were Gone* (New York, 1946), where various contributors discuss everything from comic strips to union activity.

As the issue of mobilization of civilian manpower was always a sensitive political problem, the student can find considerable debate in the *Congressional Record*. More specialized treatment of McNutt and the WMC can be located in the following congressional documents: House of Representatives, Fifth Interim Report by Select Committee Investigating National Defense Migration, pursuant to HR 113, *Recommendations on the Mobilization of Manpower for the All-Out War Effort*, August 10, 1942, 77th Cong., 2d sess., 1942; House of Representatives, Fifth Interim Report by Select Committee Investigating National Defense Migration, *Changes Needed for Effective Mobilization of Manpower*, October 1942, 77th Cong., 2d sess., 1942; House of Representatives, Committee on Military Affairs, hearings on *Mobilization of Civilian Manpower*, 69th Cong., 1st sess. (HR 1119), 1945; Senate, Committee on Appropriations, hearings on *Investigation of*

Manpower, 78th Cong., 1st sess., 1943, 3 pts.; Senate, hearings on *Investigation of the National Defense Program*, 78th Cong., 2d sess., pt. 26, 1944; Senate, Committee on Military Affairs, hearings on *Mobilization of Civilian Manpower*, 69th Cong., 1st sess. (S. 36, HR 1752), 1945.

Congressional involvement in economic mobilization for war can also be traced in more recent literature. Roland Young, *Congressional Politics in the Second World War* (New York, 1956), provides an overview and restricts his sources to public documents such as the *Congressional Record*. Donald H. Riddle, *The Truman Committee* (New Brunswick, N.J., 1964), presents a very favorable account of this important group, using a political science frame of reference. The congressional struggle with the draft can be studied in John J. O'Sullivan, "From Voluntarism to Conscription: Congress and Selective Service, 1940-1945" (Ph.D. dissertation, Columbia University, 1971).

Monographical treatment of the social and psychological effect of war on the home front has not reached the level of scholarship of several other topics. For readers interested, however, consult Therese Benedek, *Insight and Personality Adjustment: A Study of the Psychological Effects of War* (New York, 1946), which pursues a Freudian thesis. See also Frances E. Merill, *Social Problems on the Home Front: A Study of Wartime Influences* (New York, 1948). Several anthologies exist which deal with the more abstract dimension of war's effect on civilians: Leon Branson and G. W. Goethals, eds., *War: Studies from Psychology, Sociology, Anthropology* (New York, 1964); Morton Fried, Marvin Harris, and Robert Murphy, eds., *War: The Anthropology of Armed Conflict and Aggression* (New York, 1968). A contemporary study from a social science perspective which treats such topics as the family, crime, and morale is William F. Ogburn, ed., *American Society in Wartime* (Chicago, 1943).

Several valuable studies have emerged on the topic of economic mobilization in the United States during World War II. Leonard P. Adams, *Wartime Manpower Mobilization* (Ithaca, N.Y., 1951), focuses on the effect of mobilization on the Buffalo-Niagara Falls region and does a masterful job. No one has devoted more attention to the problem than Albert A. Blum. In addition to his study of conscription in *Drafted or Deferred: Practices Past and Present* (Ann Arbor, Mich., 1967), he has also contributed the following articles: "Sailor or Worker: A Manpower Dilemma during the Second World War," *Labor History* 6 (Fall 1965), pp. 232-43; "The Farmer, the Army and the Draft," *Agricultural History* 38 (January 1964), pp. 34-42; and "Birth and Death of the M-Day Plan," in *American Civil-Military Decisions*, Harold Stein, ed. (Birmingham, Ala., 1963), pp. 61-96. Blum's conscription studies focus on the view from the

War Department. Another source which rests primarily upon War Department documentation is *The Army and Industrial Manpower* (Washington, D.C., 1959), by Byron Fairchild and Jonathan Grossman. A volume in the official Department of the Army history of World War II, the work is a model of institutional history with valuable references to government documents. Another first-rate study of wartime institutions is by Herman M. Somers, *Presidential Agency: OWMR, The Office of War Mobilization and Reconversion* (Cambridge, Mass., 1950), who worked with the agency for sixteen months. A more critical view of economic mobilization during World War II is presented by Paul A. C. Koistinen in "Mobilizing the World War II Economy: Labor and the Industrial-Military Alliance," *Pacific Historical Review* 42 (November 1973), pp. 443-78. Koistinen takes what amounts to a New Left view of the collaboration between big business and the military during the war. A general study of the government regulation of the economy is Lester V. Chandler and Donald H. Wallace, eds., *Economic Mobilization and Stabilization* (New York, 1951).

The standard work on the role of labor in economic mobilization is now almost twenty-five years old. But until a new work appears the reader must be satisfied with Joel Seidman, *American Labor from Defense to Reconversion* (Chicago, 1953). Despite the author's sympathy for unions, the book provides an admirably balanced account. To supplement this work the reader is urged to consider several important essays: Milton Derber, "Labor-Management in World War II," *Current History* 48 (June 1965); Robert K. Murray, "Government and Labor during World War II," *Current History* 37 (September 1959); and Bruno Stein, "Labor's Role in Government Agencies during World War II," *Journal of Economic History* 17 (September 1957). An older work which proved valuable was Carol Riegelman, *Labour-Management Co-operation in United States War Production* (Montreal, 1948), which used many official documents. For the controversy over national service legislation, the most recent study is George T. Mazuzan, "The National War Service Controversy, 1942–1945," *Mid-America: An Historical Review* 57 (October 1975), pp. 246-58, which makes use of the papers of Grenville Clark at Dartmouth College. Nelson N. Lichenstein, "Industrial Unionism under the No-Strike Pledge" (Ph.D. dissertation, University of California, Berkeley, 1974), argues that unions sold out to the state during the war.

The subject of blacks and World War II has received attention in recent years. An older work, Louis Ruchames, *Race, Jobs and Politics: The Story of the FEPC* (Chapel Hill, 1948), can still be examined with profit. More up-to-date information can be found in a series of recent articles. Allan M.

Winkler, "The Philadelphia Transit Strike of 1944," *Journal of American History* 59 (June 1972), pp. 73-89, describes the reaction to attempts to integrate one city's transportation system. H. Sitkoff, "Racial Militancy and Interracial Violence in the Second World War," *Journal of American History* 58 (December 1971), pp. 661-81, explores the character of racial tension. Lee Finkle, "The Conservative Aims of Militant Rhetoric: Black Protest during World War II," *Journal of American History* 60 (December 1973), pp. 692-713, suggests that radicals may have been sold out by moderate black leaders seeking accommodations with the white power structure. The most recent scholarly survey of the entire question is Neil A. Wynn, *The Afro-American and the Second World War* (London, 1976), which contains a good bibliography.

In 1963 Betty Freidan published her book, *The Feminine Mystique* (New York, 1963), which raised many questions about the modern woman. The question of women's role in World War II was explored thoroughly by William H. Chafe, *The American Woman: Her Changing Social, Economic, and Political Roles, 1920–1970* (New York, 1972). Chafe contends that the war was a major turning point in the emancipation of women. The thesis that the war wrought a revolution in the status of women is also the thesis of Chester W. Gregory's dissertation, "The Problem of Labor during World War II: The Employment of Women in Defense Production" (Ohio State University, 1969). Chafe admits that women still faced serious problems of discrimination during the war, but argues that the economic consequences of their employment would contribute to permanent changes in their status. Modifying this thesis, Eleanor Straub, "Government Policy toward Civilian Women during World War II" (Ph.D. dissertation, Emory University, 1973), proves the continued discrimination against females by the federal government. She marshals considerable evidence to prove that the American home front during World War II was no bed of roses for females seeking employment or a voice in their own destiny. Several older works, much in the nature of official reports, proved useful on the subject of women and war: Helen Baker, *Women in War Industries* (Princeton, N.J., 1942), traces the problems encountered in the first year of war. International Labor Office, *The War and Women's Employment: The Experience of the United Kingdom and the United States* (Montreal, 1946), provides first-rate statistics on working women down to the state level. Several official publications by the Department of Labor (Women's Bureau) provided important information: Margaret K. Anderson, *Women's Wartime Hours of Work: The Effect on Their Factory Performance and Home Life* (Washington, D.C., 1947); Mary E. Pidgeon, *Changes in Women's Employment during the War* (Washington, D.C., 1944); Ethel Erickson, *Women's Employment in the Making of Steel* (Washington, D.C., 1944). For the story of women who decided to make a direct contribution to military victory see Mattie E. Treadwell, *The Woman's Army Corps* (Washington, D.C., 1954). Josephine von Miklos, *I Took a War Job* (New York, 1943), is a readable memoir by a forty-year-old, ex-dress designer, who followed McNutt's advice. Elizabeth Hawes, *Why Women Cry or Wenches with Wrenches* (New York, 1943), is an early propaganda piece for women's liberation. For the social impact of women's mobilization the reader may benefit from a perusal of such manifestations of popular culture as the *Woman's Home Companion* and *Ladies Home Journal* for the war years.

On the subject of reconverting wartime labor and integrating veterans the most recent study is David R. B. Ross, *Preparing for Ulysses: Politics and Veterans during World War II* (New York, 1969). Ross focuses exclusively upon the problem of the veterans. Alonzo L. Hamby, "Sixty Million Jobs and the People's Revolution: The Liberals, the New Deal, and World War II," *Historian* 30 (August 1968), pp. 578-98, treats the ideological dimensions of reconversion as another stage in the reform movement. Older works on the subject include the special report prepared by Bernard Baruch and John M. Hancock, *War and Postwar Adjustment Policies* (Washington, D.C., 1944), which laid the groundwork for much of the debate over the timing and character of reconversion. J. Carlyle Sitterson, *Development of the Reconversion Policies of the War Production Board* (Washington, D.C., 1945) is the official history by that wartime agency, which should be supplemented by Nelson, *Arsenal of Democracy*.

In periodical literature the two most useful journals for the subject of manpower mobilization were *Business Week* and the *Monthly Labor Review*, the latter a publication of the government with excellent statistical summaries. All modern historians are indebted to the recent compilation by George Gallup, ed., *The Gallup Poll: Public Opinion, 1935-1971*, 3 vols. (New York, 1972), which makes easily accessible this vital information on American attitudes. No one can hope to work in recent American history without recourse to the *New York Times*. The papers at the Roosevelt Library are critical for a study of this period, but two edited collections have brought some of this material to the researcher: Samuel I. Rosenman, ed., *The Public Papers and Addresses of Franklin D. Roosevelt*, 13 vols. (New York, 1938-1950), gives the major state papers and executive orders; *The Complete Presidential Press Conferences of Franklin D. Roosevelt*, 12 books (New York, 1972) provides verbatim coverage of these important exchanges. For more detailed information on sources the reader is referred to the appropriate notes in the text.

INDEX

ABOUT THE AUTHOR

George Q. Flynn is Professor of History at Texas Tech University in Lubbock, Texas. He has written numerous articles on recent American history, and is the author of *American Catholics and the Roosevelt Presidency, 1932–1936*, and *Roosevelt and Romanism: Catholics and American Diplomacy* (Greenwood Press, 1976).